Welsh National OPERA

INTERNATIONAL MUSIC THEATRE AT ITS BEST

Another first for one of the country's most exciting opera companies. On tour Summer 1990.

THE WORLD PREMIERE OF

TORNRAK

A new opera by John Metcalf with libretto by Michael Wilcox, commissioned by WNO.

The magical spirit culture of the Arctic meets the conventions of Victorian England in this story of love across a great cultural divide.

Set against the wide open spaces of the Canadian Arctic, an Inuit (Eskimo) woman saves the life of a shipwrecked sailor, and returns with him to his native Wales. The moving story of their doomed love affair contrasts the beauty, dignity and savagery of Inuit culture with the conventions and attitudes of the 19th Century Britain.

Premiere at Cardiff New Theatre 19 May 1990 (also 30 May), then touring to Liverpool, Birmingham, Southampton, Manchester, Bristol and Oxford.

Phone WNO Marketing on (0222) 464666 for full details of this and future plans.

THE GENERAL

31

Editor: Bill Buford
Commissioning Editor: Lucretia Stewart
Assistant Editor: Tim Adams
Managing Editor: Angus MacKinnon
Assistant to the Editor: Ursula Doyle

Managing Director: Caroline Michel
Financial Manager: Robert Linney
Subscriptions: Gillian Kemp, Carol Harris
Office Assistant: Stephen Taylor

Picture Editor: Alice Rose George
Picture Research: David Brownridge
Design: Chris Hyde
Executive Editor: Pete de Bolla
US Associate Publisher: Anne Kinard, Granta, 250 West 57th Street, Suite 1316, New York, NY 10107.

Editorial and Subscription Correspondence: Granta, 44a Hobson Street, Cambridge CB1 1NL. Telephone: (0223) 315290. Fax (0223) 358165. Subscriptions: (0223) 311951.
A one-year subscription (four issues) is £19.95 in Britain, £25.95 for the rest of Europe, and £31.95 for the rest of the World.
All manuscripts are welcome but must be accompanied by a stamped, self-addressed envelope or they cannot be returned.
Change of address: From 25 March 1990 *Granta* will be at 2–3 Hanover Yard, Noel Road, Islington, London N1.

Granta is photoset by Cambridge Photosetting Services, Cambridge, England, and printed by BPCC Hazell Books Ltd, Aylesbury, Bucks.,

Granta is published by Granta Publications Ltd and distributed by Penguin Books Ltd, Harmondsworth, Middlesex, England; Viking Penguin Inc., 40 West 23rd St, New York, New York, USA; Penguin Books Australia Ltd, Ringwood, Victoria, Australia; Penguin Books Canada Ltd, 2801 John Street, Markham, Ontario, Canada L3R 1B4; Penguin Books (NZ) Ltd, 182–90 Wairau Road, Auckland 10, New Zealand. This selection copyright © 1990 by Granta Publications Ltd.

Cover by the Senate. Photo: François Lochon (Frank Spooner Pictures).

Granta 31, Spring 1990

ISBN 014-01-3855-2

JOURNALISM

IN

GRANTA

To coincide with the publication of Isabel Hilton's 'The General', Granta is offering the following book-length pieces of its best journalism at a special price:

- ■ 'The Fall of Saigon' by James Fenton (*Granta* 15).
  'One of the finest pieces of reportage I've ever seen.' Godfrey Smith, *Sunday Times*.

- ■ 'The Snap Revolution' by James Fenton (*Granta* 18).

- ■ 'In Pursuit of Guzman' by Nicholas Shakespeare (*Granta* 23)
  'An enthralling piece of investigative reporting in the tradition of Graham Greene and his travels in Mexico'. Mick Brown, *Sunday Times*.

- ■ 'Gibraltar' by Ian Jack (in 'The Murderee' *Granta* 25)
  What really happened on 6 March 1988? **'His investigation shakes the central pillars of the government's case.'** *The Scotsman*.

Each issue is available at £5 each. If you buy three, we will give you the fourth one free. This offer expires on 30 June. Send the coupon below (or details written on a separate sheet of paper) to Granta, 44a Hobson Street, Cambridge CD1 1NL.

- -

Please send me the following back issues:

☐ 'The Fall of Saigon' in *Granta* 15 at £5.
☐ 'The Snap Revolution' in *Granta* 18 at £5.
☐ 'In Pursuit of Guzman' in *Granta* 23 at £5.
☐ 'Gibraltar' in *Granta* 25 at £5.
☐ All of the above at £15.

Name _____

_____

_____ Postcode _____

Payment: ☐ cheque enclosed
☐ credit card (subscriptions only) Access/American Express/
Diners Club no._____ (Visa not accepted)

Credit card orders can be accepted by phone: (0223) _____
For foreign orders, add £1 for postage for each issue.

ff

MARIO VARGAS LLOSA

The Storyteller

'One of the
world's outstanding
contemporary
narrative masters.'
Newsweek

0 571 15208 2   £12.99

CONTENTS

CLASSIC RUSSIAN CINEMA AVAILABLE ON VIDEO

BATTLESHIP POTEMKIN

STRIKE

OCTOBER

TIME IN THE SUN/BEZHIN MEADOW

ALEXANDER NEVSKY

IVAN THE TERRIBLE

THE BOYARS' PLOT

MOTHER

END OF ST. PETERSBURG

STORM OVER ASIA

FALL OF THE ROMANOFF DYNASTY (DOCUMENTARY)

TEN DAYS THAT SHOOK THE WORLD (DOCUMENTARY)

RUSSIAN CLASSICS

SPECIAL MAIL ORDER OFFER

Each programme is available at £14.95, including postage and packing (U.K. and EIRE).

As a special offer, Hendring will be shipping free of charge the two documentaries if all ten films are ordered. The documentaries are, of course, available outside this offer at the price of £14.95.

Please pay by Cheque or Postal Order or International Money Order (Do not send cash) payable to Hendring Limited, and send along with this coupon to:
Hendring (Russian Offer), 29 Beethoven St, London W10 4LG.

Postage: UK and Eire – free; Europe – £2.00 extra per tape; Outside Europe – £6.00 extra per tape.

Please note that all tapes are PAL TV system only and not suitable for use in USA, Canada or Japan. Only VHS format available.

Payment may also be made by Amex/Access/Visa. Please call Credit Card Hotline 01-960 1871.

Please fill in below in block capitals.

NAME_____

ADDRESS_____

_____ POSTCODE_____

	QUANTITY	PRICE
BATTLESHIP POTEMKIN		
STRIKE		
OCTOBER		
TIME IN SUN/BEZHIN MEADOW		
ALEXANDER NEVSKY		
IVAN THE TERRIBLE		
THE BOYARS' PLOT		
MOTHER		
END OF ST PETERSBURG		
STORM OVER ASIA		
THE FALL OF THE ROMANOFF DYNASTY		
TEN DAYS THAT SHOOK THE WORLD Narrated by Orson Welles		
SUB TOTAL		
P&P		
TOTAL		

A Letter for our Subscribers

Dear Subscriber,

Over the past year the size of *Granta*'s readership has grown at a phenomenal rate. To ensure a fast, efficient service, there are a number of things to bear in mind:

■ If you have problems with your subscription, please let us know as soon as possible.

■ We can deal with your queries much more quickly if you quote your subscriber number when writing. You will find this on the top line of your mailing label.

■ Should you change your address, please inform us in good time. Hundreds of copies of the magazine are returned after each dispatch because subscribers have moved without telling us.

■ Please use your postcode in all communciations with us. This will ensure that your copy of *Granta* reaches you without unnecessary delays.

■ We occasionally exchange our mailing list with other publications whose aims are broadly similar to our own. If you would rather not receive mailings from these publications, simply write and tell us, and your name will not be included.

Yours sincerely,

Gillian M. Kemp
Subscriptions Manager

P.S. *If you're not already a subscriber, isn't it about time you became one?*

ISABEL HILTON
THE GENERAL

Photo: T. La Penna (Rex Features)

I can see now where this story ended, although for a long time I was playing with other endings, reluctant to let go. It ended with that moment of cinema, crossing General Stroessner's spongy lawn and looking back to see him, framed in the doorway, waving. I waved, went through the gate and into the General's car, and the world rushed in around me, hotels, luggage and airports—everyday people, everyday lives.

I didn't go back—that was one possible ending, that I would return—I told myself there was no time and it was true. But the story wouldn't go away. The kitchen telephone would ring and it would be Gustavo Stroessner, the General's son, bellowing in that strange accent down a fuzzy line from Brazil, like an unruly fictional character nagging for a larger part in the plot.

'Hello, Colonel. How are you? How is the General?'

'Do you need any material?' He would answer. 'How is the work going?' None of the 'material' ever arrived, but it didn't matter. I knew what it would have been and was glad he hadn't sent it.

But where had the story begun? It had been there for years, but I always found something else, wars, elections; Latin America was never short of events clamouring for attention. Except in Paraguay. Paraguay was a situation, rather than an event. It was wrapped in a layer of clichés, and, when events poked through, they seemed only to reinforce the clichés. Josef Mengele was in Paraguay; fascist army officers from Argentina fled to Paraguay when their *coup* plots failed; Indians in the Paraguayan jungle were hunted by fundamentalist American missionaries with rifles. Stroessner had been there for ever and always would be.

Then, suddenly, in February 1989, he wasn't.

I wasn't there either. I was in Jamaica, watching a more orderly change of government. I called my newspaper from Kingston, cursing my bad luck—a journalist in the wrong place. It was too late. Stroessner had been hustled out of the country and had gone to ground in Brazil, where he sat in his beach-house, under siege from

General Alfredo Stroessner with his wife Dona Eligia at a mass celebrating the anniversary of the independence of Paraguay, 14 May 1986.

a press corps in bathing-suits. No interviews, no comment, no recriminations. Nothing.

He had never been a great one for interviews, but now he had a further excuse. He was in asylum and that imposed silence. After an interlude of disorderly scenes at the beach-house—photographers on step-ladders peeping over the wall, helicopters chartered by TV companies chattering overhead—he was moved. Some said to São Paulo; others said Brasília. At any rate, he had vanished behind another set of walls, another set of guards. He was rumoured to be ill and had a brief spell in hospital, then silence.

Six months later, I decided I would try to find him, to talk to him, and I had mixed feelings about the prospect. I knew nobody had and I didn't really see why I should be different, though I also knew that the unpredictability of Latin America could precipitate you as easily into a president's office as into a jail. I had set out on similar quests before and knew that they followed no timetable and that you just had to go where they led you until you either gave up or found yourself pushing an open door. I also knew that the last door always opened on to another, that it was hard to stop going through them and that there was never going to be enough time; I would end up, I feared, with one of those hollow-hearted stories which reconstructs the drama without the main character.

But even with that risk, it was a tempting drama. I knew that Stroessner's Paraguay had featured a kind of rampant official gangsterism, racketeers masquerading as high officials, contraband pretending to be business. There was a constitution, a state structure; there were laws, elections: but none of them was real. What was real was power, cronyism, corruption, the righteous men in jail and the criminals in government. At least, that's what I had been told. I didn't doubt it, exactly, but I hankered, foolishly, for evidence. I wanted to meet someone who had been cheated and robbed; I wanted to know exactly who had done it. I wanted to follow a thread to the Presidential Palace.

I set off for Asunción at the beginning of September 1989 with a suitcase of research I had only just begun to read and a list of names and numbers. Apart from one detailed academic political study and some slim volumes published by human rights organizations, there was remarkably little about Stroessner's Paraguay. It was, as someone was to say, in the et ceteras in the list of nations. It was like the silent planet, on a different radio frequency from the outside world. It fought savage wars with its neighbours, in which thousands died; created passionate myths and legends, but who cared? It changed presidents so often that when Alfredo Stroessner staged his coup, in May 1954, then sanctified his newly acquired throne with rigged elections, he must have seemed like just the latest man through the revolving door.

When he fell, thirty-five years later, he held a number of records. He was the longest-serving dictator in the western hemisphere and the second longest in the world: only Kim Il Sung outlasted him. The world had lived through thirty-five years of history, but three-quarters of the population of Paraguay had known no other leader, and there was not an institution or political party in the country that had not been shaped by his presence.

I had read that his image and name were everywhere. A neon sign flashed the message in the Plaza de los Heroes in Asunción: 'Stroessner . . . Peace . . . Work . . . Well-being'—on, off; on, off; on, off, twenty-four hours a day. Television began and ended with his heavy features and a march named after him. There was a Stroessner Polka, for more light-hearted occasions. The airport was named after him. The free-port on the Brazilian frontier was called Puerto Stroessner. There were Stroessner statues, avenues and roads, and official portraits of him hung in every office and school.

When I got to Paraguay, six months after he fell, he had been painted over. The portraits had gone, the airport was renamed, the march was no longer played and some of the statues, at least, had disappeared.

Democratic ideals were now the height of fashion. General Andres Rodriguez—who had led the February *coup* against Stroessner, his old friend, mentor and relative by marriage—had sanctified his position, like Stroessner, with electoral holy water: he got seventy-four per cent of the votes. Everybody knew there had been fraud, out of habit, if nothing else, but since Stroessner used to get over ninety per cent, Rodriguez looked like an honest man. Many people, I was to discover, liked to think that Rodriguez's less than perfect elections were free and fair. There had been something so grubby and humiliating in the last years, to be living in

Stroessner's Paraguay, that people fell upon the idea that this was now democracy and used it to wash away some of the slime. So large had the tyrant loomed that it only required his removal to encourage the hope that democracy was possible. From there it was a short step to pretending it had arrived.

Rodriguez was immensely popular. He was cheerful, where Stroessner had been bad-tempered; vigorous, where Stroessner had been in decline; available, where Stroessner had been withdrawn. Rodriguez never troubled to hide the fact that he had grown immensely rich in Stroessner's service but he had been forgiven his sins for this one act of deliverance. Only a few, with a natural bent towards scepticism, reflected that in May 1954 it had seemed like a new dawn too.

I was shown to a room in the Hotel Excelsior, proprietor Nicolas Bo, friend of General Stroessner. It was pitch-dark.

Was there another one? I asked.

Yes, but a room with daylight is extra.

I paid extra and got a view of a huge building site across the road. Every morning, at seven, I would be woken by the clink-clink of hammers on concrete. While I was there, the building rose a whole floor. I used to look out of my window, wondering who was out there in the city who could help me and what I had to do to find them.

It was Saturday when I arrived, the traveller's dread weekend. I looked through my list of names and numbers. The shops were shut, the town was quiet, the phones didn't answer. I began to read again, trying to absorb the country's tortured history.

Asunción—still sleepy, but sleepier then. When Stroessner came to power only one square kilometre of Asunción had running water. The rich lived in colonnaded houses along Avenida Mariscal Lopez, rattan chairs set out on deep verandas. Water and milk were sold off mule-carts, and the life of the town centred round the railway station where the peasants came in from the country to sell vegetables and chickens.

Outside the capital, red dirt roads turned to mud in the tropical rains. The wars that had kept the country backward had affected its society too. In Bolivia or Peru, there were enough of the Spanish-speaking élite to colonize, to relegate the Indian population to a despised under-class. In Paraguay, although tribal Indians were being steadily exterminated, their culture had always been accommodated in the past, even absorbed. The indigenous language, Guarani, is as important as Spanish, spoken by every populist politician. And, in spite of the strength of the Church, the need to repopulate the country after the worst of the nineteenth-century wars had left a legacy of *de facto* polygamy.

I would get to know Asunción a little, peeling back its layers of history: single-storey homes and grid-patterned streets running down the hill to the river; flashy high-rise buildings in the centre and, scattered through the outskirts, some giant institutional relics of a building boom in the late 1970s. Nobody had been very interested in roads or drains, it seemed. The streets were full of pot-holes, and had been scoured and carved up by the tropical floods that coursed down them. A few ostentatious hotels, décor somewhere between an ersatz gentleman's club and a high-class brothel. On the shores of the river, there were the shanty towns, squalid, but not as many as in Lima or Rio de Janeiro.

It was a quiet town, still. It woke up at six in the morning and went home at noon for lunch and a long siesta. At five business started again and by seven or eight it was all over: the rich went to their dinner parties and cocktails; the poor hung about under street lamps, where there were any; the modestly comfortable listened to lyrical Paraguayan music in bars. They sang in Guarani, because, they said, it was more expressive and passionate than Spanish. There was very little crime on the streets—less than the crime in the police or the government. Women sold their babies to foreigners who favoured Paraguay because the babies were less likely to be black than in Brazil; and they sold themselves in several well-known sites around town. On Sundays, everyone went to mass.

I bought all the newspapers. There seemed to be several free shows in town: political rallies at which factions of factions of parties attacked each other before thin crowds; the law courts where a succession of fallen grandees of the Stronato, Stroessner's system, bandits all, appeared in court protesting their innocence against charges of grand larceny. One general, who swore he never stole a centavo, nevertheless offered, as a gesture of solidarity to the new government, to donate—on a purely voluntary basis—one million dollars to the public purse. Many of the names in the newspapers were familiar from the books I had read: those who had jumped early enough and were still cruising town in their chauffeur-driven cars, still making deals; and those, the famous figures from the opposition, who had been jailed or exiled, and who were now in Congress, making politics.

The weekend wore on in the half-life of the hotel. On Sunday, a telephone number finally answered—some friends of friends, intellectuals. We had lunch and talked about Stroessner. They were not the sort who knew him or wanted to. They had tried to live their lives in spite of him, to create a cultural island in a bandit state. Did I realize, they said, that in thirty-five years Stroessner had never thought of building a national museum or a gallery? Sitting in their house, listening to music, I picked up the telephone book and looked up Stroessner, Alfredo. He was there, followed by 'Stroessner, Frederico' and 'Stroessner, Graciella', all with numbers and addresses. I imagined a citizen ringing the president to complain about the drains.

On Monday morning, I started in earnest down my list—politicians, journalists, other people's contacts. Talking to people who hated him would be easy, I thought. Talking to those who had been close was the challenge. Of those, Conrado Pappalardo's name stood out.

2

Conrado Pappalardo, a friend had told me, knew everything. He had been Stroessner's political intimate and presidential secretary for years. Pappalardo was also a survivor. He had switched sides at the eleventh hour; he remains presidential secretary, now to President Rodriguez.

The presidential palace lies down near the river, a low, grey building that could never quite make up its mind which architectural style it was imitating: Greek classical? Colonial? Was that square tower English? There were palm trees and dark-suited security men, immobile, their hands hanging by their sides or clasped behind their backs: whatever way I approached the presidential palace, I had to pass one of them.

It was very early in the morning, but there was already a gathering at the door: television and radio reporters, rural officials, the claque of the local press.

To get to Pappalardo, I had first to make a courtesy call on the press office where I found Oscar, the presidential press officer.

Oscar used to be on television, but this was much better. He was very proud to be serving democracy. No, he had no material about Stroessner, but as many copies as I liked of General Rodriguez's speeches.

I took a copy, and thanked him. A photograph of President Rodriguez hung behind his desk. I asked him what had happened to the thousands of portraits of President Stroessner.

He didn't know, he said.

Along the corridor from Oscar's office, near the main entrance and overlooking the river, was a vast salon where petitioners sat, waiting for an audience with the president. Whether that audience was granted depended on the decisions taken in the last room between them and the inner sanctum, Conrado Pappalardo's office, where power was discreetly, but enduringly, exercised.

Pappalardo was smooth, rich, and elegantly dressed; his manners were impeccable; he was the perfect servant. Someone told me that, as well as having once been Stroessner's secretary, Pappalardo was also Stroessner's godson. Stroessner, patriarch of the nation, had many godsons.

I made my speech of introduction and dropped a name, the son of a former Argentine ambassador who had known Pappalardo quite well. Pappalardo made careful note on a piece of presidential notepaper, under my name. He checked, several times, that he had spelled it correctly, then asked a few questions to determine how seriously he should treat the name-drop.

Pappalardo viewed Stroessner with affection and with sadness, the sadness of having watched his greatness decline into the foolishness of a sclerotic old age. He had been a great governor, Pappalardo told me, who had raised the people's living standards and insisted on raising educational levels to those of Italy. 'So obviously, once that happened,' Pappalardo said, 'the people

Above: General Alfredo Stroessner wearing a poncho given to him at an inauguration parade in June 1959.

wanted more liberty and Stroessner didn't want to give it. Until 1982, I was behind him. He was always polite, never angry, never irritated.' But in 1982, Pappalardo sighed, something went wrong. 'He seemed to grow bored, and the militants took over the government. His son, Gustavo, began to emerge. He spoke badly of his father, disloyally.

'Gustavo was always complaining,' Pappalardo added. 'He complained that there were women and children everywhere.' I had heard that that Gustavo, the heir apparent, and Pappalardo, the godson, didn't get on, that they were jealous of each other.

I had also heard that it was Pappalardo who managed the payroll for Stroessner's many mistresses, distributing the money on Fridays.

Was it true, I wondered? Stroessner acknowledged his children, didn't he?

Pappalardo frowned and sucked his teeth for an instant. 'No . . . He neither denied them nor acknowledged them.' Pappalardo started describing how Stroessner lived—'like a soldier, you know, a very spartan life, For years there was no hot water system in that house. He had one of those little showers that heated the water when you needed it.' We talked about Stroessner's house and Stroessner's marriage: he never paid much attention to his wife, Dona Eligia. 'He lives alone now,' said Pappalardo. 'Perhaps he's too proud to call his wife to ask her to join him.'

It was really only power, Pappalardo added, that interested Stroessner.

There was a red telephone on Pappalardo's desk, the presidential line. It rang and Pappalardo jumped. It was not a jump that implied any fear on his part, but rather a demonstration of his own importance and his gift for perfect service. When the president needed him, he must attend.

'Immediately,' he said into the telephone and left the room. People started entering his office, gossiping, waiting for a good moment to whisper a request to the fixer of fixers. Outside, in the public salon, more people gathered; I could hear the shuffling of their feet to mark the passing time. Pappalardo returned and continued his story, from time to time interrupted by his other duties, in and out of the President's office.

He himself had realized, Pappalardo said, that the old man had to go, and he told him so in 1982. 'Stroessner didn't reply, but he never really spoke to me after that. I offered him my resignation every year, but he never accepted it.'

What could the perfect servant do, but carry on?

But things had changed, he said. Stroessner became remote and lost his concentration. The government was run by low-grade advisors and scheming ministers. 'Stroessner spent only one hour here each day and he spent the rest of the time at home, reading. Nobody knew because everybody was so loyal to him that it was hushed up.'

Pappalardo mentioned other personal titbits. Stroessner, who was afraid of illness, cultivated the myth that he had perfect health. Once, said Pappalardo, he had an operation for skin cancer and refused an anaesthetic, preferring pain to the impotence of unconsciousness. Stroessner hated being touched, Pappalardo told me, and never embraced anybody. He never threatened or lost his temper, but then I doubted that Pappalardo had ever given him the chance.

Pappalardo was coming to the end of what he wanted to tell me. He gave me a copy of General Rodriguez's speeches. 'This will be of great interest to you,' he said.

I hid Oscar's copy under my handbag and said thank you.

I asked him if I could see Stroessner's house.

That, he said, would be difficult.

I asked him if I could see Stroessner.

He smiled. He had no contact and could not tell me who might have.

I asked if I could see those former ministers who were now in jail.

That, he said, would be up to the Ministry of Justice but he thought it would not be possible.

I knew I was becoming a nuisance and in danger of being dismissed. Then the door opened and a man came into the office. Pappalardo saw his opportunity. 'This is the man you should talk to,' he said. 'Ambassador to the Presidency, Miguel Angel Gonzalez Casabianca. This is the new Paraguay,' Pappalardo said, in the manner of a Harley Street gynaecologist modestly displaying the healthy outcome of a rather difficult breech presentation. 'Dr Casabianca was in exile for many years and now he is part of the government. You should get to know him. He could become president.'

The Ambassador to the Presidency made a face and sat down heavily at the table, pulling out a packet of cigarettes.

Dr Casabianca was a tall man with a large, heavy face, drooping eyes, the creased skin of a chain-smoker. He had a gloomy watchful air that I later decided resulted from having subordinated most other things in life to a political struggle that must have seemed, for most of that time, hopeless. I waited, not yet knowing where Casabianca fitted so not sure where to begin.

The door opened again, and a delegation of local party bosses shuffled into the office. They had come to invite the president to their folk festival. They were small, dark and weather-beaten, dressed in the dateless style of the South American cowboy. They would have figured as fittingly in a 1911 daguerreotype as in a street-corner band. Pappalardo stood up and received them graciously, paying elaborate tribute to the beauties of their town.

Pappalardo returned for a moment and I tried my luck with one more direct question: Were the stories of Stroessner's promiscuity true?

Pappalardo answered. There was more to it than showed in public, he conceded. 'Never in public and never orgies.' And then he deftly shifted the subject again. 'But he talked very little about his personal life . . . He was never concerned about his children. He was only interested in power,' he repeated. 'He wasn't,' added the man who had served Stroessner for more than thirty years, 'all bad. Whenever a Paraguayan drives on a paved road or comes into that airport, or switches on a light, they should be grateful to him. Yes there was contraband . . . But people here don't think of that as a crime. If you brought the Queen of England to Paraguay she would run contraband too. Up to 1982 he was a good president, but then he began to weaken.'

A bugle sounded outside his office, and there was a rush of footsteps. The president was leaving the palace. Pappalardo swept up his briefcase and glided definitively out of the room. The palace had emptied as if by magic. It was like a stage set after the show was over.

It rained most of the day, a chilly rain, and in the evening I met up again with Dr Casabianca at a German *bierkeller*. Casabianca drank whisky, chain-smoking Kents and talked about the years of hopeless exile politics, watching twenty-five years of life slip by and the dictatorship remain as firm as ever.

While Pappalardo had been oiling the wheels of the Stroessner machine—'He's a hard man for a government to do without,' Casabianca had said earlier, smiling one of those private, exile's smiles, 'so many years here, helping everybody'—Casabianca had been one of those whom the machine had all but crushed.

And how had that been machine made?

Before Stroessner came to power, there had been eleven presidents in nineteen years—Stroessner had conspired against five of them—and if there was a lesson in Paraguay's bloody history it was that weakness was the only political crime. Since the late nineteenth century, few Paraguayan presidents had had more than a few months in office, a year or two at most. Stroessner set out to be different.

There were two potential pillars of power in Paraguay—the army and the right-wing Colorado Party—and it was Stroessner's trick to use each to dominate and control the other. Stroessner became president as the Colorado Party's candidate—he was already commander-in-chief of the army and he then consolidated the army's obedience by making membership in the Colorado Party compulsory for all officers. But the party was the problem: the only reason he had been nominated was because the members of each one of several factions thought they could use Stroessner to destroy the others.

In the first few years, Stroessner set out to purge the party, helped by a young member of it, Edgar Ynsfran. Edgar Ynsfran later became first his chief of police and then his minister of the interior. Ynsfran, supported by a network of informers, turned out to be ruthless. The year after Stroessner was elected he created the legal instrument Ynsfran needed—the 'Law for the Defence of Democracy', under which opposition activity was labelled communist. Stroessner also continued the state of martial law, which suspended all constitutional guarantees and allowed Ynsfran's police to detain and torture whomsoever they chose. Martial law had been in force since 1929.

By the late fifties, however, Stroessner's greatest challenge came from yet another faction in the Colorado Party, whose members wanted an end to the police state and demanded political normalization. Casabianca was among them. He had been a student leader and then a congressional deputy and had supported demands for political reform—an amnesty, a new electoral law, press freedom. The leadership of the Colorado Party then backed the demands as well, and Stroessner appeared to agree.

Shortly afterwards there was a student demonstration, and Stroessner took advantage of it to throw everything into reverse The demonstration was violently repressed and turned into a pitched battle between students and police. When Congress complained, Stroessner dissolved Congress. A reign of terror began. The state of siege, which had been briefly lifted, was reimposed, and a vast round-up, master-minded by Ynsfran, began. Over 400 Colorado politicians who opposed Stroessner were jailed or fled into exile, where they founded the Popular Colorado Movement.

With the crack-down Casabianca went into hiding in the Uruguayan embassy in Asunción. Six months later he left the country. He had always been one of Stroessner's favourites, but thereafter Stroessner persecuted Casabianca wherever he went. 'Stroessner was always very indulgent but finally he would never forgive you if he thought you had betrayed him.' He had a long arm, Casabianca said, and a long memory. Casabianca scraped a living in Buenos Aires, working in the central market, eventually working his way up to be supervisor of supplies to the city's markets. But then, following the *coup* in Argentina in 1976, Casabianca was suddenly thrown out of his job again. 'After that, I did whatever I could, buying and selling, an estate agent for a while. Now here I am, working alongside the people responsible for all those years of persecution.'

Casabianca is a public figure now. He has a huge office in the presidential palace and is greeted with respect in restaurants. He drank several more whiskies and sent the coffee back, complaining it was cold. 'All the waiters here used to be police informers. Now some of them work with us. Now all my friends who weren't around all those years are reappearing. Still, you can't blame people for that. The consequences are too serious here.'

Above: Argentina's President Juan Péron (left) is welcomed to
Paraguay by General Alfredo Stroessner in August 1954.

Driving home, the Special Ambassador to the Presidency fiddled unsuccessfully with the car heater. 'They just gave me this,' he said, 'I still don't know how it works.'

The next morning, I went back to my list of names and numbers. Pappalardo had started as my best hope. Seeing him had left me flat. I needed some allies, some strategic advice. I had the number of a lawyer, Felino Amarillo. I had been told that he would make me laugh and that he could introduce me to the Asunción underworld. I rationalized my need to laugh with the thought that perhaps, if the government wouldn't help, the gangsters might. I never met them; but I did meet Felino.

After a long telephone chase, he turned up at my hotel, lounging there in one of the pompous leather chairs, a slim young man with his black moustache, looking round a lobby that was overflowing at the time with society women rehearsing for a charity fashion show.

I introduced myself.

'Why do you stay in this brothel?' he said.

I rode down to Plaza Independencia on the back of Felino's newly acquired motor bike. He rode a motor bike, he told me later, because he couldn't afford a car. At least, he couldn't afford a legal car. Half the cars in Paraguay were not legal. They had been stolen in Brazil and driven over the border. They are called mau cars, because, like the Mau-mau, they came in the night. It was one of the army's sidelines.

Why didn't he buy one of those?

He gave me a pained look. 'In the first place, I wouldn't buy a mau car. And in the second place, as soon as someone like me did buy a mau car, the police would come and arrest him for having it. You can only drive a stolen car if you are in the police or if you're a friend of a policeman.'

We took the lift to the fifth floor. Someone had scratched the name Felino Amarillo in the paint-work. 'Young people,' Felino observed, 'no standards.'

'Hey, Gordo! [Fatso!]' he yelled, when we got into his office. There was a groan next door. 'Stop sleeping and come here!'

A man appeared, rubbing his face. 'I wasn't sleeping, I was reading.'

Felino bellowed with laughter. 'May I present Dr Rafael Saguier. Rafa, this distinguished English journalist wants to know about Stroessner.'

'*La puta madre*,' said Dr Rafael Saguier.

'Scottish journalist,' I said.

'Make yourself at home,' said Rafael. 'Stroessner. *La puta madre*. We must take her to the *escribano*.'

I never quite understood why I had to see the *escribano*, except that he was considered to be both wise and knowledgeable. For Rafael and Felino it was clearly imperative, in any case, that I did, so I found myself out in the street again, dodging along the narrow pavements, Rafael on one side and Felino on the other, both talking at me, shouting scurrilous Stroessner anecdotes over the roar of the traffic.

It was my turn to be self-conscious. I kept my eyes front, wondering who was watching, who could have seen from a passing car. It was a feeling that I was to have often. Asunción was a small town in which everybody knew everybody. Every time I talked to someone, I wondered who would find out about it, what they would hear. I felt no closer to finding Stroessner, but there was the sense that behind one of those windows there might be people who could, if they chose to, if I could convince them, open the door.

We got to the *escribano*'s office. He sat under a slowly revolving fan in a room shuttered against the sun. 'In Paraguay,' he said, 'the usual gap between the Third World and the developed world is even greater. So what is the aim of ideology? In the underdeveloped world ideology is a system of lies which stimulates people to survive. Truth and science are the monopoly of the developed world. Stroessner was thirty-five years of no truth and no science.'

3

Back in his office, Felino said, 'I'm going to lend you, lend you mind, a real treasure.'

He reappeared a few minutes later with a book. He was hugging himself with glee. He read out the title, *The Golden Book of the Second Reconstruction*, and fell back in his chair, bellowing with laughter. For the Stronato historians, Felino explained, the first 'reconstruction' was that of Bernardino Caballero, a nineteenth-century tyrant who fathered over ninety children and, at the end of his reign, left the country with sound finances, a trick rarely repeated in Paraguayan history. The second 'reconstruction' was Stroessner's. And it was this that *The Golden Book* described.

The prose of *The Golden Book* strains against the outer limits of adulation. When mere words are inadequate to describe the greatness of Stroessner, a common failing apparently, the very type is forced to unnatural extremes. Felino began to read:

> We have seen Alfredo Stroessner, THE LUMINOUS LIGHTHOUSE, in his various facets dissipating the shadows of PARAGUAYAN NIGHT. We have not been able to embrace the totality of his life because that would be a labour requiring more breath than we have . . . We will not enter into an analysis of whether he had or has defects. It is human to have them in the midst of the great virtues which he possesses. But, yes, we consign to you what he once said: 'One cannot be perfect because perfection belongs only to God, but we must try, as far as possible, to reach a degree of perfectibilty which will take us closer to God.'

'What's the book about?' said Felino. 'What's anything about in this country: money and corruption.' Felino showed me the back pages, which were advertisements, the paid and signed subscriptions to the cult of the dictator: '___ _____ would like to congratulate the author on his luminous work of history . . . '
'___ _____, patriot and outstanding citizen, salutes President Stroessner.'

'Outstanding citizen,' snorted Felino, 'he paid to have that advertisement put in. About himself!'

'Look at this one,' Felino said, flipping through the pages, pointing to another advertisement: '*Obra util*. Useful book: declared such by that minister means that every school then had to buy this useful book.'

˙ I took *The Golden Book* back to my hotel and continued to read it, wincing with pain. Every page revealed the writer's effort. There was, for instance, the challenge of turning Stroessner's unremarkable parentage and early life into the nation's destiny. This is what I read of the first meeting between Stroessner's father Hugo, an immigrant German brewer, and the local girl he was to marry:

> A fifteen-year-old girl passed [Hugo] one day and powerfully attracted his attention. In romantic terms, he had been struck by an arrow. He united himself with her. It was an instantaneous decision. HERIBERTA MATTIAUDA, thus was the name of the young woman who moved [Hugo's] most intimate fibres. She was a descendant of a well-known family in the area, and in her were united the features of wit and beauty and the gallantry and the presence that belong to Paraguayan women . . . Heriberta had once read about Charlemagne in a novel, and her suitor was like a Blue Prince, since his eyes were blue.

I read on, by now enjoying the pain. Two sons and a daughter were born, and briefly mentioned. Then came the birth of Alfredo, whose cries 'already seemed to announce a new dawn for Paraguay,' and who, in the eyes of his father, 'had some connection with the product of his labours, seeing him as blond as the liquid product of his noble sacrifices.' I read the sentence again, in disbelief: Alfredo was as blond as a pint of German beer?

Sadly, the effort of this prose proved too great to sustain, and most of *The Golden Book* is a tedious transcription of the official diary. Not a ceremony missed, not a decoration unrecorded. There were many ceremonies, an embarrassment of decorations: natural tributes of a world rushing in to honour the greatness of Alfredo Stroessner. For the outside world, Stroessner was not an unwelcome figure. The United States pumped in military and economic aid, and trained the officers of Stroessner's police and armed forces. He was, after all, a staunch anti-communist. For the Brazilians he was a loyal friend, stability on their southern flank. For his fellow dictators in the 1970s he was a compadre. The international approval rolled in—Order of Merit of Bernardo

O'Higgins, Chile; Order of the Condor of the Andes, Extraordinary Grand Cross, Bolivia; Collar of the Order of the Liberator, Venezuela; Order of Aeronautical Merit, Grand Cross, Venezuela; Grand Cross with Diamonds of the Order of the Sun, Peru; Golden Wings of Uruguay; Honorary Aviator, Chilean Military Medal; and from General Sam Shephard, US Army, the Medal of the Inter-American Junta of Defence. In a lull in the proceedings, he gave himself the Paraguayan Diploma and Brevet of the Naval Pilot.

There was more: the United Arab Republic, Holland and Japan. In 1961, Queen Elizabeth remembered the General and gave him the Order of Victoria (the Caballero Grande, as *The Golden Book* describes it). Prince Philip, Duke of Edinburgh, followed with the Grand Cross of the Knights of the Order of St Michael and St George in 1962, and General de Gaulle pinned the Legion d'Honneur on to what was, by then, one of the most crowded chests in South America.

I trudged on—past sinister photographs of the members of Stroessner's cabinets being sworn in with a straight right arm salute, of a multitude 'delirious with enthusiasm' acclaiming its leader at a rally—searching for some coded trace of reality, some acknowledgement that not everyone had applauded. There was none. There was no mention of the opposition, the dissenters—no name was allowed to challenge the omnipresence of Stroessner's. There were, instead, a number of familiar faces. There was, among them, Conrado Pappalardo in 1969, slimmer and wearing a moustache. 'State Director of Ceremonial,' read the caption, 'a man who, from the first moments was and is at President Stroessner's side.' And there was another name, one that ran like a counterpoint through the diary, heading a delegation here, presiding over a ceremony there, leading the applause at meetings, standing in for the absent president when he went abroad. Over and over again, the name of Juan Ramon Chaves.

Juan Ramon Chaves—his nickname, I learned, was Juancito the Liar—was on my list and I had been trying to find him. Juancito was the man who had run the Colorado Party for Stroessner, frightening off the opposition, delivering the renominations, managing the conventions that rewrote the constitution to prolong

Stroessner's rule. Juancito had been president of the party for twenty-five years, Stroessner's political right arm, until Juancito came out on the wrong side of a party split in August 1987. But when Stroessner was overthrown, Juancito, like Pappalardo, got his old job back. I was told that he was nearly ninety now and was running the party again.

The Colorado Party headquarters is a vast building in the centre of town. Like the Communist Party palaces of Eastern Europe, it is a testament to years of domination and robbery. You approach it up a steep flight of steps from the street and then enter a cavernous hall. Once Stroessner had subdued the internal opposition, the Colorado Party enjoyed huge revenues based on a compulsory subscription from the salaries of all public servants. Everybody had to join, from the humblest army cadet to the beauty queens. It was the patronage machine: local section bosses ruled like petty kings—they enjoyed *mbarete*, or 'clout', and, in return, delivered raised hands at convention time.

Juancito Chaves ran all this, Stroessner's system, one organized along fascist lines with branches in every village and with a network of paid informers. They reported chance remarks, unwise jokes and, of course, conspiratorial intentions. If the penalties for disloyalty were absolute, the rewards for service were great.

The security apparatus, the adjunct to the party network, consumed thirty per cent of state revenues and was sustained by military aid from the United States and from development aid, some of which also went to build the roads and bridges that Stroessner always pointed to as the emblems of his 'modernization' of Paraguay.

In his modernized Paraguay, there was, above all, peace, but it was a peace punctuated with episodes of savage violence directed against peasant organizations, trade unions, the Church or anyone who showed a capacity for organization outside the Colorado Party. The price of peace—a phrase that became part of official terminology—was the division of spoils: monopolies of contraband pacified the military and police—whisky, cigarettes, electronic goods, cars stolen in Brazil—and high officials took a percentage of every government transaction. The Party enjoyed the privileges of the one-party state. And holding it all together, at the centre of the web, the all-pervading image of Stroessner.

He held it all together through fear, but fear was not all. As I talked to people, I realized that Stroessner's domination was a subtle balancing act between co-option and terror, sometimes within the same individual. Those who served him feared him, but serving him was also the quickest way to get rich. And those who were closest to Stroessner were not serving him out of their fear of him, but because they wished to share a little of the power and a lot of the money. Fear was just what the opportunity cost.

He maintained a cynical show of formal legality. When he needed to reinforce the appearance of democracy, he tempted the opposition into co-operation with the promise of participation, then snatched it away. The constitution was amended twice to allow him a further term in office, in 1967, at a constitutional convention attended by almost all political parties—except, of course, the banned Popular Colorado Movement—and again in 1977, to perpetuate his rule for life. Both these conventions were run for him by Juancito the Liar.

Juancito's daily routine was a legend in Asunción. He left his house at dawn and got into his car. He appeared briefly at the party headquarters and then returned to his car. From then until evening, he roamed the town. If Juancito didn't want me to find him, Felino had said, I wouldn't. The only man in Asunción who knew how to find him was the man who brought him cheese from the market.

I made appointments, but he didn't keep them. In the end, I just sat, conspicuously, and waited with the others in the huge hall outside his office, under the eye of his door-keepers, watching his machine at work.

A woman began a litany of complaint. 'They don't let you see the president. They won't let you talk to him. They'll make you wait fifteen days, come back tomorrow, come in the morning, come in the afternoon.' Barefoot shoeshine boys polished the boots of party members. Others appeared, also barefoot, selling the party paper, *Patria*, for years the most unconditional supporter of Stroessner: under Stroessner, all public servants used to subscribe; the money was deducted automatically from their paypackets.

Then came the nod.

Juancito's office was vast. At the far end, crouching next to a bank of telephones behind an immense desk placed beneath an outsized portrait of President Rodriguez, was a shrunken old man. Little Juan the Liar.

'Well, Señora?' He rasped out his words. In the pauses, a little lizard tongue flicked across his lips. 'What do you want, Señora?'

'To talk about Alfredo Stroessner.'

'Who?'

I thought perhaps he was hard of hearing. 'Alfredo Stroessner,' I repeated, louder.

He waved his hand impatiently. 'Oh, I can't talk about that, that's all past. It's a local subject, a subject for us.'

'But you knew him well.'

'No. I didn't admire him. I didn't admire him. I opposed him.'

'But you were close to him for many years.'

'No, no, I opposed him. Let's talk about now, today, about the future.'

He launched into his set-text for foreign journalists—all about the excellent situation of Paraguay now that it had been liberated from the tyranny of Stroessner. Four lines about the economic programme, four lines about the political situation. I dutifully took notes.

'The situation is good, it's democratic, without authoritarianism.'

He slowed down, watching my pen move across the paper, making sure that I kept up, that I got it down precisely.

I had expected a defence, a justification of those long years at Stroessner's side, self-serving but reasoned. An explanation of how, at the end, Stroessner had crossed some final line of tyranny. I was not prepared for his flat denial of involvement.

'Did you know the coup was coming?' I asked him.

He waved his hand in a gesture of dismissal. 'I can't talk about that. It would take too long. But he didn't fall by himself, did he? He fell because something happened. But I can't talk about the past. There is complete freedom of the press here.' He glared at me myopically. 'Nobody bothers you, do they? You can come here in absolute freedom, can't you? Well then.'

The lizard tongue again. The old man's fidgeting. 'Stroessner!' He spat the word out. 'We didn't support Stroessner, we struggled against him for years.' He looked at me, perhaps wondering what I knew. 'At the beginning, he was a man of much hope. But then he made mistakes and made a bad government.'

'Which year was that?' I asked. I knew that Juancito had never defected. He had just been elbowed aside, at the next to the last moment, by the new crowd, the *militantes*.

'I don't remember exactly which year it was. We opposed him for many years. The militants had the power. We had none.'

Juancito had been thrown out of the party presidency on 1 August 1987, at a famous party convention. His faction, the traditionalists, had tried to fight off a takeover by the militants, the young turks who saw their chance to use the last powers of the ageing president to secure the party and the government. They were friends of Stroessner's son Gustavo, and he, it was said, was their candidate for the throne. The traditionalists lost.

'But before that you had power,' I insisted. 'You were a key man through most of the Stroessner years.'

He spluttered with rage. 'No, no. It was Stroessner who had power, who had all the judicial and executive power. We didn't have power. I wasn't a key man in the Stroessner years. I was a key man in the opposition.'

'Did you approve of nothing he did then?' I asked, wondering how far this fantasy would go.

'A few things perhaps,' he said. Stroessner had, he acknowledged, built a little. 'But material things are not the only thing that matter,' said Juancito. 'What matters are the spiritual values of democracy, liberty and justice.' I looked at his huge desk, his bank of phones, trying to find a way through this monstrous lie, some small admission that Juancito might once, perhaps long ago, have supported Stroessner. In the face of this flat contradiction, I would have felt it a victory. But Juancito was a hard man to induce to reflection. His look was growing more venomous. He had begun to chew the air, an old man's habit. The flunkey was entering the middle distance, headed in my direction. Time was running out.

'But your photograph is in *The Golden Book*,' I said.

'*Golden Book*? What *Golden Book*? No such thing. Never

existed.' And then a thought clearly struck him. 'You've seen it? Which one have you seen . . . all three?'

'Yes,' I lied. Three *Golden Books*? I hoped I didn't have to read the other two.

'You've seen all three?' he said. Now he was thinking, talking fast, wondering whether to make an admission. He didn't wonder for long. 'I'm in it, you say? Really? I have never seen it. I didn't know anything about it. Is my signature there? Do you have it with you?' I didn't, and he embarked on his bamboozle-the-jury performance again. 'Someone must have forged my statement. My photograph? I don't know anything about photographs. Talk about the future. That's what matters, not the past.'

He turned the outsized leather swivel-chair towards a phone and picked it up. The grim flunkey gestured me to the door.

'Well, what did he tell you?' asked Felino later. 'He said he was a key man in the opposition,' I said. I thought Felino would never stop laughing.

In the end, there wasn't a politician in Paraguay who had not been formed by Stroessner. For those who played the game, there was a seat in Congress and a share of the spoils. For those who didn't, there was ruin, torture, imprisonment, exile or death. And there were very few who didn't play the game, at least at first. Talking to people in Paraguay is like peeling an onion. The outer skin is anti-Stroessner. Perhaps the next two layers are layers of persecution. But get to the centre and you will come across a layer of co-operation. Juancito the Liar and Pappalardo are collaborationist onions covered over with the thinnest skin of repudiation. But so many of Paraguay's famous opposition figures, heroes of the later years of struggle, have, buried inside, that core of collaboration.

Looking through *The Golden Book* I had found an entry that surprised me: in 1962, it said, President Stroessner inaugurated Radio Nanduti.

I was taken aback. There were two media in Paraguay whose closure had caused an international scandal, and one of them was Radio Nanduti. I remembered running the story at the time, as a short item in the newspaper. It had been a violent affair, in 1986.

CENTRAL SOUTH AMERICA

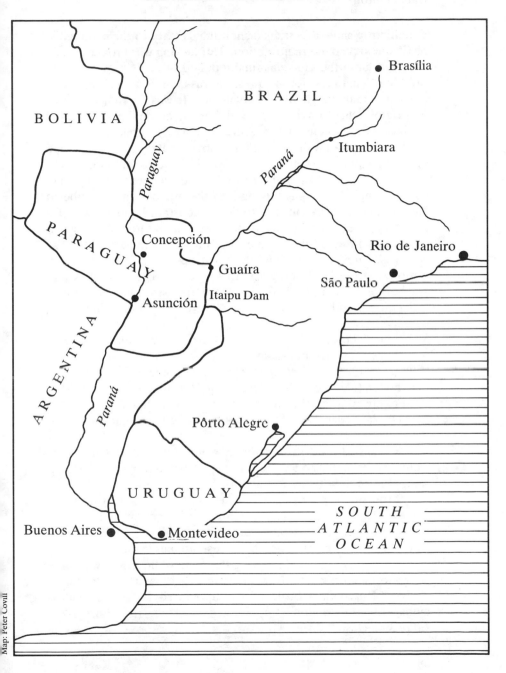

The military arrived in trucks, shouting, 'Death to the communist Jew,' and sacked the radio station. The sacking was broadcast as it occurred, until the plug was finally pulled.

The 'communist Jew' in question was Humberto Rubin, one of the names that everybody had given me. He was the radio station's proprietor, chief broadcaster and known as an intelligent and implacable opponent of Stroessner's. I had planned to see him anyway, but now I wanted to ask him how was it that Stroessner had opened his radio station: just who was Humberto Rubin in 1962?

I was shown into a small shambolic studio where a bearded man with a rumpled face was talking into the microphone. Humberto Rubin seemed to live in the studio, in constant dialogue with his huge audience. The only way to interview him was to be interviewed by him, on air, and squeeze questions into the commercial breaks.

Yes, Rubin said, he had invited Stroessner to open the radio station, not just because he was *El Presidente*, but because Rubin had believed in him. He had believed in Stroessner first because he was grateful and then because he hoped Stroessner would bring democracy.

'Look,' he said, 'from 1947 until Stroessner came to power it was chaos here, parents against children, brother against brother. When someone arrived saying we were now going to live in peace all of us hoped there would be at least some security. Democracy didn't even matter that much. All that mattered was that there were no tanks in the street. Until Stroessner came we never knew who had the power.'

Rubin had thought that things would be hard, but that they would get better. 'The Stroessner chapter was unfortunate,' Rubin said, 'but he didn't create it alone. We all helped.'

Stroessner's other famous closure was that of *ABC Color*, the biggest newspaper in Paraguay before it was shut down in 1984. It has an equally famous proprietor and editor, Aldo Zuccolillo. Zuccolillo comes from one of the richest families in the country. His enemies make a point of insisting that Zuccolillo's family fortune comes from trading in contraband sugar with Paraguay's old enemy, Bolivia. Zuccolillo's brother was appointed by Stroessner as ambassador in London—appointed in fact shortly before *ABC Color* was closed down.

Stroessner closed the paper because it had annoyed him. It had annoyed him because it was publishing about Itaipu.

Itaipu was the most grandiose of many grandiose projects. Its beauty was that it combined several of Stroessner's fetishes—the friendship with Brazil, a project of Pharaonic proportions, electrification and almost unlimited opportunities for corruption.

It was sold as a triumph. The Guaira Falls on the Parana River had been a source of tension between Paraguay, who claimed possession, and Brazil, who occupied them in 1964. In 1966, Stroessner signed the Act of Iguazu with Brazil, agreeing to joint exploitation of the enormous hydro-electric potential of the falls and thus implicitly relinquishing Paraguay's claim to sole possession. In 1973, with the Treaty of Itaipu, construction of the dam was agreed. It was to be financed by loans raised by Brazil, and Paraguay was to pay off its share by selling back to Brazil, at preferential rates, most of the electricity produced.

Many Paraguayans believed the treaty made Paraguay into a virtual colony of Brazil. Paraguay had little control over the cost of the dam, which rose from the original estimate of 1.8 billion dollars to seventeen billion. And in return, Paraguay received only about fifteen per cent of the contracts.

But the impact of that fifteen per cent on the tiny economy of Paraguay was staggering. The money had never rolled so freely. 'Before Itaipu, the Paraguayan upper classes' idea of a good time was to go on a trip to Buenos Aires,' said Felino. 'Then they suddenly had so much money they didn't know what to do with it.' Asunción became a sybaritic society. Petty officials who had lived in miserable little houses suddenly had two cars and domestic servants and Asuncion had more Mercedes than any other capital in Latin America. 'We were all corrupted,' said a friend. 'We all got used to drinking French wine and eating Dutch cheese, to having dishwashers and videos.' Mass opposition was tranquillized by the flood of money. 'If Stroessner had retired in 1980,' said Paul Lewis, author of a study on Stroessner, 'he would probably have gone down as a great president.'

Paradoxically, for Zuccolillo, Itaipu was a catalyst that forced him into taking up with the opposition and that led to the closure of his newspaper. He told me his story, one that I was finding increasingly familiar: how at first he had supported Stroessner; how, in the late 1960s, that support had become a qualified one, followed by disillusionment and then opposition and finally repression. Even so, *ABC Color*'s record is one of courage. In the seventeen years the paper published, Zuccolillo's journalists were jailed on thirty-two occasions. It became the practice for everyone to keep an overnight bag in the office, in case of arrest, and Zuccolillo himself was in jail twice. The end came in March 1984, also a familiar story: fifty police with machine-guns, a man with a piece of paper on which was written the charge—promoting hatred amongst Paraguayans.

Between the closure of *ABC Color* and the coup, every paper in the country that wasn't owned by a Stroessner friend or relative was either closed or its staff harassed. The opposition weeklies *El Enano*, *El Radical*, *Dialogo*, *La Republica* and *El Pueblo* all went. The staff of *Nuestro Tiempo*, a church-backed monthly, was persecuted. Radio Caritas, also backed by the Church, tried to fill in some of the space left by Radio Nanduti and was told to stick to prayer.

After the February coup, *ABC* came back and Zuccolillo had fun exposing the crimes of his fallen adversaries. He published a series of articles on the fabulous mansions built by Stroessner functionaries, and his guided tour—'the tour of Asunción's corruption,' as he calls it—is on the itinerary of every visiting journalist. The tour includes the market, where the contraband ranges from cases of Scotch to plastic buckets from Brazil; the Central Bank building, which contains an Olympic-sized swimming-pool and a theatre, true cost unknown; the mansions of the Stroessner clan, family and mistresses, former ministers and army officers. Zuccolillo's own home is also a mansion; in fact it is a mansion as large as most of those on his tour, as his wife was the first to point out to me.

The tour also includes General Rodriguez's French château, though that was left out of the newspaper series.

I asked him why.

'Because of what he did in February,' he said. 'I have forgiven all his sins.'

4

I was still looking for Stroessner.

Juancito Chaves hadn't helped, even with his memories; in their way, both Rubin and Zuccolillo had, but they didn't know Stroessner's whereabouts. I had searched through the official histories for clues to the man behind the deadly prose. I had walked around his city, trying to imagine how it was when his presence filled it. Nobody would admit to being in touch with him. Those who wanted me to talk to him couldn't help. Those who might have helped didn't want to.

But I was beginning to understand why he fell. After the easy money that followed the Treaty of Itaipu, his own system had begun to rot. By the time the dollars stopped flowing in, his two pillars, the army and the party, were crumbling. But there was also something else. There was social protest.

There were peasants demanding land, citizens demanding human rights and the Church, steadily, quietly, preaching solidarity and justice. In the land of no-science and no-truth, there were now groups burrowing away in the structure of the big lie, collecting information, writing news-letters, worrying the system. The Data Bank was one of them.

The Data Bank's members always knew that information was subversive, but they never knew what information exactly would bring the police down on them. When Stroessner's police finally raided, they didn't just take away the people; they stripped the place bare. Typewriters, photocopiers, even the electric wiring out of the walls—all of it went (and when they raided a home, they took everything down to the last pair of socks). Even afterwards, no one could be sure what it was that they had done, this time. José Carlos Rodriguez, a sociologist at the Data Bank, one day found himself on the run with an order out to shoot him on sight. He escaped by hiding in the belly of the beast, taking a military flight to the Brazilian border, then hitching a ride with a police chief. 'Nobody checks the papers of anybody who's with a police chief,' he said. Back home, the police followed his child for six months, waiting for the father to make contact.

Rodriguez at least knew he was guilty, even if he wasn't sure of what. But there were many who were genuinely innocent: when the Data Bank was raided, a passer-by, who had gone inside to use the lavatory, was arrested with all the others. Who could know when he would be released? A famous case is Nelson Ortigoza's. What he did, if anything, is now so lost in myth and counter-myth that it has ceased to be the point of the story. Nelson Ortigoza was in solitary confinement for twenty-five years. For the last two, his cell was bricked up. He was eventually released into house arrest, but escaped, helped in fact by my two friends Felino and Rafael. They say that when Stroessner heard the news he had a coughing fit that lasted four hours.

The resistance was growing, nevertheless, and, as more and more people were prepared to protest, more lawyers were emerging prepared to defend them. One of them was Pablo Vargas. Vargas had been in prison sixteen times, beginning in 1956 when he was thirteen. He was tortured four times, the first time when he was sixteen. In one session in 1969 he lost a kidney.

Vargas worked for the Church Committee, an inter-denominational body that had been set up in response to a particularly brutal repression of a peasant organization in 1976.

I asked him if his work had been dangerous, and he gave me a weary look. We were sitting in a cool, whitewashed room, shafts of sunlight filtering through the shutters. I waited for him to answer, half-listening to the murmur of the street below. My question, I realized, must have sounded banal.

'I saw many people die under torture,' he said finally. 'People used to ask me why didn't I write about it, but I never wanted to because torture is something that nobody can describe. At one time I went to see all the films in which there was torture to see if it could be portrayed, but I found it was romanticized, idealized. What I saw on the screen seemed to me like a game for children.'

A person who is tortured, he said, becomes an animal. 'It's the most miserable thing there is. They tell you, "Rest. We will come for you at three o'clock." And you watch the time pass. If they don't come you pray that they have forgotten or that they have gone for somebody else.'

Inside those jails, the routine of torture had its own ritual, one that the prisoners got used to. When they heard loud music, they knew that, for somebody, the dance had begun. 'I remember the *pileta*,' he said. The *pileta* is popular in Latin America. It is simple, cheap and effective. It consists of holding a prisoner's head down in bath water until he is nearly drowned. Then you haul him out. Then you put him back. Sometimes the water is clean, sometimes it's sewage. 'It was just a metal bath,' said Vargas. 'It had feet like lion's claws. How often did I lie on the ground, looking at those feet?'

He was hunched over in his chair, looking at his hands. He stopped suddenly and looked round. The room was silent.

'Why am I talking about this? I have never talked about this.' He shrugged, his chair creaked. 'When they begin,' he continued, 'you are naked. Your hands and feet are tied. The bath had one tap, and I would lie there, listening to that tap running, to the sound of the water changing as the bath filled, trying to guess how deep it was.'

He looked up. 'The *picana* [electric prod] and the *pileta* don't hurt, you know. People think they do, that the torture is pain. It's not pain. It's worse than pain. It's like a small death each time: you long for pain in the end. It's better to feel pain than that absolute despair. When they use the *picana*, you think you are going to explode.'

'You talk to your torturer,' he continued, 'about anything. About fishing or food, trying to postpone the moment. The torturers tell you that they don't like doing it and ask you to help stop it, to tell them something. But there's nothing you can tell them. I have seen people tortured for twenty-nine days on end.

'I could guess from the way they walked which one was coming for me. They were all different. Normally an interrogator would torture a man for half an hour at a time; then there would be another one, and then it would be back to the first. Sometimes they would torture two at a time, all the while comparing observations. And sometimes there were sessions that lasted four to five hours at a time, and during them they would talk about your performance. They killed a man once within the first half-hour, and they were very contemptuous of him. They'd had a girl of eighteen who had survived hours of it. "What kind of a man would die after half an hour?" they said. A good torturer doesn't kill. You knew, if they broke somebody's bones, it was because they were going to kill him.'

Torture had left him with bad dreams, he said, but he wasn't unusual. 'In Paraguay, fear was like a second skin, something we all wore on top of our normal skin.'

Today, Vargas is a senator. He is forty-six. Of the seventeen people who were in the leadership of his party when he was twenty-two, five are still alive. 'You feel like an old man, at forty-six,' he said. 'Stroessner stole thirty-five years of my life. Thirty-five years of systematic human rights violations while the rest of the world was completely silent. One of my friends was arrested at nineteen and got out at forty. There were people who were in jail for twenty-two years without trial. There were cases of mistaken identity in which the accused were released after six months, but there were others in which they were forgotten for ten years.'

Like the man in the lavatory of The Data Bank, I thought, wondering how long it would be before he was set free.

I walked back towards the centre of town, to get some air, and found myself in the square, looking at the neo-classical Congress building. In front of it was a little Bolivian tank, a trophy from the Chaco War, painted the same municipal green as the benches and the little bronze statues that had been imported from France. The heat was suffocating except for a light breeze.

I sat on an empty bench and looked at the statue of Mariscal Francisco Solano Lopez, president of Paraguay from 1865 until his death in the disastrous War of the Triple Alliance in 1870. Lopez had nearly wrecked Paraguay, having been lured into a war against Argentina, Brazil and Uruguay; and, by the end, half of Paraguay's population was dead. The last battles were fought by children from the cadet school, with painted-on moustaches.

Someone told me that his rearing horse had started out on ground level—it now rests on an oversized plinth—but the children used to daub him with paint. I liked the idea of the children's revenge.

Behind me was the police headquarters. It takes up an entire block. The torture chambers were 300 yards from where I was sitting. Could the street noises be heard in the cells? What would it be like, to listen to the footsteps, people coming and going, indifferent? Almost everybody I met seemed to have been in jail. It was almost a commonplace, but few paraded their suffering.

Sometimes there would be a look: it was like the look you imagine crossing a soldier's face when a kid asks, 'What's war like?' Sometimes you could tell that there were questions that were being thought but not asked: Where were you when it was happening? Were yours among the indifferent pairs of feet I listened to from my cell? Why do you come now, wanting to know, when it's all over? Where were you with your questions when my son was kidnapped outside my front door, when my brother was exiled, when I was in the *pileta*?

I went to have a coffee with Felino.
'You want to know where they tortured people?' he asked.
'Everywhere.'
I wanted a list.
We went out on to the balcony and looked down on the city. It was late afternoon, and the roofs were bathed in a rich, golden light. Felino began to point out the buildings which had cells and torture chambers. After five, I stopped taking notes.

Rafael had been in most of them, said Felino. The windows of Rafael's office, next door, had much the same view. I wondered: what did he think when he looked out?

'Jail wasn't so bad,' said Rafael. 'All the nicest people were there. One time I met a kid whose only crime was that he was a brilliant basketball player. His team was coming up against a general's team, so the general had him arrested.'

I was getting depressed, wondering what I was going to say about Stroessner's Paraguay that didn't make it sound like a bad novel with an exotic backdrop: the comic opera dictator with the oversized hat, covered in gold braid. And where was the man, at the heart of it all? Nobody could tell me. They all had their own, oversized image. I was beginning to hear the same stories.

What made him laugh? I asked.

People stared back.

I phoned home, upbraiding them for the pain of my own absence, for the frustration of the story. My daughter had had an accident, in the playground, a cut over her eye. She was fine, I was told. I put the phone down and began to cry with the shame of not being there.

I turned over my notes, wondering if I had enough to stop.

I could see how it had all begun to fall apart, around the ageing dictator. He grew tired and no longer put in the hours. He began to ramble on old themes, to go off and play cards and chess with his cronies, to visit his mistress. His health began to give him trouble, and he didn't like it.

What I didn't know was how he felt about it. Whether he knew that he was losing his grip. What did he think about when he took off the gold braid and climbed into bed? Did he worry about his paunch? Did he notice his legs were growing thin? Did the decay of his body disturb him as he took those young women to bed?

I felt I hadn't made sense of the women and it annoyed me. I wanted to know what it was like to be debauched by Stroessner. Did his subjects admire him for his appetite for teenage girls or detest him for his insistence on his rights as the national stud?

And why so many? Had he mixed up his appetite with his sense of national destiny? It wasn't an entirely idle question. There had never been enough settlers in Paraguay. There had been too many wars, too many exiles. Everybody had a story of a grandmother, an aunt or even a mother abducted when a schoolgirl by a predatory male.

Stroessner's neglected wife, Dona Eligia, was more pitied than resented. Behind the official first family pomp, people said, was a *campesina* who chewed tobacco, a concubine from his days as a junior officer whom he kept on as a wife, a prisoner of his insistence on the myth of official respectability. She could be got into evening dress for state occasions, but mostly she kept in the background, bringing up their three children, Gustavo, Freddie and Graciella in the official residence on Avenida Mariscal Lopez. Stroessner had separate quarters at the back.

Stroessner did not build lavish mansions on every corner. The public myth is of a man who lived ascetically, though, as someone pointed out, why bother, when the whole country is yours? But his way of affirming the reality of his possession, his absolute right, was through the women. The younger, it seemed, the better. His annual pilgrimage round the high schools presenting diplomas was mentioned in *The Golden Book*. The President, it said, took a keen interest in education. From the school platforms he would inspect the rows of schoolgirls and, when he spotted one he liked, she would be delivered to him.

In the early years, a Colonel Perreira acted as procurer for Stroessner. There was little point in resisting, and, in any event, the girls and their families were well rewarded. 'You had hit the jackpot if your daughter came to the notice of a *capo*,' said Rafael, 'and if it was Stroessner, well, your dreams were made of gold.' Nobody knows exactly how many girls there were, or how many children he had by them. When he tired of the girls, Stroessner had them married off to army officers who swallowed their pride and acknowledged his children as their own. But one or two lasted long enough to become public figures in their own right. I had tried to find some of these women. I talked to one on the phone, but she wouldn't meet me. I talked to people who knew them, slightly, but it was gossip, funny stories of other boy-friends hiding on the roof when the General called unexpectedly. Nobody seemed to know or care what they really felt.

Then I met a woman who did, a friend of Maria Estela Legal, known as Nata, Stroessner's most famous mistress. 'I'll tell you about her,' she said. 'But don't use my name. I was just her friend, nothing political. Just her friend.'

Nata's story, she told me, was a very Paraguayan one. She was the natural child of parents who each married somebody else. Stroessner picked her out of a school procession, when Nata was fifteen, and her mother gladly sold her.

Since she was too young to be given a house of her own, Nata was sent to live with one of Stroessner's generals and his wife. The girl spent the first few months weeping with misery, but gradually resigned herself to her situation. In any event, there was no choice.

Stroessner talked to her regularly, took her on fishing trips. 'He probably showed her the first real kindness she had known,' said her friend. Nata became pregnant, and after her first daughter was born she was given her own house, where Stroessner would visit, every afternoon. She had a second daughter two years later.

Nata could have anything she wanted—cars, money, jobs for the relations who came flocking round. Her friend insists she didn't abuse her power. She was nearly arrested once, by a zealous and ill-informed policeman who pointed out that the car, a present from the president, had no number-plates. She didn't make a fuss, said her friend, and would have gone to the police station, but a street-wise kid selling chewing-gum alerted the policeman to the fact that he was on the brink of an important career error.

But it was a lonely life. In official circles, the done thing was to support the myth of the first family. At Nata's parties it was always the same crowd, a couple of generals, a senator, her doctor, a plastic surgeon and two or three friends. Nevertheless Stroessner was devoted to both her and the daughters.

He went shopping at the supermarket himself and then went round to cook them meals. He helped the girls with their homework and was always there for birthday parties, answering the door himself. 'He loved them, in his way,' said her friend, 'but I couldn't have stood it. He was so authoritarian. They were never allowed to wear trousers because he said it was unfeminine. And he was fantastically jealous. Whenever Nata went out, he had her followed. I have seen him following her himself, all alone in a black car.'

Nata, as she grew older, tried to escape several times. Once, after a row about one of Stroessner's many other amours, she left. She went to Switzerland and married an Italian antique dealer. Stroessner was desperate. He did everything to get her back. He hung on to the daughters, then aged eleven and thirteen. Nata was away for six months and then returned to visit her children, intending to stay for two weeks. She stayed three months. The Italian husband became jealous.

It was an impossible situation and eventually she came back. She had been married about four years. 'It was so sad,' said her friend. 'She had been such a different person in Switzerland. She was able to go out, have a coffee, talk and laugh, just like anyone else.'

She was back but she was still lonely. Eventually she persuaded

Stroessner that she needed to marry. A husband was found, an architect. The wedding was held in a house she had shared with Stroessner by the lake in San Bernardino, fifty kilometres from Asunción. The guests, on entering, walked under a large portrait of the president hanging in the entrance. None of Stroessner's friends went.

After the marriage, it was business as usual, except for the husband, whose presence clearly irritated the General. Stroessner continued visiting the house that he had built for Nata on the airport road, always after the regular Thursday meetings of the army chiefs that he chaired as commander-in-chief, but on several other days too. At first the husband waited on the veranda but finally he was told to remove himself further and he took to playing bingo in a hall near the house. As it happened, the bingo hall belonged to Gustavo Stroessner. Stroessner was visiting Nata when the *coup* started.

5

People had begun to feel that change was coming. Dr Casabianca felt it. He had returned to Paraguay in 1983 after the newly elected President Alfonsin in Argentina had interceded on behalf of the exiled members of the Popular Colorado Movement. (Stroessner said that of course there was no problem, the members of the Movement had always been free to return, and that they should have asked sooner.) Dr Casabianca returned the next week and then spent the next five years being followed, harassed and arrested. When he was in prison in December 1988—one of the last political prisoners of the Stronato—he said he felt then there was a change coming. 'The police were polite to me. It was as though they knew it couldn't last.'

The issue, finally, was the succession.

In most ways, Andres Rodriguez was the natural successor to Stroessner. For years he had been part of the corrupt inner circle. He had grown rich in the drugs traffic and had invested in land, breweries and a currency-exchange empire. By the 1980s he had shown signs of becoming nearly as respectable a businessman as Paraguay permits. He was commander of the cavalry, a key army corps, and he had a dynastic connection through the marriage of his daughter to Stroessner's son, Freddie. For all these reasons, he was seen by the militants as the principal threat to Gustavo's succession.

Gustavo had acquired a reputation for brutishness and greed, which might not have done him any harm, but also for homosexuality, which certainly did. If the father lived austerely, the children squandered lavishly. Local journalists estimate Gustavo's winnings—culled from gambling, the drug trade and a string of 'business' interests—at 100 million dollars. His rise in the armed forces was viewed with resentment, and it ate away the foundations of Stroessner's second pillar of power.

The militants—new money and friends of Gustavo—had won control of the party at the disastrous and violent convention in 1987. Juancito the Liar and his friends were ignominiously thrown out, and Sabino Montanaro was elected the new party president. He was also minister of the interior, had part of the stolen car concession, sold passports and dabbled in narcotics. He had been excommunicated at one point, for torturing priests.

The plan, people now say, was to call another constitutional convention and make Gustavo vice-president, ready to shove him upwards when the vacancy appeared. Gustavo's friends and several die-hard militants deny this; some thoughtful bystanders wonder if Gustavo wasn't so unpromising that even the militants had their doubts. Whatever the plan, it was true that this was the last, truly decadent stage of the Stronato, a combination of grand larceny and radical violence in the face of decay and no control.

The displaced Colorados plotted their revenge and the times were with them. Things were moving on the streets, strikes and demonstrations, backed by a Church led by the wise and courageous Archbishop Abimael Rolon. In January 1989, Gustavo was promoted to colonel and 150 officers above him were retired. Many of them were Rodriguez's cronies, and Rodriguez began to smell a rat. The junior officers, for their own reasons, were bordering on a revolt. Rodriguez realized he was about to be caught between his junior officers—he would be engulfed in their revolt— and the new militant faction. And then Rodriguez was warned— people say that it was Pappalardo—that Stroessner planned to retire him. That was why, the story goes, Rodriguez pretended to have broken his leg and did not attend the usual Thursday general staff meeting, the week of the *coup*.

They moved the next day.

Ammunition and radios for the *coup* had been supplied by some wealthy industrialists, as, even in his decline, Stroessner was too canny to hand out too many bullets to his own army. In the afternoon, Nata's house was attacked: Stroessner was there having his customary siesta. His bodyguard gave the old man enough cover to allow him to escape, and he went off with his own élite unit, the presidential guard, although even here, few fought with any conviction. His generals had so long neglected military affairs that they could scarcely remember how to give orders, and the tanks in the élite unit couldn't move because the man with the keys was out of town. Only around the police headquarters was there serious fighting. By the next morning, Stroessner and his family were packed off on a flight to Brazil, and there was dancing in the streets.

Felino told me how he went out looking for a statue to topple. 'They were surprisingly hard to find. After thirty-five years we finally noticed he didn't put up statues.'

Felino found one in the end and knocked it over.

Some peasants occupied the cathedral hoping now that the dictator had gone they might get some land. The chief of police accused them of being communists and produced as evidence a tin of Russian prawns that he claimed they had been eating.

Nata put to rights the house and grounds that had been ravaged by the assault and sat down to await developments, consoling her daughters, who were, perhaps, the only people in Paraguay who genuinely mourned the exile of their father. The younger one stood out in the wrecked garden, it was reported, watching Stroessner's plane fly off, tears pouring down her face.

6

I had a pile of notebooks; I had a new circle of friends; I was even beginning to fall into the routine of life in Asunción. But I hadn't found Stroessner. I felt frustrated: I wasn't really any closer to finding him than I when I arrived. I had one last hope—the militants

Above: General Alfredo Stroessner at a military parade in 1982.

who had kept the faith. The important ones were in jail, and I wasn't allowed to see them. But there were one or two others, lesser figures, who had not been arrested. One was Benitez Rickman.

Benitez Rickman is a notary public, but in the last fifteen months of the regime he had been the minister of public relations. I couldn't say, from the evidence, that he had done a brilliant job, but it had become a hard item to sell. I had seen him once before in his office, a room filled with German military regalia, mementoes of his grandfather, and Stroessner souvenirs: photographs of Rickman and the General, newspaper cuttings about the great man. Rickman had advanced the theory that Stroessner had been punished by both the Russians and the Americans. I was sure he had stayed in touch.

I had listened sympathetically and was rewarded with an invitation to his house, to look through his library. I went, thinking that perhaps I could pass some test and be given Stroessner's telephone number in Brazil. My appearance at the gate of his mansion sent his Alsatian dogs into a tedious frenzy. I began to feel that I should have known better.

There was another guest sitting in the study, an Argentine man in his sixties from the provincial town of Salta. His hair was dyed an implausible chestnut. He wore an extravagantly double-breasted brown suit; a shirt with red, white and blue stripes; and a paisley cravat. He talked incessantly, between long pulls of beer, in a voice like a band-saw, fidgeting from chair to chair. He was introduced as an old friend of the family.

The maid brought some red caviare. 'What's this?' the family friend croaked. 'Red caviare. Shouldn't caviare be black? Is it Chinese?'

I made a joke about Russian prawns, but nobody laughed.

The Argentine talked on and on, about the purity of the Argentine 'race' and his own European ancestry. Then he got on to Jews.

Benitez Rickman's Stroessner library was the largest collection I had seen of official eulogy: *The Golden Books* (all three), *Panorama* magazine, glossy brochures for the public works, treatises on Latin American genealogy that were beached on the further shores of social Darwinism.

Could Rickman really be serious?

The evidence suggested that even my host, who must be among Stroessner's most ardent admirers, had not managed to get very far through his own collection: *Alfredo Stroessner, Politics and Strategy of Development*; *Stroessner, Defender of the Democratic Institutions*. There were Stroessner's acceptance speeches on his many nominations. There were the rally speeches: Stroessner on democracy and communism; Stroessner on communism and democracy. There was a commemorative volume published in 1987, the centenary of the founding of the Colorado Party, with chapter headings like 'The Unity of the Colorado Party is the Basis of Public Peace.' 'Never again,' ran the text, 'must it be admitted that a Colorado is the enemy of another Colorado. The best friend of a Colorado is another Colorado.' *Stroessner, Imbatible*—this title was heavily underlined, especially at the beginning. I pictured Benitez Rickman, in an evening of especial piety, sitting down to study and learn, even to memorize passages. But the underlining stopped abruptly after the first twenty pages. I felt touched. It had defeated him, too.

There were souvenirs as well. Benitez Rickman showed me a bottle of champagne, presented to Stroessner. 'That champagne costs 400 dollars a bottle,' he said, laying the bottle carefully back in its presentation case.

Meanwhile, the Argentine was becoming embarrassing.

Our host fidgeted. 'My friend is a bit of a Nazi,' he said with a laugh. Then he lapsed into silence, visibly dejected by the impossibility of shutting up his guest without breaching the rules of hospitality. He shrank into his leather armchair and stared at the wreckage of the red caviare. The Argentine poured another glass of beer which foamed over on to the tray. I picked up yet another book, *Stroessner City, the Construction of the Century*.

'Can you put me in touch with President Stroessner?' I asked Benitez Rickman.

'Why?' he said, as had so many others. I always thought it was an odd question. 'What do you want to talk to him about?'

'His thirty-five years in power,' I said.

'He isn't seeing anyone. He can't talk about politics in his situation.'

I had asked so many people the same question. I had asked a friend of Gustavo's, a businessman who had told me about the exemplary family life the Stroessners led.

Was he in touch? Would he send a letter for me? A copy of *Granta*? The editor had thought it would help.

The businessman promised he would, but his expression of studied innocence told me that it probably wouldn't get further than the waste-paper basket. I had begun to give up hope of getting at Stroessner through Paraguay. I had begun to give up hope of getting at Stroessner.

It was the next morning when the phone rang in my room. It was a call from Brazil, where I had some lines trailing in the water. I had become so discouraged in Paraguay that I had almost forgotten them. Suddenly it seemed as though there was a way of delivering a letter, if I was still interested.

I had a letter. I had carried it around, trying to find a way of sending it. It was letter from the editor of *Granta*, to Stroessner. At the time it had seemed like a good idea. I took it out and read it through, wondering whether I really wanted to send it. Tactically, I had to admire it, but it still made me squirm.

I visited Felino.

'Does Stroessner read English?' I asked.

Felino spluttered into his *mate*. 'No! He's underdeveloped. Like me.'

Well, you'll have to help me translate this, I told him.

But then I had to give up on Felino. Even as a joke, he couldn't bring himself to get the tone right. We called in Rafael's wife Solange.

She read the letter and gave me an ironic look. 'You want to talk about his achievements? Is this for real?'

I fidgeted. Well, I said, I want his point of view.

'You'll get it, I'm sure,' she said tartly. 'Except that he won't see you.' Solange added some touches of her own.

Do you have a doctorate? she asked.

No, I said, I never completed my thesis.

What was it about? she asked.

Metaphysical Chinese poetry in 1920s Shanghai, I said. That, I added, was why I never finished it.

'I think you deserve a doctorate,' she said, inserting '*Doctora*' in the text.

I took the letter back to the hotel to fax it to Brazil. The receptionist stared at me but decided against comment.

That night I went out to dinner with Rafael and Solange, to the Yacht Club, a grandiose development where the rich and their children idle at the weekends. 'You could drop a bomb on this place,' said Rafael, 'and not damage humanity one bit.' At dinner Rafael and Solange told stories about their adventures in the opposition: how Rafael went into the cathedral on the day of the March for Life, one of the last, great demonstrations, disguised as a woman. His wife began to laugh and soon none of us could stop.

'You should have seen him,' said Solange, tears rolling down her face, 'in my fish-net tights and a skirt he borrowed from his mother, tittupping along in high heels. He was just like Benny Hill. Everyone who saw him said, "Look, there's Dr Rafael Saguier dressed as a woman."'

'There were supposed to be more of us,' said Rafael, trying to rescue his dignity. 'A group of seminarists was supposed to come but the bastards pulled out. So there I was, all by myself, in the darkest corner of the cathedral, carefully taking off my fish-net tights, when this priest finds me and threatens to call the police if I don't leave immediately. Call the police! They were ten-deep outside. You can imagine what it would have done to my reputation to be arrested disguised as a woman.'

'But why, Rafa?' I gasped, helpless with laughter myself, 'why did you go to the cathedral disguised as a woman?'

'To occupy it, of course.'

'*Gordo*,' said his wife, wiping her eyes and putting her arm round him. 'You were a lovely woman . . . '

The story was almost over and I missed my children. I had been told for two weeks that Stroessner was unseeable, and I was resigned to a few days of boredom in Brasília for form's sake. I said goodbye to my friends.

'Come back soon,' said Rafael, 'and we'll write a book

about Napoleon Ortigoza and his twenty-five years in solitary confinement.'

I promised I would.

7

Stroessner had begun his exile, appropriately enough, in Itumbiara, as the guest of Brazil's electricity company, but the locals complained and the governor was hostile. There had been too much contraband, he said, too many murders. Stroessner moved to his own beach house in Guaratuba, but that didn't last either: it turned into one of the most popular stake-outs in the history of journalism, a long beach party. They moved on again, while Gustavo looked round Brasília for a house. Stroessner's wife and family went to Miami. Perhaps Dona Eligia, like Nata, saw her chance of freedom. Gustavo, for whom there was an implausible extradition request, stuck close to his father, counting on the Brazilians to look after him. Stroessner was reported to want to go to the United States, but it was made clear that he would be turned down.

I had forgotten what a vision of hell Brasília was: the illegitimate offspring of an intellectual love affair between an architect and a dictator. Everyone must have cheated on the contracts, because what had once been intimidatingly new was now shabby and peeling. I was in Metropolis, locked in the past's vision of the future. I felt nostalgic for Asunción's haphazard charm. I chain-smoked and looked out of the window of my hotel, watching the traffic accidents five floors below. It was a landscape of modernist blocks marching across bleak open spaces. In the afternoon, the sky blackened and a deluge hosed all the people off the landscape.

I looked down the list of people I might call, at least to avoid eating alone for three days. But first, I rang my contact.

'It's all fixed,' he said.

'What do you mean, fixed?'

'The gentleman you want to see has said yes. Let me give you his telephone number.'

'He said yes?' I repeated foolishly.

I began to feel as though I was in a bad film. I rang the number
and got Gustavo. He was extremely affable. There had been some
awful casting error. It was the wrong movie.

'We were expecting your call. When do you want to come? Are
you alone? I think I should come and meet you at your hotel to
discuss how to proceed.'

The catch, I thought. He'll come. He'll smell a rat.

But he kept on phoning after that. He dropped the idea of
coming and rang instead with questions that, asked by someone
else, would have been endearing. 'Would it be all right if we don't
wear suits?' he asked.

Quite all right, I said.

'You won't take pictures, will you, if we're not in suits?'

Wouldn't dream of it.

They would send a car, he said, to my hotel. He rang back
again, to reconfirm the time.

I was alone in Brasília. There was nobody I could tell. I turned
on the air-conditioning unit, and it fell out of the wall. I phoned
Cambridge. I phoned London. I phoned Florida to talk to Paul
Lewis. What would he ask Stroessner? I asked him. I found myself
worried. I imagined myself forgetting to ask the most obvious
question, paralysed by the absurdity of the situation.

I went out to buy a camera and got soaked, somewhere in no
man's land. That night I went through my notebooks. I couldn't
think of a single thing I could ask him that he would possibly want to
tell me.

I waited in the lobby for the car. It was a long wait of a kind I
had had before, a woman hanging around a hotel lobby, trying
simultaneously to look out for one particular stranger yet avoid eye
contact with all the others. A blue Chevrolet Commodore pulled up
outside and a burly Brazilian got out. He struggled with my name at
reception. We pulled out into the traffic and took the road to the
South Lake Residential Zone, over the bridge and into Sector Nine,
medium to senior bureaucrat-grade villas with small swimming-
pools and hibiscus hedges. We pulled up, the car's nose pointing at a
high metal gate. The driver hooted his horn. The gate opened, and
we drove straight into a garage.

Gustavo was there, waiting in the garage. He opened the door of the car, and we greeted each other warmly. He was effusively welcoming.

'Are you sure,' he asked, 'that you don't mind the sneakers?'

He apologized his way up a path of stepping stones that had been set into a spongy tropical lawn. 'You must excuse the conditions in which we have to receive you. We still haven't got all our things yet. It was all rather hurried, leaving. We are rather camping here, birds of passage, you might say.' The front door opened on to a living-room, furnished with brocade chairs. It was tasteful, I thought, and realized I was childishly disappointed. Opposite the door, French windows stood open on a garden, and I glimpsed a swimming-pool. It was very quiet, except for the crickets.

I turned round from the garden at the moment the General made his entrance. It was as though the photographs had come alive. That heavy face, the pouchy blue eyes, the full underlip beneath the moustache and the slightly receding chin that folded into a flabby neck. His blue-silk suit was carefully buttoned over a paunch. The General was clearly not given to sneakers.

'Welcome,' he said, 'a great pleasure to receive you.' We shook hands, and he gestured me to one of a group of chairs arranged around a glass coffee-table. He sat, quite still, on an upright chair while Gustavo lounged and fidgeted in an armchair opposite me.

Stroessner cleared his throat and began to make a speech. 'In Paraguay,' he said, 'there was democracy. A fully democratic system, with absolute independence of the judges and the parliament. Then there was great progress. Great progress. Development.' He stopped.

I fished the tape recorder out of my bag and put it on the table. Gustavo was still fussing.

'This isn't going to be published here, is it?' he asked. 'We . . .'

The General interrupted. 'We can't make any statements here. We can't talk about the internal politics of Paraguay.' My heart sank. 'A lot of people have asked for interviews, but we have said no. This is a special case. But we are in political asylum. We have to be careful.'

I wondered why they had made an exception. Occasionally, walking down a street in Asunción, there had flashed into my mind the preposterous thought that my package had reached them and that the two of them were sitting poring over *Granta*. It had made me laugh out loud. I recalled once sitting in the Moneda Palace in Santiago, Chile, in deep conversation with one of Pinochet's close political advisors, certain that at any moment someone would burst through the door and bundle me out of the room, shouting that it was a case of mistaken identity. Now, I kept expecting the telephone to ring, and some security man to tip them off, or perhaps a loyalist in Asunción who had seen me laughing in a café with the wrong people. I wondered if he knew anything about me, about the people I had been seeing. At any moment, I felt, the director would shout, 'Cut!' But he didn't.

Stroessner showed no signs of resuming his speech. Perhaps that was it. His statement had been made.

'Where shall we begin?' I said. 'Perhaps you could tell me something about your early life, your childhood.'

Stroessner cleared his throat and returned to his formal manner. 'I have visited many countries in Latin America . . .'

'Your childhood,' Gustavo interrupted, 'she wants to know about your childhood.'

The old man closed his eyes in exasperation. 'No, no, this is up to me now.'

He started again. 'I have visited many countries. Here in Latin America. I am not going to quote them all because I have visited almost all of them, including . . .' He tailed off, paused and started on a different tack. 'I have received many visits from the great personalities of the world, heads of state who include General de Gaulle. Also that . . .' He stumbled, searching for the name. I felt my stomach tensing. 'General Péron,' he said. I relaxed again. 'On two occasions as head of state. Also Chile, General Pinochet, and Ibanez del Campo, and I have been in all the countries like Ecuador, Venezuela. And I have been in Brazil I don't know how many times, on many occasions.'

He was clearly a man for lists. The recitation seemed to have tripped him back into his speech 'Paraguay and how I built It.' 'Now,' he went on, 'with support and co-operation, Paraguay developed considerably. And had peace, peace and respect for the constitution and laws.'

'You know this is being recorded,' said Gustavo.

'I know, I know. I am not going to—I am going to be careful.' He resumed in a firm tone. 'Now I am going to tell you. Paraguay was always a patriotic country. And it had a lot of internal and external problems. From 1904 to 1940 it had twenty-one presidents, an average of one each year and a half. For each government. This was all they had. From 1940 to 1948, I was the eighth president. So when I became president, I took'—he corrected himself—'we took measures to do what the country needed.' He was both stumbling and unstoppable. I wondered how much they had talked about what they were going to say.

'Asunción had no running water,' he was saying, 'and we made the road to Paraná, to the Friendship Bridge. With the co-operation of Brazil we built the Friendship Bridge, and we also built the hydroelectric plant Icarai, and the bridge was finished by Brazil. We also used the Brazilian road to reach the Atlantic, for exports and imports to Paraguay. We fostered the production of soya, cotton and all the agricultural products. And we built a lot of roads, a lot of roads, that . . .' He tailed off again, and Gustavo jumped in.

'In Paraguay,' he said.

'Yes, yes,' said Stroessner, 'I'm talking about Paraguay.'

I smiled encouragingly.

'Five thousand kilometres of roads,' said Gustavo.

'Asphalted,' said Stroessner.

'No,' said Gustavo, 'No. Asphalted, 700 kilometres. And 6,000 kilometres of dirt roads.'

'No, no. More, Gustavo.'

'Well, 10,000 kilometres of dirt roads then.'

'No. Asphalted.' He began to list them. 'The TransChaco road, how long was that? The road to Encarnación, how long was that?'

'Well, let's say 1,500 asphalted. Let's say that,' said Gustavo.

The old man ignored him and continued to recite his rosary of roads.

'Well, let's say 1,500 kilometres,' Gustavo said, louder, with the air of a man forced to pay more for a car than it was worth, but bored with the bargaining.

'And the road to . . .' The General had forgotten where the road was to. He paused and moved on to the next item on his mental agenda. It was the economy.

'And we managed to balance the budget. Balance it. We did that. It was possible. And we managed not to have too much external debt. It was under control. So it's not a pressing problem for the country today.'

'And the electricity. And the water,' said Gustavo, hurrying on to his own shopping list.

'I have already said that,' snapped his father. I felt a certain sympathy for the General creeping up on me.

'Now,' he continued, 'we built bridges with the co-operation of Brazil on the Paraná. The co-operation of Brazil on the Paraná, the Friendship Bridge . . . And the bridge over the Paraná is under construction with Argentina.' I began to wonder if it was me or him. It was hot, and the effort of remaining affable and interested was telling. Was there anything in there? I wondered, and how was I to get to it? 'And then the one over the Paraguay River. I should also mention the co-operation of Spain. And then the bridge at Concepción towards the Chaco.'

I began to wonder if I had enough tape.

Stroessner was still going. 'Now as to energy. The country didn't have any. The truth is when we built Icarai with the . . . also Itaipu'—he paused, realizing that he had left off an item on an earlier list—'Yes, Itaipu, which is now, which will be, the biggest dam in the world. Also Yacyreta, with Argentina. And we were doing studies about another dam. And this is thanks to the co-operation of world financial institutions like the World Bank and Inter American Development Bank.'

I asked him how he achieved his economic stability.

Gustavo answered. 'Twenty-two years,' he said.

I asked the question again. He had nothing to say, I realized later, to questions like how?

'There is no doubt,' said Stroessner—it was one of his verbal mannerisms, like 'Now I'm going to tell you . . .'—'that the exporters asked for a larger quantities of the local currency in exchange for the export dollar.' They certainly did. Fiddling the export dollar was one of the many means of growing extremely rich in Paraguay. Even the Central Bank was on the fiddle. I found myself wondering if it was a game, after all. If he was ticking off a list of possible accusations and offering his pre-emptive defence, closing off the issue to further exploration.

He went on about the stable exchange rate, told me how he had never needed to knock off zeros. That was true, too. I recalled the restaurant in Buenos Aires that was wallpapered with worthless currency, a citizen's satire on incompetent government. But not in Paraguay.

He had jumped again, without pausing, to another subject— the next accusation on his imaginary prosecutor's list. 'If I was there for several terms of office,' he said, 'it wasn't because I wanted to be. It was because the people insisted. The country was developing, and it was necessary that President Stroessner continue.' He had slipped into the third person.

He got back on track again, listing endorsements this time, tailoring some of them, it seemed, to please me. 'Now what comes to my mind is that I had many friendships. Good friendships.

'I received a book from General Alexander, who was Montgomery's commander, and I read it. There was a book about Cunningham. I always read a lot. We had many delightful visits. I was also in Europe, in various countries—in Spain, in France. In France,' he repeated, losing it slightly, 'it was Pompidou who was president then. I was in Italy as well. I was also in Bavaria, in Germany, to see my relatives, my father's family. He was from Hof. He was born on 17 May 1867. He came to Paraguay as a tourist, to see Iguazú, the waterfall. Then he went to Encarnación and he saw that circumstances were very good and he stayed and built a brewery at the beginning of the century. I was also in Asia, in Japan and in Nationalist China, Taiwan, South Africa, always with the idea of developing the country.' It had come neatly back to his central mission.

'Morocco,' said Gustavo. We both looked at him. 'Morocco,' he repeated. 'You were in Morocco.'

'Yes, I was in Morocco,' Stroessner admitted, irritably. 'But just to see it. Just a visit.'

I was still trying to provoke some opinion, something beyond this. I asked him who had impressed him, of the leaders he had met.

He began another list. 'I also met President Nixon . . . and Eisenhower.'

'Ford,' yawned Gustavo, from deep in the chair.

'Ford. And that one, what was his name—who replaced Kennedy?'

Gustavo was silent.

Johnson, I volunteered.

'President Johnstone. I was invited to the US specially by him. Now there is no doubt, that of all the heads of state who impressed me . . . '

'Franco,' said Gustavo, firmly, but perhaps unwisely.

'Him too,' said the old man. Now I knew he was second guessing me.

'Franco,' insisted Gustavo, oblivious of his *faux pas*. 'And Pompidou, you said . . . '

'I have already mentioned him.' Stroessner was trying to cut him off. I pictured a little boy at his father's knee, being told about the great General Franco. But Pompidou?

'But she asked who most impressed you,' Gustavo insisted.

The old man became stubborn. 'Well, they all did; they were all impressive. Now General de Gaulle, in Asunción, he had a very good impression of the country because he saw the youth, the army, the people. He said things about Paraguay.' He straightened himself in his chair, as though he was going to recite a poem. 'He said the following: he said very short things. He said, "A great people, a great government and . . . and . . ."'

'A great race?' said Gustavo.

The old man ignored him, rummaging in his memory, trying to put it in order, to make it come out right. 'He said.' He began again. 'What was it he said? He said three things. "A great race, a great government . . . a great . . ."' He couldn't remember, but then he cheered up. 'But he said other things about other countries that I am not going to repeat,' he concluded.

'I knew the president of Panama,' he added, as an afterthought.

He started to tell me about the great English personalities who had visited Paraguay, then veered off again. 'Why don't they serve coffee, Gustavo?' We dropped the English personalities and turned to his military career.

'Now there is no doubt,' he resumed, 'that I entered the Military College in 1929.' Well that's a relief, my inner voice whispered, childishly. It was beginning to mock me, that voice. I struggled on.

Why had he chosen a military career? I asked.

His were patriotic motives, he said. Then he jumped to the civil war, the rebellion, as he called it.

There was a long pause, but, as I drew breath for a question, he came to life again. 'Well, I became president,' he suddenly said. 'There was half a political party in the government. Then we made the electoral law. And there were more parties in the government. Because the government is the high political body that runs the country. One definition. That's all I can say.' He veered straight off again, on to the great increase in Paraguay's exports under his rule.

I tried his childhood again.

'I liked the primary and secondary schools,' he said. 'I read a lot. I read everything, everything I could when I was a child.' And that was the end of that.

'Now I always cared about the country,' he continued, 'I always believed that the laws should be respected. I always tried to instil in school-children and university students . . . I was always in contact with the people. And I always held audiences for the public. Not just for officials but the general public.'

'So people would come to the Palace,' I said. I realized I was humouring him. I wondered if he had noticed, but it didn't seem likely.

'Oh, yes. And they would wait, and if there was time . . . A lot of people came. Problems of every kind. Education problems. They came. And I would talk to the education ministry. Land problems or personal requests. Yes.' He spoke in bursts, then would sink into what was almost a reverie. He pulled himself up again. 'So I,' he began. 'There is a phrase that we used: "He uselessly strives who tries to please everybody." ' He smiled, the patriarch, happy with this piece of political wisdom, wiser than his brood, children who thought you only had to ask and it could be given.

'So I satisfied as many people as I could, of those who came with their requests. And when they invited me to the interior, I said, "If I come I want a school to be painted or finished." Because we built a lot of schools . . . ' I thought of the generals, building him little projects so that he could go there and untie the ribbons—such a small price to pay for what they got in return.

'Secondary schools,' said Gustavo, rolling the words slowly round his mouth. 'Universities.'

I shifted in my seat, trying to shake off my drowsiness. Gustavo was suddenly attentive. 'Would you like to change your chair? Are you comfortable?'

The whole room started to take on the qualities of a dream. The light seemed to come and go. I could feel my own will to find a way through to this man slipping away into the warm air.

'Going back to that difficult time,' My voice sounded suddenly loud, 'before you became president—'

'That was the politicians,' said Stroessner, 'creating problems. Ambition for power, to dominate. Beating the people, quarrelling among themselves. It's a very long story. Books have been written about it, all the intrigues of that time.' I recalled Juancito the Liar snapping the same phrase at me, trying to dismiss me when I had asked him about the *coup*. 'None of them lasted. They were there only a short time. The movements, the intrigues, the barracks revolts.'

How had he put a stop to all that? I asked.

By development, he said, building things. I looked at him, puzzling over the connection. 'Insisting on peace,' he added, 'insisting on what the country needed, not the senseless political movements. Political movements—' He was searching for a phrase again. 'Avoiding negative political movements.'

A uniformed maid appeared with a tray of coffee and orange juice. In the break, Stroessner allowed himself a comment. 'She seems familiar,' he said to Gustavo, looking at me, 'as though I knew her from somewhere.'

Gustavo had come back to life. 'We are going to write history together,' he boomed. 'History!'

There were the sounds of voices in one of the other rooms.

His mother and sister, Gustavo explained. A family reunion. I wondered if they were tempted to listen at the door. The house didn't seem that big. Were they sitting in the kitchen, waiting for me to leave?

'I hear you have been in Asunción?' Gustavo said.

Stroessner suddenly focused. 'In Asunción? When were you in Asunción?'

I told him I had just come from there. 'But I wasn't there very long,' I added, limply, dreading the questions that would follow.

'And do people remember the General?' asked Gustavo, eagerly. I felt like a drowning man.

'Oh, yes,' I said.

'And what do the people in the street say?'

I searched my mind for an acceptable quote. I couldn't find one. My smile was becoming rigid. 'Some remember you with great affection,' I said, thinking of Benitez Rickman. 'Although the politicians are different.' I heard the tone in my voice, appeasing, and hated it.

Gustavo joined in. 'The politicians speak badly of him. They say the works were Pharaonic projects, that people stole.' He recited the case for the prosecution.

Yes, things like that, I said.

'It's not true,' said Gustavo.

'They say those things to inflame,' said Stroessner.

'Some of the people who say those things were at his side for a very long time,' I ventured, prodding for a reaction.

Gustavo pulled the shutters down. 'That's all right,' he said, 'they were good people.'

But Stroessner was interested. 'She said people who were at his side.'

'Yes,' said Gustavo. Then to me: 'But they didn't betray him. Very few betrayed him. They were all good people. They were called to co-operate and they did. They were not traitors. We don't consider those who are co-operating traitors.' Gustavo didn't want any trouble.

'There might be some,' said the General. 'There might have been some.' The General and I looked at each other, and I began to wish Gustavo would go to the lavatory.

'That is what we have said, in general.' Gustavo was trying to steer back towards the harbour.

'A few are against us,' said Stroessner, giving in. 'The rest are with us.'

Above: Asunción mural of General Alfredo Stroessner during his campaign for a fifth term of office in 1988.

'What do the humble people say?' asked Gustavo. He genuinely seemed to think this was safer ground. 'Twenty-two years without inflation?' he prompted me. 'All those things?'

'The universities,' said Stroessner, 'the Catholic University . . .'

He began the list again, without waiting for the humble people's view. The airports. Asphalted. Energy. Electric light.

We talked about his great obsessions, stability and the communist menace. When he first came to power, he said, his main concern was just to keep power, day by day, worrying about whether he would make it to the end of his term of office.

'To get through the first year,' interjected Gustavo, 'the first month . . .'

'The first month then the first three months. Then the first year,' resumed the old man. They mused on, in their querulous duet.

I asked him about communism, and the threat posed to the continent by the Cuban revolution, a subject to which he had devoted the bulk of his speeches for thirty-five years, drawing heavily on the Cuban threat in order to milk defence dollars from the United States. I braced myself for a harangue. I had read it, but I wanted to hear him say it.

He seemed surprised to be asked about the effect of the Cuban revolution in Paraguay. 'In Paraguay, we always talked about democracy. I don't know if they had democracy there.'

Cuba? I thought. Democracy? Had he heard me correctly?

'Cuba was a very long way from Paraguay,' said Gustavo helpfully. 'So it didn't have a lot of influence.' His father agreed.

'Did it have no repercussions for you?' I asked. I felt suddenly off-balance. I pictured Benitez Rickman's library of Stroessner's speeches on the communist threat; all those State Department reports of Stroessner's complaints that his strategic country's fight against Cuban infiltration was underfunded.

'No,' said Stroessner, 'in Paraguay there was a stable regime. Stable.'

'But there was so much talk,' I insisted, 'of the danger of communism in the continent.' This was a subject on which I had come prepared to be bored, to be lectured, to be treated to banalities. This was the man who had hosted conferences of the

World Anti-Communist League, attended by the real hard core. The White Hand from Guatemala, d'Aubuisson, the killer from El Salvador. The Argentine dirty warriors, the South Koreans, the Taiwanese, the South Africans. This was the man who had teased the world over Mengele. I couldn't believe this was happening.

'Yes. That's what Vice-President of the United States said,' the General said. 'That Vice-President. What's his name?'

'Nixon,' I said, still in my own thoughts, in my memories of Stroessner, the well-paid subaltern on the western front of the Cold War.

'Quayle,' said Gustavo.

'Quayle?' I said. What did Quayle have to do with it?

'He said there were three problems,' said Stroessner. He remembered all three this time. 'Drugs, communism and the debt. Yes.'

And what do you think? I asked, clutching at this implausible straw.

'Listen,' said Stroessner, clearly bored with my insistence on communism. 'I am a democrat and I have always demonstrated it.' My head began to swim.

But the attempted revolutions in Paraguay? The guerrillas? I couldn't let it go. I was sounding like him. He was sounding like me.

'A few,' said the old man. 'But they were very small in number. They were of no importance.'

I thought of those peasant massacres, armed assaults on people seeking land-reform, tortured oppositionists, all condemned as communists. Of Archbishop Rolon, Humberto Rubin. Of the language of the Cold War, preserved in the rare air of Asunción. And he didn't believe it? Never had?

'There was no reason for a revolution in Paraguay,' Stroessner added, by way of explanation.

I tried a few other ways of asking the question and gave up. Stroessner simply refused to worry about communism.

I tried another line of questions, on the problems of authority. Did he feel, always, that he was being told the truth by those who served him?

'Yes, always,' he said. Another dead end, I thought. 'Though,' he added, after a pause, 'one can always be wrong, given what happened.'

I looked up at him. He was smiling at the floor. I hadn't expected irony.

He seemed to be thinking about it, talking from inside at last. 'I was always confident that I knew. I never expected this . . . this'— he searched for the word—'this *cuartelazo*.' For reasons that are not hard to find, there is, in Spanish, more than one word for a *coup d'etat*. The most derogatory is '*cuartelazo*', a barracks revolt, a rabble got out of hand.

'But the people,' he said, 'the people had no part in this. The people were always at the margin of these events.'

Gustavo had wandered off, at last. He had answered the telephone, then loped into a room at the back of the house. The General's tone had changed, his voice had dropped, had become more personal without his shambling minder to steer him back from forbidden ground.

How did he feel about it, I asked him, wondering how long I had.

'Look, what can you do in these circumstances . . . "*A lo hecho, pecho*"—take it on the chin. It happened. Taking into account all the other things that happened in the past, what happened to me is not extraordinary.'

He returned to his consolatory recital. 'Paraguay had a long period of progress, tranquillity and peace. It took giant steps.'

Gustavo came back and the morning drifted on. I could smell their lunch. I had my own plans and I wanted to get out. I left, arranging to return later, when the day was cooler.

'It's too hot to wear a suit in the afternoon,' said the General. I looked at Gustavo's sneakers. I wondered how long his father had nagged him about them and why Gustavo had held out.

8

Outside, I felt normal again, but needed someone to talk to. I had an arrangement to meet a Brazilian diplomat. He was the perfect companion, full of charm and cynicism. He also knew something about Stroessner: he had been the one sent from the foreign ministry to meet Stroessner on his arrival in Brazil.

We met for lunch. After the Stroessner's household, Brasília was suddenly bustling, nearly human. According to my companion, the restaurant was the best one in town, not for the food but for the politicians. 'They come here to plot. So all the journalists come here to watch them. So all the politicians come here to be seen by the journalists.'

He told me about going to meet Stroessner. It had been the beginning of carnival, he pointed out, a fact that I, in my Anglo-Saxon way, had overlooked: not the best moment for a diplomatic crisis. The capital had emptied, and he himself was about to leave for Rio when the minister called. A plane was waiting, the minister said, to take him to Itumbiara. He had no idea where it was; when he got there he still didn't. After having to fight his way past all the journalists, he finally found Stroessner, poring over a map.

He then sat there on behalf of the Brazilian government, listening to the radio with Stroessner and his family, occasionally going out to answer some questions for the press corps. There were solidarity visits from some right-wing politicians who wanted to get their pictures in the papers. Considering all things, he said, Stroessner was holding up well. 'Imagine,' he said, 'it's not as though he'd had time to pack or go to the bank.' Stroessner read the papers and watched the television news, but couldn't lose the habits of control: afterwards he would come in, upset and angry, saying: 'Do you see this? They're calling me a tyrant. A tyrant!' Then he would walk up and down, muttering to himself, 'This has got to be stopped. This has got to be stopped.'

The car was late for my second appointment. I began to wonder. Had he changed his mind? Had I said something that afterwards struck him as unfriendly? Perhaps I had been indiscreet on the telephone.

I was about to call when the car appeared, forty-five minutes late, pulling up in in front of the hotel.

The route was the same. You turned left off the main drive from the lake, went over the speed bump and then stopped by the corrugated steel fence. I opened my own door; it wasn't armour-plated. In his own exile, did Stroessner recall the fate of Tacho Somoza, blown to pieces on a street in Asunción under the noses of the security services?

Gustavo was waiting again, and we walked through the door from the garage, across the small garden and up the stone path. The General was dressed in the same dark blue silk suit.He was wearing a red tie. 'Be careful of this rug,' he said, taking my elbow. 'It can sometimes trip you up.'

'No it doesn't,' said Gustavo.

I heard voices and sounds of another meal in preparation, occasional laughter. At one point Gustavo called in his wife to be introduced: a small, fair-haired, fine-boned woman, very good looking with blue eyes, dressed in shorts. Gustavo made her tell me about the time she attended a horse show at Olympia and another time at some other place that we decided must have been Windsor. She excused herself as soon as she could. 'I shall leave you to work.'

And then we sat down—Stroessner in the same upright chair again, with the same disciplined stillness.

Occasionally he grew impatient and made as if to rise or dismiss me, but it seemed to me that it was only the old dictator's habit of rationing his audiences. When I misjudged one of his pauses, left the silence unfilled too long, he would put his hands palms down on his knees and say, 'Well, we have talked a great deal,' or, 'I think we have covered everything,' and I would have to rouse myself to a new line of questioning.

It must have been odd, to have this stranger sitting there, hour after hour.

This was his last display. The General had dusted off the president, put on a suit and performed for history as well as his rambling old age would allow. Gustavo, with his fears, his bad conscience, was playing the minder, fearful that reality might break through the recitation of roads, airports and electric lights, and that the General might say something which would annoy Asunción, stimulate someone there to reach out for Gustavo and mean it this time. At odd moments, when Gustavo was answering the telephone or had simply fidgeted his way out of the room, the General would almost seem to want to talk, to drop the show, to gossip. He couldn't disguise his interest in what had been said of him by his former collaborators—Pappalardo, Juancito the Liar, Ynsfran.

'He said that?' he spluttered, when I told him of my interview with Juancito. 'Chavez said that? He was always the first and loudest in his praise, the most obsequious. Well,' he said dismissively, 'it's best not even to think about that one any more.'

But these were exceptional moments. I had come for my second interview wanting to get some sense of how the General felt about the *coup*—what led to it? why he thought it had happened? did he think that things could have turned out differently?—but I was not to have much success.

There were so many things Stroessner clung to: that the army had not been unhappy; that he had never insisted that officers join the Colorado party (I had seen a photocopy of the regulations, but what was the point of insisting?); that those who ousted Stroessner were members of a small clique who did it for no other reason than that of squalid personal ambition.

Under Stroessner, life in Paraguay had always been marked by peace, order and an absence of serious social conflict. The problems with the Church were a matter of a few individual priests. The problems with the United States were some minor difficulties (with one ambassador). The problems with the 'exiled' opposition were exaggerated ('There is no doubt that you can't satisfy everybody, but the truth is that they [of the Popular Colorado Movement] came back, were in the country, had all their liberties and guarantees'). The problems with the press were only because some members of it had been advocating violence. Paraguay, under Stroessner, was a fully democratic society.

I reminded him that he had closed down newspapers.

He disagreed. 'Only *ABC*, and only because it was advocating violence.'

'Disorder,' boomed Gustavo, from deep within his armchair, and Stroessner agreed, this time, with the interruption.

'Yes, disorder. They would say things like: "Tomorrow the chief of police will be replaced," when the chief of police wasn't going to be replaced. Things like that, things that were completely untrue. Free expression has its limits and reaches only to where the freedom of another begins.' A decision was taken, he said, by the

Supreme Court, a legal decision, because subversion cannot be allowed in a democracy. 'But there were all the other newspapers. Paraguay never had so many newspapers as now. And they said what they liked about my government. I read them every day. There was no censor.'

It was true that there had been no censor. A censor is a hard thing to explain away in a fully democratic state. Besides, a censor implies someone to argue with. One of the beauties of Stroessner's state of terror was the very uncertainty about what was permitted.

I was starting to see that, at the heart of it all, there were just too many things that could not be reconciled: a clear white space between the Paraguay of Stroessner's vision and the Paraguay I had got to know. There were also two Stroessners: one, the beloved father of the people, progressive and popular; the second, the man who, for thirty-five years, ran a state of terror in the name of national security and the fight against communism. Now, in exile, he chose to forget the second Stroessner; or, at least in my company, he had chosen to forget him, and there seemed to be little that I could do about it.

I asked about the conflict with the Church, but that hadn't existed either. His government had looked after the Church; it had funded the parochial schools. How could there be a conflict with the Church? Only a few, a very few, individuals, misused the pulpit for purposes that were not religious.

'A few, who disagreed with the government,' explained Gustavo.

'There was some resistance,' admitted Stroessner. 'Some . . .' he groped for the word, 'politics.'

'They wanted an accelerated agrarian reform,' said Gustavo.

'And you have to impose order,' Stroessner said. It wasn't a word he shouted, but it was one whose sound he liked. There seemed to be something reassuring about the way he said it. '*Orden*,' he would say in the Spanish. '*Orden*,' rounding out the first syllable, rolling the 'r' slightly.

We talked about the Pope's visit to Paraguay, and Gustavo explained liberation theology to me. Priests in Paraguay, he said, agitated among the poor, suggesting that they were entitled to other people's land. 'The peasants believed them. The Church should have talked to the rich first and convinced them that they had to donate part of their wealth to the poor, not just teach the poor to shout at the rich.'

'Yes,' he repeated, pleased with his idea. 'Rather that the rich give to the poor in good grace . . .'

I asked about Archbishop Rolon.

Stroessner started to say that the Archbishop had always acted correctly, but Gustavo chipped in. 'No,' he said, 'Rolon hadn't acted correctly for a long time.'

Stroessner started to argue.

'There were confrontations,' said Gustavo, sticking to his guns.

'Not confrontations,' said Stroessner.

'She has already interviewed Rolon,' said Gustavo.

'Is that true?' said Stroessner.

'Yes,' said Gustavo, 'she's said so.'

'*That* Rolon?' asked Stroessner, as though the idea that he could be sitting with someone who had interviewed the archbishop was too bizarre to grasp.

'Yes,' said Gustavo.

Stroessner changed his tack. '*That* Rolon has some family members who are in politics, and he couldn't keep his nose out of it. But we didn't have any conflicts. It might be that he thought in a certain way, but this happens sometimes.'

'There was no personal problem,' said Gustavo, perhaps recalling the unfortunate excommunication of Sabino Montanaro, the one who tortured priests.

'Oh, no. Nothing.' said Stroessner. 'We always had . . . I always went to mass. To the military chaplain.'

Gustavo began to explain that the Church itself was divided, and that part of it supported the government, and part of it was against it.

Stroessner, however, was already trying to claw back the argument. The Church was not divided, he said. 'There were just a few priests who . . . It was a personal thing.'

A short silence fell.

Gustavo broke it. 'Did Monseignor Rolon say there was any conflict?'

Yes, I said.

Archbishop Rolon, who was entitled to a seat in the State Council, had refused to take it up because he did not want the Church to be associated with the government. I had seen Rolon in Asunción, and he had explained all this to me. He also recounted explaining all this to an emissary that Stroessner had sent to see him, and in the end the emissary had pointed to the crucifix on Rolon's chest and said, 'You should wear a hammer and sickle, not a cross.'

Gustavo tried to make the best of it. 'It's not that Rolon went to the State Council the first time and then refused to go after that,' he said. 'From the very first day Rolon didn't go. Never.'

'But what I'm saying,' said Stroessner, his voice growing harder, 'was that Rolon was sworn in, as a member of the State Council.'

'But he never, never went,' insisted Gustavo.

'I've already told her that,' snapped the General.

'And that's what I'm saying!' Gustavo turned to me: 'You see we never had a disagreement with Rolon,' he said, trying to help, 'because we never saw him at the Council.'

'And that was what was unconstitutional,' said Stroessner, making a bid for the last word. 'You have to obey the constitution and the laws as a citizen, really.'

There was an uncomfortable pause.

Then Gustavo said: 'My nephews are in an English school, an Anglican one.'

I thought he was changing the subject.

'The headmaster is a Mr Venables.' Mr Venables and the Anglican school were famous in Asunción for managing to impose some discipline on Stroessner's grandsons. Zuccolillo's wife and daughters had lots of stories about it. I remembered the one about one of Stroessner's grandsons throwing all the toilet rolls into the lavatory and being made to pick them out again.

'I am very keen on religion,' Gustavo was saying, still trying to mend relations with the Church. 'I am a friend of lots of priests.' He laughed. 'But we never talked politics.'

'Well, that's enough of that,' said Stroessner.

I rather agreed.

I gave up on the Church and turned to the army—surely here the old soldier would recognize that things had gone wrong?—but he held firm to the vision of himself as the beloved patriarch. It was a mystery, really, how the *coup* could have come about.

He started to tell an anecdote that got nowhere, about a British general in Africa, waiting for information and smoking. 'Just smoking and smoking,' he said, 'waiting for information that never arrived.' I pictured a general, in his khaki shorts, waiting for information. 'A *coup d'état*,' Stroessner said, 'is something that one doesn't expect. It's about a lack of information.' This was related to the British general in Africa but I was not entirely sure how, except that the British general, like Stroessner, did not expect what happened next.

I tried another approach.

How had he interpreted the demonstrations in the last months of his regime?

'Oh, they were,' said Stroessner, 'an entirely normal thing in a democracy. Entirely normal.'

'Did you not object to them?' I asked, recalling descriptions I had heard of how savagely the police had responded to the exercise of these democratic rights.

'No, never.' he said.

I tried again. 'On reflection,' I asked, 'was there something now, knowing what you do, that you would have done differently?'

It was still no. He had been firm, had never weakened and had always acted against corruption.

He decided to explain the *coup* to me. 'What happened was this,' he said. 'I'll tell you. When the Convention came, the Colorado Party had three factions [*listas*]. And one of the factions won. And the others lost. And those who lost began to conspire— that's what it was. It wasn't anything else. The losers conspired.'

Had he known at the time that the losers were conspiring?

He had not. He had noticed that they had been complaining— even expressing their complaints in the press—but it was, as they say, a free country. Those were the reasons for the *coup*.

'The *cuartelazo*,' Gustavo corrected him.

'The *cuartelazo*,' he agreed.

Gustavo went out of the room and returned. He had been

looking for a book but he couldn't find it. It was written by a man called Levin. He didn't remember the title, but it was about Paraguay and had been, he said, very successful both there and in Argentina.

Might that be Lewis, I suggested, Paul Lewis?

'What was it called?' asked Gustavo.

I told him.

He claimed to have read it. He said that he had liked it.

The General said, no, he hadn't read it. Neither seemed to recall that they had banned it for years.

9

That night, in the hotel, I listened to my tapes. The next day would be my last. I had a ticket to return to London, and Stroessner had agreed to see me again in the morning before I left. I had little to lose, I thought, in confronting him with some realities. That's what I decided I would do: I would make Stroessner confront Stroessner.

I would talk to him about torture.

I began by citing Amnesty International. A simple statement: that Amnesty International had consistently reported that in Paraguay there was torture.

'Rupture?' said Stroessner. 'No there was no rupture. We always answered the questions.'

There was never a rupture or there was never torture? I asked, deflated by this attack of deafness.

'No,' he said, 'never a rupture. We answered all the questions quite normally.'

But what about the allegations themselves? I said. The physical mistreatment in the prisons?

'No. Absolutely not,' he said. 'I don't remember any such allegations. Or any such information coming to me through such organizations.'

'So the behaviour of the Paraguayan police was—'

'—Correct,' he interrupted.

'Correct?' I said.

'Correct,' he repeated.

What about the state of siege? I asked, determined to poke my finger through the ideal democracy of Paraguay. 'Did not the state of siege act as an impediment to justice?'

I had made him irritated.

'Look,' he said. 'The state of siege was necessary. There was subversion in Latin America. It was more of a preventive measure. It wasn't used much.' He, he said, would have preferred to have lifted it. It was not what he wanted.

But I had crossed the line.

'These are things that have already been judged. Things in the past,' he said. 'I have to think of my status as a resident in this country. But I do insist that in Paraguay there was order [*orden*]: the judiciary had the power of complete independence; justice was fully exercised.'

I asked him if he regretted the way things had turned out.

'Oh, yes,' he said. 'I went in by the front door and had always wanted to leave by the front door. But circumstances didn't allow it. But I don't want to make any accusations. Everything that happened, happened, and, if I had known—well, we are all wise after the event . . .'

'Well,' he said abruptly, 'I think we have talked quite a lot. I was at the head of the government—by popular choice—and Paraguay progressed. That's all I can say, Isabel Hilton,' he said, his pronunciation of my name laboured. 'The chain of hotels. Is it written the same way?'

Gustavo came to life suddenly and gave me a short lecture on the Latin antecedents of Conrad Hilton. It did not interest the General.

'I think I have given you all the time necessary,' he said. 'We are fine here in Brazil, but it is transitory. I am not used to Brazil. The climate is good, but I miss Paraguay, the ambience. You get used to your friends. It's easier there. But I have a lot of company here.'

'More or less,' muttered Gustavo, 'more or less.'

I wondered how deposed dictators go about building a social circle.

'We have nothing to complain about,' said his father sharply.

'Do you still play chess?' I asked.

'No,' he said, 'I have nobody to play chess with.'

We chatted about the weather and fishing. I thought of my Paraguayan friends and made one last try. I asked him about Jimmy Carter.

'Carter,' he said, 'had asked me what I had seen at the NASA space museum. A lot of interesting things. I was given some moon-dust, you know.'

And what had he thought of Carter's human rights policy?

'I thought it was very good,' said Stroessner. 'I have always thought that human rights are very important for the whole world.'

Had he read what human rights reports said about Paraguay?

He couldn't remember the details, he said. 'But we were always concerned about human rights on a permanent basis.'

It was over.

The General had said his last word. He showed me to the door, pointing out again the dangerous rug. He clasped my hand and thanked me. Gustavo walked me across the lawn, and I took advantage of the moment to ask him whether there had been a plan to make him president.

Absolutely not, he insisted. Never.

As we were talking I glanced back at the house and realized that the General was still standing there, waving, as though seeing off a visiting head of state, patiently waiting through this unexpected hitch in protocol.

Embarrassed, I waved again and we retreated out of sight.

It was absurd to feel sorry for him in his loneliness, I told myself. He had always been lonely, despising those close to him, taking refuge in his relationship with Nata and a series of court-jesters, human familiars whom he adopted.

Meanwhile, Gustavo was chattering on, tumbling over himself in his strangely ingratiating manner. How had I become their last hope of vindication? Because I had invited them to think that, I supposed. I didn't like it.

Gustavo followed the car out into the road, shouting 'Goodbye! Have a good journey!' I set off back to the hotel behind the taciturn Brazilian driver. I thought of the people I had met in Paraguay, the overwhelming kindness of strangers. I thought of all those people who had suffered at Stroessner's hands. I wondered what they would have done, if they had sat down for three days with him. I thought of all the people who had clung to him when he was in power, who had grown rich for the sacrifice of a few scruples and a little pride. 'Stroessner didn't do it on his own,' Rubin had said. 'We were all in it.'

His greatest gift had been his power to corrupt. His great good fortune that so many were willing to be corrupted. He had distorted meaning so far that finally there was none. How long would he last, I wondered, in this little domestic prison, adding up the mileage of asphalted roads?

What did he say? people asked me. What was he like? I found it impossible to describe. 'I saw Stroessner,' I said to one friend, a man who knows as much about Latin American dictators as anybody.

'Did he say much?' he asked.

'No,' I replied.

'I'm not surprised,' he said. 'They never do.'

Above: General Alfredo Stroessner in the garden of his house in Brasília in September 1989.

**John Gregory Dunne
HARP**

Harp: the word describes a musical instrument. Harp the word is like kike or nigger or fag, a word of abuse, sharp and short and nasty, used for Irish Catholics living in America.

Harp - an autobiography? a writer's memoir? a novel? – is about both harps. It is about being a Catholic in a country of Protestants, an immigrant among Anglo-Saxon do-gooders, an anarchist in the suburbs.

'A book that welcomes you in, talks to you wonderfully for a while, takes you into its confidence, **Harp** is rather like the life story of an Irish writer as you might hear it in a single long night in a bar, especially if you were Irish too, and the writer could take the corresponding liberties.'
Los Angeles Book Review

'What style Dunne shows here! What muscle! What a voice! He sounds like an Irish Norman Mailer.'
Detroit News

'A marvellous, funny memoir.'
Kathleen Tynan, *Observer*

March publication, hardback, £13.99

ISBN: 0 140 14210 X

GABRIEL
GARCÍA MÁRQUEZ
THE FUTURE OF
COLOMBIA

Above: Pablo Escobar Gaviria.

In October 1989, the press revealed one of Colombia's best-kept secrets: that for over a year, authorized representatives of the government of Colombia had been holding formal talks with authorized representatives of the country's drug-traffickers. When the government denied the report, the drug-traffickers then confirmed it, subsequently forcing the government to admit reluctantly that it was true. There was no further explanation. There has been no further explanation, and in the end the press disclosure has revealed only one thing: the pattern of a drugs war that has relentlessly repeated itself, with no prospect of solution.

The first known attempt at dialogue was in Panama in May 1984, when one of the leading drug-traffickers, Pablo Escobar Gaviria, head of the Medellín cartel, used an intermediary to convey a proposal to President Belisario Betancur. It stated that Escobar and the other drug-traffickers would withdraw from the drugs trade, would destroy their processing plants, would re-invest their immense capital legally in local industry and commerce and would share with the state the burden of the foreign debt—if in return, the drug-traffickers were tried in Colombia and not extradited to the United States, under the terms of a treaty that, although dormant for several years, was then about to be revived.

It is interesting that Escobar and the drug-traffickers did not seek to be pardoned, even though the idea of an amnesty had already been established: on the day he took office, President Belisario Betancur had offered an amnesty to members of the armed guerrilla movements, some of whom had been sheltering in Colombia's mountains for more than thirty years. President Betancur has always held to a policy of dialogue, and so he greeted the drug-traffickers' offer in a positive spirit. Attorney General Carlos Jimenez Gómez, who for the past year had been holding secret talks with the main drug barons in search of an honourable agreement, set off to meet them in Panama once more. It has not been proven that this meeting was authorized by the president, but I believe it was. However, that was as far as things got. On 4 July, the newspaper *El Tiempo* learned about the meetings and denounced them, whipping up public opinion against any possibility of agreement. President Betancur found himself obliged to back off and to deny that he had anything to do with the matter. With the hindsight of six years, it is clear that Colombia missed the opportunity to spare itself many of the horrors now afflicting it.

It now seems possible that the negotiations had been sabotaged by the United States, for reasons which had much more to do with Ronald Reagan's anti-communist fantasies than with drug-trafficking itself. The man appointed to deal with the problem was the United States ambassador to Colombia, Lewis Tambs, leading figure of the Santa Fe group and the militant right of Reaganism. It became evident that Tambs was against the negotiated peace that the Betancur government had set its hopes on. Tambs was obsessed with bringing into effect the treaty signed by the previous Colombian government, which included the shameful clause sanctioning the extradition of Colombian citizens to the United States. Ambassador Tambs's draconian manoeuvres seemed to suggest that to the United States the drug-trafficker and the guerrilla were one and the same thing, and he coined an important term: the narcoguerrilla. Thanks to the extradition treaty, it would be an easy step therefore to send US troops to Colombia where, with the excuse of prosecuting the drug-traffickers, they would in fact be fighting the guerrillas. One way or another, it seemed, it would be possible to extradite virtually any Colombian to the United States.

That was the impression I received when I had lunch with Ambassador Tambs shortly after his arrival in Bogotá, and time has proved me right. Tambs was later transferred to the US Embassy in Costa Rica and played a leading role in Irangate, helping Oliver North build a secret airport for the Nicaraguan contra forces.

We Colombians still wonder why the traffickers proposed the armistice, and whether the proposal was genuine. I believe it was. What the traffickers said, stripped of its rhetoric, is revealing: 'We prefer a tomb in Colombia to a cell in the United States.' They were frightened by the extradition treaty, but that is not the whole explanation. I think the main reason was cultural: by birth and background, the drug-traffickers were unprepared for life outside Colombia. Their Ali Baba riches were no use to them anywhere else, and it was in Colombia they felt secure and best able to flaunt their wealth, spending it among their lifelong friends, joking in their slum dialects and eating good Colombian cooking from their very own pots. What they yearned for most was the only thing they did not have: a place in Colombian society. When the attempt at a dialogue failed, however, the drug-traffickers tried to win this place for themselves through a range of despicable methods, methods that would eventually rebound against them.

When the dialogue failed, it gave the traffickers the time they needed to secure their survival. If anyone had wanted them arrested, a policeman on the beat could have done it. But on the whole, Colombian society viewed them with an interest and a curiosity verging on complacency. They were the talk of the moment. Journalists, politicians, industrialists, businessmen or the simply curious all flocked to the perpetual feast at Pablo Escobar's ranch Napoles on the outskirts of Medellín. Escobar had his own private zoo with giraffes and hippopotami shipped from Africa for his guests' entertainment. The airplane displayed at the front gate which ferried the first cargo of cocaine to the United States had become a national monument.

The traffickers had wealth, but they wanted more: they wanted power as well. Escobar was elected to the reserve list for the House of Representatives and became a patron of human rights seminars. Carlos Lehder ran extravagant discos, erected a statue of John Lennon in the pleasure-loving city of Armenia, organized a political movement and published a far-right nationalist magazine printed in green ink as a homage to marijuana. He attended Congress with his armed bodyguards, laughing through the sessions with his feet up. Jorge Luis Ochoa of the Medellín cartel and Gilberto Rodríguez Orejuela from Cali, nowadays mortal enemies, used to roam together around the world buying up thoroughbred horses, looking for European partners for their legal businesses. Once they were arrested in Spain and then extradited to Colombia, where they were set free. With so much in their favour, none of the traffickers' politician friends bothered to advise them that the crimes they were perpetrating had become horrendous and were in fact terrible political blunders.

Their first big mistake was to kill justice minister Rodrigo

Lara Ponilla in April 1984. Unfortunately, President Betancur's response was also a mistake. Harassed by accusations of doing nothing, and perhaps feeling revulsion at the crime, he allowed the extradition treaty to be used for the first time, even though he repudiated it then and possibly still does so now deep in his heart. No doubt he was driven to implement the treaty because he had no other sufficiently powerful legal instrument immediately available to him; to use the treaty in this way, however, meant it was no longer a measure of the law; it had become a weapon of revenge.

Carlos Lehder is now serving an extravagant 'life' sentence of over 135 years in the United States. By the end of October 1989, some twenty Colombians and three foreigners resident in Colombia had been extradited. The drug-traffickers have never denied they were the ones ultimately responsible for the death of what is by now an incalculable number of Colombians, although they have always denied the murder of justice minister Lara Bonilla which began the whole war of opinion against them. At least 800 members of the left-wing party *Union Patriotica* (Patriotic Union), including its candidate for president, Jaime Pardo Leal, have already fallen victim to their ruthless campaign of extermination. The slaying of the inimitable Guillermo Cano, editor of the *El Espectador*, was a personal tragedy for me and I still have difficulty accepting it. Equally difficult are the subsequent attacks on the newspaper itself, where I spent my best years as a journalist. Judges and magistrates, whose miserable salaries were barely enough to provide for the education of their children, were faced with an impossible choice: either to sell out to the traffickers or be killed by them. The most admirable and heart-rending thing is that over forty of them, and many journalists and officials as well, chose to die.

What is incomprehensible is this: amid all this slaughter, the traffickers never ceased proposing dialogue with the government. We shall probably never know how many attempts were made. In Mexico at the end of 1985 I talked to an emissary from Pablo Escobar, who was anxious to re-affirm the offer made to the Colombian government in Panama, but with one remarkable change: discussion of the extradition treaty, which until then had been at the heart of any dialogue, was now to be left until after agreement had been reached. This effort came to nothing, as did so many others.

few months later, the Colombian Supreme Court declared the extradition treaty unconstitutional, but the killings continued unabated. It is not unreasonable to suppose that there are reasons for this butchery that have never been made public, but nobody has taken into account to what extent the social and political situation of our great, ill-starred Colombia, with its centuries of rural feudalism, its thirty years of unresolved guerrilla conflicts, its long history of governments which have failed to represent the wishes of the people, has bred the drug-traffickers and all that they stand for. In 1979, when Panama's General Omar Torrijos visited the livestock ranches in the Sinu valley of Colombia's Caribbean region, he was surprised at how many cattle ranchers were protected by armed civilians. He recalled that El Salvador showed similar symptoms of collapse of social order just before its troubles started. Torrijos was right. Not many miles from the prosperous farms he saw—in the middle reaches of my legendary River Magdalena—the social structure was breaking down so badly that in a few short years a parallel order would be created, but it would be one controlled by the drug-traffickers.

In the 1960s, the guerrilla arm of the Communist Party, the Revolutionary Armed Forces of Colombia (FARC), had set themselves up to defend the unarmed peasants against the rapacious landowners. This original idea swiftly degenerated, and to finance their war the guerrillas raised money from the cattlemen through kidnapping, blackmail and extortion. The landowners responded by recruiting private armies, some of which were even given legitimacy by the government on the grounds that they were 'self-defence' groups. At first, everything was directed towards the physical elimination of communism, one journalist who visited the region wrote six years ago. But then they started on cattle rustlers, then criminals in the towns, and even began killing beggars and homosexuals. The cattlemen who survived not only lost much of their fortunes, but found themselves threatened by gangs of outlaws whom they themselves had first given arms to.

It was these ruined ranch-owners who contacted the drug-traffickers. Between them they created the Magdalena Medio of today, a huge empire of 50,000 square kilometres that is twice as big as El Salvador and more heavily armed than the country General

Torrijos knew in his youth. This has all taken place in the past few years, less than 300 kilometres from Colombia's presidential palace and within a stone's throw of the local army barracks, and yet it only became known last year when a deserter told the whole story.

The drug-traffickers provided money, know-how and their undisputed business acumen. Their reprisals were violent and scientifically planned, with paramilitary squads from training schools run by mercenaries bought for gold in London and Tel Aviv. The schools recruited adolescent criminals from the poorest shanty towns of our cities, who would then grow up to spread terror and death throughout Colombia. Thanks to some uncanny dialectical joke, what the FARC had planned as a revolution turned out to be one in reverse. The Magdalena Medio became a world apart, not simply with self-defence groups, but with proper police forces accountable to mayors and local councillors elected by the inhabitants. Their plans for housing, health and education seem to be a direct challenge to the central government. The proud local leaders have their own extreme right-wing political party. Its symbol is a telescopic rifle sight.

By the time the rest of Colombia learned of this desperate reality, it was too late. The state within a state, no longer satisfied with the fertile plains and romantic sunsets of the Magdalena, was expanding, working its way into every imaginable corner of the nation.

An observer of our reality has said that the whole of Colombian society is addicted to drugs. Not to cocaine— which is no great problem in Colombia—but to a far deadlier drug: easy money. Our trade and industry, our banking system, our politics, press, sport, all our science and arts, the state and all our public and private organizations are with few exceptions bound up in a network of illicit intrigue, impossible now to unravel. In the past three years an incredible 1,700 members of the army and police forces have been tried or dismissed for their links with the drug-traffic; twenty-five full-time politicians are on a list published in the United States of direct recipients of drugs money; copies of the confidential minutes of our national security council meetings have been found in a trafficker's brief-case; the telephone infidelities of top public officials have been illegally tapped; raids on houses have uncovered the names of many prominent Colombians linked to innumerable shady deals. This stealthy, uncontrollable hydra is nowhere to be seen, but present everywhere; it insinuates and corrupts all it touches, far beyond the boundaries of our country. Even the government is probably unaware of how far these illegal funds have helped them by easing social tensions.

The most conservative estimates put investments from drugs at a billion dollars a year. They could easily be five times as much. According to calculations published in the press, the three main drug bosses in Colombia have personal fortunes of over three billion dollars each. It is inconceivable that with a purchasing power of this magnitude they could ever be satisfied with the fleeting passion for material things; it is clear that they have sought, and managed, to penetrate into even the dark recesses of the minds and wills of their countrymen.

But the real obsession of the drug-traffickers, their Freudian obsession, has been to buy land, land, ever more land. A while ago they threw a huge party to celebrate the one hundred and fifty thousandth hectare that they had purchased. It is as though they are trying to buy up the entire map, with its condors and rivers, the yellow of its gold and the blue of its seas, so that no one can ever move them from where they want to be. Faced with this crazy reality, the voice of the presidential candidate Luis Carlos Galán seemed to offer a faint hope when he again called publicly for the drug-traffickers to surrender. The almost ritual manner of his death, shot in public surrounded by heavily armed bodyguards, finally forced the Colombian government to confront its tremendous historical responsibility. Although slow and unpredictable, President Virgilio Barco's reaction could not have been more forceful.

Like President Betancur before him, Barco's first move was to use the special powers of a state of siege to reinstate the unconstitutional extradition treaty. The drug barons seemed to have been taken aback by such determination from a man previously so little disposed to action. Barco then ordered raids on their mansions and ranches, confiscating their drug-transporting yachts and their revealing files. Barco's actions were effective enough that they will surely be reflected in the production and sale of cocaine. The drug-traffickers' worst enemy, however, is still their own methods, which will, once again, turn the whole country against them.

Perhaps the Colombians' most surprising trait is their capacity to get used to everything, however good or evil. Their powers of recuperation verge on the supernatural. Some, perhaps the most sensible, appear oblivious to the fact that they live in one of the most dangerous countries in the world. On the Sunday of the funeral for Luis Carlos Galán, whose death had moved the whole nation, ecstatic crowds poured into the streets to celebrate the Colombian football team's victory over Ecuador.

In the centuries' old tradition of violence in Colombia, urban terrorism is something new. Casual bombings which kill innocent people, and anonymous telephone death threats that persistently disrupt daily life, are bound to end by uniting friends and enemies against this invisible terror. People can perhaps live with the fear of what has happened, but nobody can live with the dread of what might happen: a bomb blowing children to bits at school; being machine-gunned by mistake while leaving a cinema; vegetables exploding at the market; an airplane disintegrating in mid-flight; your family poisoned with the tap-water. No: terrorism has never won a war.

For his part, President Virgilio Barco must know that what he had hoped would be a blitzkrieg will in fact be the most difficult and hazardous enterprise of his life: his many-headed enemy keeps itself forewarned and forearmed by shadowy informers who operate within the power structure and have ears to hear everything and eyes that see all there is to see; his government's resources are ludicrously inadequate compared to those of the enemy.

It is all very well for the United States to accuse Colombia of dragging its heels in the war on the drug-traffickers, even though more drugs are sold on its city streets than on ours, and though they keep secret the lists of their untouchable countrymen involved in the trade. There must be many in a nation which last year alone consumed 270 tons of cocaine. In the end, however, the aid the United States is giving Colombia for the present emergency cannot compare with the two billion dollars in official and clandestine funds allocated to the Nicaraguan contras over a period of eight years. Nor are we likely to see any more as long as President Barco refuses to allow US troops into Colombia, even if their sole aim is to crush the drug-traffickers.

All this suggests that the war against drugs in Colombia will be lengthy and costly, with little prospect of success. And worst of all, it is irreversible. Unless something unforeseen and glorious suddenly happens: one of those inspired impossibilities which have so often saved Latin America in the past. If dialogue is not the answer, then almost anything else is worth trying, provided that it costs no more lives. It is unthinkable that before this unfinishable war is finished, we might finally finish off our country: that is the only encouraging forecast I can muster in an attempt to avoid ending this chronicle on a note of catastrophe.

Translated from the Spanish by Nick Caistor

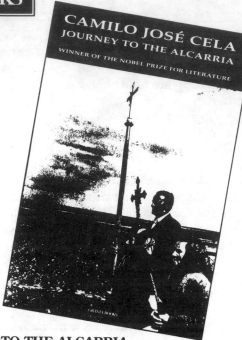

JOURNEY TO THE ALCARRIA
Camilo José Cela

In the summer of 1946, seven years after the end of the
Spanish Civil War, Camilo José Cela set out on foot to
discover the heart of Spain. He chose the Alcarria,
because he believed it was a place where nothing
ever happened, a place remarkable for its Spanishness.

This is travel writing at its best - picaresque in the
tradition of Cervantes, elegiac, verging on nostalgia.
Regarded as Cela's greatest book of non-fiction,
Journey to the Alcarria should help to establish why
Cela, at the end of 1989, surprised an English-language
readership unfamiliar with his work by receiving
the Nobel Prize for Literature.

First British Publication

WINNER OF THE NOBEL PRIZE FOR LITERATURE

Paperback, £4.99

ISBN: 0 140 14022 0

SALMAN RUSHDIE
IS NOTHING SACRED?

I grew up kissing books and bread.

In our house, whenever anyone dropped a book or let fall a chapati or a 'slice', which was our word for a triangle of buttered leavened bread, the fallen object was required not only to be picked up but also kissed, by way of apology for the act of clumsy disrespect. I was as careless and butter-fingered as any child and, accordingly, during my childhood years, I kissed a large number of 'slices' and also my fair share of books.

Devout households in India often contained, and still contain, persons in the habit of kissing holy books. But we kissed everything. We kissed dictionaries and atlases. We kissed Enid Blyton novels and Superman comics. If I'd ever dropped the telephone directory I'd probably have kissed that, too.

All this happened before I had ever kissed a girl. In fact it would almost be true, true enough for a fiction writer, anyhow, to say that once I started kissing girls, my activities with regard to bread and books lost some of their special excitement. But one never forgets one's first loves.

Bread and books: food for the body and food for the soul—what could be more worthy of our respect, and even love?

It has always been a shock to me to meet people for whom books simply do not matter, and people who are scornful of the act of reading, let alone writing. It is perhaps always astonishing to learn that your beloved is not as attractive to others as she is to you. My most beloved books have been fictions, and in the last twelve months I have been obliged to accept that for many millions of human beings, these books are entirely without attraction or value. We have been witnessing an attack upon a particular work of fiction that is also an attack upon the very idea of the novel form, an attack of such bewildering ferocity that it has become necessary to restate what is most precious about the art of literature—to answer the attack, not by an attack, but by a declaration of love.

'Is Nothing Sacred?' is the text of the Herbert Read Memorial Lecture delivered by Harold Pinter at the Institute of Contemporary Arts in London on 6 February 1990. It was also published by *Granta* as a pamphlet.

Love can lead to devotion, but the devotion of the lover is unlike that of the True Believer in that it is not militant. I may be surprised—even shocked—to find that you do not feel as I do about a given book or work of art or even person; I may very well attempt to change your mind; but I will finally accept that your tastes, your loves, are your business and not mine. The True Believer knows no such restraints. The True Believer knows that he is simply right, and you are wrong. He will seek to convert you, even by force, and if he cannot he will, at the very least, despise you for your unbelief.

Love need not be blind. Faith must, ultimately, be a leap in the dark.

The title of this lecture is a question usually asked, in tones of horror, when some personage or idea or value or place held dear by the questioner is treated to a dose of iconoclasm. White cricket balls for night cricket? Female priests? A Japanese takeover of Rolls-Royce cars? *Is nothing sacred?*

Until recently, however, it was a question to which I thought I knew the answer. The answer was No.

No, nothing is sacred in and of itself, I would have said. Ideas, texts, even people can be made sacred—the word is from the Latin *sacrare*, 'to set apart as holy'—but even though such entities, once their sacredness is established, seek to proclaim and to preserve their own absoluteness, their inviolability, the act of making sacred is in truth an event in history. It is the product of the many and complex pressures of the time in which the act occurs. And events in history must always be subject to questioning, deconstruction, even to declarations of their obsolescence. To revere the sacred unquestioningly is to be paralysed by it. The idea of the sacred is quite simply one of the most conservative notions in any culture, because it seeks to turn other ideas—Uncertainty, Progress, Change—into crimes.

To take only one such declaration of obsolescence: I would have described myself as living in the aftermath of the death of god. On the subject of the death of god, the American novelist and critic William H. Gass had this to say, as recently as 1984:

> The death of god represents not only the realization
> that gods have never existed, but the contention that
> such a belief is no longer even irrationally possible: that
> neither reason nor the taste and temper of the times
> condones it. The belief lingers on, of course, but it does
> so like astrology or a faith in a flat earth.

I have some difficulty with the uncompromising bluntness of this obituary notice. It has always been clear to me that god is unlike human beings in that it can die, so to speak, in parts. In other parts, for example India, god continues to flourish, in literally thousands of forms. So that if I speak of living after this death, I am speaking in a limited, personal sense—my sense of god ceased to exist long ago, and as a result I was drawn towards the great creative possibilities offered by surrealism, modernism and their successors, those philosophies and aesthetics born of the realization that, as Karl Marx said, 'all that is solid melts into air.'

It did not seem to me, however, that my ungodliness, or rather my post-godliness, need necessarily bring me into conflict with belief. Indeed, one reason for my attempt to develop a form of fiction in which the miraculous might coexist with the mundane was precisely my acceptance that notions of the sacred and the profane both needed to be explored, as far as possible without pre-judgement, in any honest literary portrait of the way we are.

That is to say: the most secular of authors ought to be capable of presenting a sympathetic portrait of a devout believer. Or, to put it another way: I had never felt the need to totemize my lack of belief, and so make it something to go to war about.

Now, however, I find my entire world-picture under fire. And as I find myself obliged to defend the assumptions and processes of literature, which I had believed that all free men and women could take for granted, and for which all unfree men and women continue every day to struggle, so I am obliged to ask myself questions I admit to finding somewhat unnerving.

Do I, perhaps, find something sacred after all? Am I prepared to set aside as holy the idea of the absolute freedom of the imagination and alongside it my own notions of the World, the Text and the Good? Does this add up to what the apologists of religion have started calling 'secular fundamentalism'? And if so, must I accept that this 'secular fundamentalism' is as likely to lead to excesses, abuses and oppressions as the canons of religious faith?

A lecture in memory of Herbert Read is a highly appropriate occasion for such an exploration, and I am honoured to have been asked to deliver it. Herbert Read, one of the leading British advocates of the modernist and surrealist movements, was a distinguished representative of the cultural values closest to my heart. 'Art is never transfixed,' Read wrote. 'Change is the condition of art remaining art.' This principle is also mine. Art, too, is an event in history, subject to the historical process. But it is also *about* that process, and must constantly strive to find new forms to mirror an endlessly renewed world. No aesthetic can be a constant, except an aesthetic based on the idea of inconstancy, metamorphosis, or, to borrow a term from politics, 'perpetual revolution'.

The struggle between such ideas and the eternal, revealed truths of religion is dramatized this evening, as I hope I may be excused for pointing out, by my absence. I must apologize for this. I did, in fact, ask my admirable protectors how they would feel if I were to deliver my text in person. The answer was, more or less, 'What have we done to deserve this?' With regret, I took the point.

It is an agony and a frustration not to be able to re-enter my old life, not even for such a moment. However, I should like to thank Harold Pinter, through his own mouth, for standing in my place. Perhaps this event could be thought of as a form of secular revelation: a man receives a text by mysterious processes from Elsewhere—above? below? New Scotland Yard?—and brings it out before the people, and recites . . .

More than twenty years ago, I stood packed in at the back of this theatre, listening to a lecture by Arthur Koestler. He propounded the thesis that language, not territory, was the prime cause of aggression, because once language reached the level of sophistication at which it could express abstract concepts, it acquired the power of totemization; and once peoples had erected totems, they would go to war to defend them. (I ask pardon of Koestler's ghost. I am relying on an old memory, and that's an untrustworthy shoulder to lean on.)

In support of his theory, he told us about two tribes of monkeys living on, I think, one of the northern islands of Japan. The two tribes lived in close proximity in the woods near a certain stream, and subsisted, not unusually, on a diet of bananas. One of the tribes, however, had developed the curious habit of washing its bananas in the stream before eating them, while the other tribe continued to be non-banana-washers. And yet, said Koestler, the two tribes continued to live contentedly as neighbours, without quarrelling. And why was this? It was because their language was too primitive to permit them to totemize either the act of banana-washing or that of eating bananas unwashed. With a more sophisticated language at their disposal, both wet and dry bananas could have become the sacred objects at the heart of a religion, and then, look out!—Holy war.

A young man rose from the audience to ask Koestler a question. Perhaps the real reason why the two tribes did not fight, he suggested, was that there were enough bananas to go round. Koestler became extremely angry. He refused to answer such a piece of Marxist claptrap. And, in a way, he was right. Koestler and his questioner were speaking different languages, and their languages were in conflict. Their disagreement could even be seen as the proof of Koestler's point. If he, Koestler, were to be considered the banana-washer and his questioner the dry-banana man, then their command of a language more complex than the Japanese monkeys' had indeed resulted in totemizations. Now each of them had a totem to defend: the primacy of language versus the primacy of economics: and dialogue therefore became impossible. They were at war.

Between religion and literature, as between politics and literature, there is a linguistically based dispute. But it is not a dispute of simple opposites. Because whereas religion seeks to privilege one language above all others, one set of values above all others, one text above all others, the novel has always been *about* the way in which different languages, values and narratives quarrel, and about the shifting relations between them, which are relations of power. The novel does not seek to establish a privileged language, but it insists upon the freedom to portray and analyse the struggle between the different contestants for such privileges.

Carlos Fuentes has called the novel 'a privileged *arena*'. By this he does not mean that it is the kind of holy space which one must put off one's shoes to enter; it is not an arena to revere; it claims no special rights *except the right to be the stage upon which the great debates of society can be conducted*. 'The novel,' Fuentes writes, 'is born from the very fact that we do not understand one another, because unitary, orthodox language has broken down. Quixote and Sancho, the Shandy brothers, Mr and Mrs Karenin: their novels are the comedy (or the drama) of their misunderstandings. Impose a unitary language: you kill the novel, but you also kill the society.'

He then poses the question I have been asking myself throughout my life as a writer: *Can the religious mentality survive outside of religious dogma and hierarchy?* Which is to say: Can art be the third principle that mediates between the material and spiritual worlds; might it, by 'swallowing' both worlds, offer us something new something that might even be called a secular definition of transcendence?

I believe it can. I believe it must. And I believe that, at its best, it does.

What I mean by transcendence is that flight of the human spirit outside the confines of its material, physical existence which all of us, secular or religious, experience on at least a few occasions. Birth is a moment of transcendence which we spend our lives trying to understand. The exaltation of the act of love, the experience of joy and very possibly the moment of death are other such moments. The soaring quality of transcendence, the sense of being more than oneself, of being in some way joined to the whole of life, is by its nature short-lived. Not even the visionary or mystical experience ever lasts very long. It is for art to capture that experience, to offer it to, in the case of literature, its readers; to be, for a secular, materialist culture, some sort of replacement for what the love of god offers in the world of faith.

It is important that we understand how profoundly we all feel the needs that religion, down the ages, has satisfied. I would suggest that these needs are of three types: firstly, the need to be given an articulation of our half-glimpsed knowledge of exaltation, of awe, of wonder; life is an awesome experience, and religion helps us understand why life so often makes us feel small, by telling us what we are *smaller than*; and, contrariwise, because we also have a sense of being special, of being *chosen*, religion helps us by telling us what we have been chosen by, and what for. Secondly, we need answers to the unanswerable: how did we get here? How did 'here' get here in the first place? Is this, this brief life, all there is? How can it be? What would be the point of that? And, thirdly, we need codes to live by, 'rules for every damn thing'. The idea of god is at once a repository for our awestruck wonderment at life and an answer to the great questions of existence, and a rulebook, too. The soul needs all these explanations—not simply rational explanations, but explanations of the heart.

It is also important to understand how often the language of secular, rationalist materialism has failed to answer these needs. As we witness the death of communism in Central Europe, we cannot fail to observe the deep religious spirit with which so many of the makers of these revolutions are imbued, and we must concede that it is not only a particular political ideology that has failed, but the idea that men and women could ever define themselves in terms that exclude their spiritual needs.

It seems obvious, but relevant, to point out that in all the countries now moving towards freedom, art was repressed as viciously as was religion. That the Czech revolution began in the theatres and is led by a writer is proof that people's spiritual needs, more than their material needs, have driven the commissars from power.

What appears plain is that it will be a very long time before the peoples of Europe will accept any ideology that claims to have a complete, totalized explanation of the world. Religious faith, profound as it is, must surely remain a private matter. This rejection of totalized explanations is the modern condition. And this is where the novel, the form created to discuss the fragmentation of truth, comes in. The film director Luis Buñuel used to say: 'I would give my life for a man who is looking for the truth. But I would gladly kill a man who thinks he has found the truth.' (This is what we used to call a joke, before killing people for their ideas returned to the agenda.) The elevation of the quest for the Grail over the Grail itself, the acceptance that all that is solid *has* melted into air, that reality and morality are not givens but imperfect human constructs, is the point from which fiction begins. This is what J.-F. Lyotard called, in 1979, *La Condition Postmoderne*. The challenge of literature is to start from this point, and still find a way of fulfilling our unaltered spiritual requirements.

Moby Dick meets that challenge by offering us a dark, almost Manichean vision of a universe (the *Pequod*) in the grip of one demon, Ahab, and heading inexorably towards another; namely the Whale. The ocean always was our Other, manifesting itself to us in the form of beasts—the worm Ouroboros, Kraken, Leviathan. Herman Melville delves into these dark waters in order to offer us a very modern parable: Ahab, gripped by his possession, perishes; Ishmael, a man without strong feeling or powerful affiliations, survives. The self-interested modern man is the sole survivor; those who worship the whale—for pursuit is a form of worship—perish by the whale.

In a very different way, Italo Calvino meets the challenge as well. His trilogy *Our Ancestors*, which he called an attempt to provide a family tree for modern man, offers us three bizarre and comical exemplary figures. There is the cloven viscount, bisected on a medieval battlefield, whose two halves live on, the one impossibly evil, the other improbably good, and both of them utterly insufferable. Only when they are rejoined, when good and evil blend and create a human being, is the viscount fit for human society again. And there is the Baron in the Trees, the ultimate rebel, who rejects the patriarchal command to eat a bowl of revolting snail soup and takes to the trees for the rest of his days. And finally there is the Non-Existent Knight, an empty suit of armour that keeps itself going by will-power and by total, unswerving adherence to the laws of chivalry. It becomes one of

105

the more illustrious *chevaliers* in the army of Charlemagne. These three fables, about the inseparability of good and evil, about the consequences and importance of refusing what one finds revolting —snail soup or tyranny—and about a (literally) hollow being sustained only by a stultifying quasi-religious code, offer us dreams of ourselves, maps of our inner natures. No less effectively, but much less prescriptively than any holy text, they show us who we are.

Joyce's wanderers, Beckett's tramps, Gogol's tricksters, Bulgakov's devils, Bellow's high-energy meditations on the stifling of the soul by the triumphs of materialism; these, and many more, are what we have instead of prophets and suffering saints. But while the novel answers our need for wonderment and understanding, it brings us harsh and unpalatable news as well.

It tells us there are no rules. It hands down no commandments. We have to make up our own rules as best we can, make them up as we go along.

And it tells us there are no answers; or, rather, it tells us that answers are easier to come by, and less reliable, than questions. If religion is an answer, if political ideology is an answer, then literature is an inquiry; great literature, by asking extraordinary questions, opens new doors in our minds.

Richard Rorty, in *Philosophy and the Mirror of Nature*, insists on the importance of historicity, of giving up the illusions of being in contact with Eternity. For him, the great error is what he calls 'foundationalism', which the theologian Don Cupitt, commenting on Rorty, calls 'the attempt, as old as (and even much older than) Plato, to give permanence and authority to our knowledge and values by purporting to found them in some unchanging cosmic realm, natural or noumenal, outside the flux of our human conversation.' It is better, Cupitt concludes, 'to be an adaptable pragmatist, a nomad.'

Michel Foucault, also a confirmed historicist, discusses the role of the author in challenging sacralized absolutes in his essay, 'What is an Author?' This essay argues, in part, that 'texts, books and discourses really began to have authors . . . to the extent that authors became subject to punishment, that is, to the extent that discourses could be transgressive.' This is an extraordinary, provocative idea, even if it is stated with Foucault's characteristic airiness and a complete absence of supporting evidence: *that authors were named only when it was necessary to find somebody to blame.* Foucault continues:

> In our culture (and doubtless in many others), discourse was not originally a product, a thing, a kind of goods; it was essentially an act—an act placed in the bipolar field of the sacred and the profane, the licit and the illicit, the religious and the blasphemous. Historically it was a gesture fraught with risks . . .

In our beginnings we find our essences. To understand a religion, look at its earliest moments. (It is regrettable that Islam, of all religions the easiest to study in this way, because of its birth during the age of recorded history, has set its face so resolutely against the idea that it, like all ideas, is an event inside history.) And to understand an artistic form, too, Foucault suggests, look at its origins. If he is right about the novel, then literature is, of all the arts, the one best suited to challenging absolutes of all kinds; and, because it is in its origin the schismatic Other of the sacred (and authorless) text, so it is also the art most likely to fill our god-shaped holes.

There are other reasons, too, for proposing the novel as the crucial art form of what I can no longer avoid calling the post-modern age. For one thing, literature is the art least subject to external control, because it is made in private. The act of making it requires only one person, one pen, one room, some paper. (Even the room is not absolutely essential.) Literature is the most low-technology of the art forms. It requires neither a stage nor a screen. It calls for no interpreters, no actors, producers, camera crews, costumiers, musicians. It does not even require the traditional apparatus of publishing, as the long-running success of samizdat literature demonstrates. The Foucault essay suggests that literature is as much at risk from the enveloping, smothering forces of the market economy, which reduces books to mere products. This danger is real, and I do not want to seem to be minimizing it. But the truth is that of all the forms, literature can still be the most free. The more money a piece of work costs, the easier it is to control. Film, the most expensive of art forms, is also the least subversive. This is why, although Carlos Fuentes cites the

107

work of film-makers like Buñuel, Bergman and Fellini as instances of successful secular revolts into the territory of the sacred, I continue to believe in the greater possibilities of the novel. Its singularity is its best protection.

Among the childhood books I devoured and kissed were large numbers of cheap comics of a most unliterary nature. The heroes of these comic books were, or so it seemed, almost always mutants or hybrids or freaks: as well as the Batman and the Spiderman there was Aquaman, who was half-fish, and of course Superman, who could easily be mistaken for a bird or a plane. In those days, the middle 1950s, the super-heroes were all, in their various ways, hawkish law-and-order conservatives, leaping to work in response to the Police Commissioner's Bat-Signal, banding together to form the Justice League of America, defending what Superman called 'truth, justice and the American way'. But in spite of this extreme emphasis on crime-busting, the lesson they taught children—or this child, at any rate—was the perhaps unintentionally radical truth that exceptionality was the greatest and most heroic of values; that those who were unlike the crowd were to be treasured the most lovingly; and that this exceptionality was a treasure so great and so easily misunderstood that it had to be concealed, in ordinary life, beneath what the comic books called a 'secret identity'. Superman could not have survived without 'mild-mannered' Clark Kent; 'millionaire socialite' Bruce Wayne made possible the nocturnal activities of the Batman.

Now it is obviously true that those other freakish, hybrid, mutant, exceptional beings—novelists—those creators of the most freakish, hybrid and metamorphic of forms, the novel, have frequently been obliged to hide behind secret identities, whether for reasons of gender or terror. But the most wonderful of the many wonderful truths about the novel form is that the greater the writer, the greater his or her exceptionality. The geniuses of the novel are those whose voices are fully and undisguisably their own, who, to borrow William Gass's image, *sign every word they write*. What draws us to an author is his or her 'unlikeness', even if the apparatus of literary criticism then sets to work to demonstrate that he or she is really no more than an accumulation of influences. Unlikeness, the thing that makes it impossible for a writer to stand in any regimented line, is a quality novelists share with the Caped

Crusaders of the comics, though they are only rarely capable of leaping tall buildings in a single stride.

What is more, the writer is there, in his work, in the reader's hands, utterly exposed, utterly defenceless, entirely without the benefit of an alter ego to hide behind. What is forged, in the secret act of reading, is a different kind of identity, as the reader and writer merge, though the medium of the text, to become a collective being that both writes as it reads and reads as it writes, and creates, jointly, that unique work, 'their' novel. This 'secret identity' of writer and reader is the novel form's greatest and most subversive gift.

And this, finally, is why I elevate the novel above other forms, why it has always been, and remains, my first love: not only is it the art involving least compromises, but it is also the only one that takes the 'privileged arena' of conflicting discourses *right inside our heads*. The interior space of our imagination is a theatre that can never be closed down; the images created there make up a movie that can never be destroyed.

In this last decade of the millennium, as the forces of religion are renewed in strength and as the all-pervasive power of materialism wraps its own weighty chains around the human spirit, where should the novel be looking? It seems clear that the renewal of the old, bipolar field of discourse, between the sacred and the profane, which Michel Foucault proposes, will be of central importance. It seems probable, too, that we may be heading towards a world in which there will be no real alternative to the liberal-capitalist social model (except, perhaps, the theocratic, foundationalist model of Islam). In this situation, liberal capitalism or democracy or the free world will require novelists' most rigorous attention, will require re-imagining and questioning and doubting as never before. 'Our antagonist is our helper,' said Edmund Burke, and if democracy no longer has communism to help it clarify, by opposition, its own ideas, then perhaps it will have to have literature as an adversary instead.

I have made a large number of sweeping claims for literature during the course of this piece, and I am aware of a slightly messianic tone in much of what I've written. The reverencing of books and writers, by writers, is nothing particularly new, of course. 'Since the early 19th century,' writes Cupitt, 'imaginative writers have claimed—have indeed enjoyed—a guiding and representative role in our culture. Our preachers are novelists, poets, dramatists, film-makers and the like, purveyors of fiction, ambiguous people, deceivers. Yet we continue to think of ourselves as rational.'

But now I find myself backing away from the idea of sacralizing literature with which I flirted at the beginning of this text; I cannot bear the idea of the writer as secular prophet; I am remembering that one of the very greatest writers of the century, Samuel Beckett, believed that all art must inevitably end in failure. This is, clearly, no reason for surrender. 'Ever tried. Ever failed. Never mind. Try again. Fail better.'

Literature is an interim report from the consciousness of the artist, and so it can never be 'finished' or 'perfect'. Literature is made at the frontier between the self and the world, and in the act of creation that frontier softens, becomes permeable, allows the world to flow into the artist and the artist to flow into the world. Nothing so inexact, so easily and frequently misconceived, deserves the protection of being declared sacrosanct. We shall just have to get along without the shield of sacralization, and a good thing, too. We must not become what we oppose.

The only privilege literature deserves—and this privilege it requires in order to exist—is the privilege of being the arena of discourse, the place where the struggle of languages can be acted out.

I magine this. You wake up one morning and find yourself in a large, rambling house. As you wander through it you realize it is so enormous that you will never know it all. In the house are people you know, family members, friends, lovers, colleagues; also many strangers. The house is full of activity: conflicts and seductions, celebrations and wakes. At some point you realize there is no way out. You find that you can accept this. The house is not what you'd have chosen, it's in fairly bad condition, the corridors are often full of bullies, but it will have to do. Then one day you enter an unimportant-looking little room. The room is empty, but there are voices in it, voices that seem to be whispering just to you. You recognize some of the voices, others are completely unknown to you. The voices are talking about the house, about everyone in it, about everything that is happening and has happened and should happen. Some of them speak exclusively in obscenities. Some are bitchy. Some are loving. Some are funny. Some are sad. The most interesting voices are all these things at once. You begin to go to the room more and more often. Slowly you realize that most of the people in the house use such rooms sometimes. Yet the rooms are all discreetly positioned and unimportant-looking.

Now imagine that you wake up one morning and you are still in the large house, but all the voice-rooms have disappeared. It is as if they have been wiped out. Now there is nowhere in the whole house where you can go to hear voices talking about everything in every possible way. There is nowhere to go for the voices that can be funny one minute and sad the next, that can sound raucous and melodic in the course of the same sentence. Now you remember: there is no way out of this house. Now this fact begins to seem unbearable. You look into the eyes of the people in the corridors —family, lovers, friends, colleagues, strangers, bullies, priests. You see the same thing in everybody's eyes. How do we get out of here? It becomes clear that the house is a prison. People begin to scream, and pound the walls. Men arrive with guns. The house begins to shake. You do not wake up. You are already awake.

L iterature is the one place in any society where, within the secrecy of our own heads, we can hear *voices talking about everything in every possible way*. The reason for ensuring that that privileged arena is preserved is not that writers want the absolute freedom to say and do whatever they please. It is that we, all of us, readers and writers and citizens and generals and godmen, need that little, unimportant-looking room. We do not need to call it sacred, but we do need to remember that it is necessary.

'Everybody knows,' wrote Saul Bellow in *The Adventures of Augie March*, 'there is no fineness or accuracy of suppression. If you hold down one thing, you hold down the adjoining.'

Wherever in the world the little room of literature has been closed, sooner or later the walls have come tumbling down.

© Salman Rushdie, 1990.

BLAKE MORRISON
AN INTERVIEW WITH
SALMAN RUSHDIE

I met Salman Rushdie at a pre-arranged location on 4 February, the week before he published his essay 'In Good Faith' in the *Independent on Sunday* and delivered his lecture 'Is Nothing Sacred?' (or rather had it delivered for him by Harold Pinter) at the Institute of Contemporary Arts in London. It was the first interview he had given in person since 14 February last year, when he spoke to CBS News immediately after Ayatollah Khomeini's *fatwa*. In the circumstances, he seemed remarkably relaxed, resilient, even jokey: after a year's silence, broken with his essay, his lecture and this interview, he seemed eager to talk. Outside the curtained window I could hear the rain falling heavily on the street; inside, we drank tea and ate Italian bread and salad. We sat on the sofa next to each other and let the tape run for nearly an hour and a half.

Salman Rushdie: This is a strange experience: I can't remember the last interview I gave, with a journalist sitting in the room.

Blake Morrison: You've chosen to break your silence over *The Satanic Verses* with a long explanatory essay. Why?

Rushdie: It's often said that writers should never explain their work, but perhaps we could agree that these are exceptional circumstances. Normally when you write a novel, it's not a thing that has simply one meaning. Some people will read a scene and find it funny or satirical, others read it and find it sad or spiritual. Usually you don't have to choose between the two versions: the writer can allow both meanings to exist. But I've been put in a position where I have to say 'what I really meant'. It's a very strange thing to be doing, because, as anyone who writes a novel knows, not all the effects are planned—things happen on a page. It's been a characteristic of this whole affair that you have to talk about *The Satanic Verses* in a language which is really not appropriate to it.

Morrison: You've waited a year. Has it been hard to keep silent?

Rushdie: Yes, it was fantastically difficult being quiet, especially since I was hearing some quite extraordinary things being said about me and my work: it was very shocking to be the object of so much hostility and falsification. I suppose the reason why I didn't quarrel with all that was that I couldn't see how to do it. There was so much of it, a whole tidal wave coming at me, and I just couldn't shout loud enough to be heard. And I thought that in a way it might be quite eloquent to say nothing: as if to say, here is someone whose business is language who is now unable to speak. But I always knew there'd been a moment when silence would no longer be useful and people would be ready to listen again.

Morrison: And you think that moment has now come?

Rushdie: It's an instinctive judgement. I'm hardly in a position to take a personal feeler on what's happening round the country. But I began to think around Christmas or thereabouts that the moment had come.

Morrison: What do you hope might be achieved by talking?

Rushdie: A number of things. The controversy has departed so much from reality that it needs to be dragged back to reality: the book that people claim I wrote is not the book I did write. I also wanted to explain that in many cases my responses to the events of the last year have been very similar to the responses of the Muslim people who have been attacking me: the attack on the Asian community makes me just as angry as it makes them feel. The idea that the National Front could use my name as a way of taunting Asians is so horrifying and obscene to my mind that I wanted to make it clear: that's not my team, they're not my supporters, they're simply exploiting the situation to their own ends. Most Muslims are reasonably tolerant and decent people, and they've been told a lot of things about my book while also being told by their mosques not to read it. I thought if I could just open up a conversation, I could begin to say that there aren't the grounds here to justify the level of upset and violence.

Morrison: Your article 'In Good Faith' seems to address Muslims here in Britain rather than those in Iran.

Rushdie: Well, I don't see how I could talk to those in Iran. It's here that the controversy is happening: it's no longer an issue in the subcontinent or the rest of Europe. This is partly because I live in Britain, of course, but partly too because things have been

115

tolerated here which wouldn't be tolerated in other countries: in France, for instance, the government has made a very strong statement against incitements to violence, and the French imam has said that French Muslims should respect the secular traditions of the country. As for Iran, the problem there has to be dealt with by processes of diplomacy and politics to which I'm not privy: there's not a great deal I can do to influence that situation, other than to express my belief as reasonably as possible that this book does not deserve the treatment it has received.

Morrison: What do you feel about the violence and the threats that have characterized some of the opposition to *The Satanic Verses* in Britain?

Rushdie: I've just read that they're not going to prosecute Kalim Siddiqui for incitement to murder on the grounds of insufficient evidence. Apparently, it is not sufficient evidence that someone is seen on national television approving of a call for another person's death, joining three hundred other people in a chant of death, and a video of all this exists. Irrespective of the rights and wrongs of the Siddiqui matter, it seems to me as a layman rather puzzling, and as the object of the attack rather upsetting, that it's all right for people to walk around the country calling for my death. I also find it hard to believe that if it were not me, but a government minister, say, the evidence would still be deemed insufficient. The real reason is presumably one of public order—which I can understand, I see the thinking. But I have a rather simple view of the subject: they're asking for me to be murdered, and I think that's a bad idea.

Morrison: What is your position on the possible paperback publication of *The Satanic Verses*?

Rushdie: I've never made any secret of my position. I think the paperback should be published. And actually, contrary to what the newspapers say, I still feel hopeful that Penguin will bring it out. I've certainly never heard from anyone there any serious suggestion that Penguin won't. In many ways this is a whipped-up issue: people have been playing their cards close to their chest, so

On 21 October 1989, Kalim Siddiqui, Director of the Muslim Institute in London, was filmed on the BBC television news in a chant of 'Death to Rushdie' in Manchester Town Hall.

journalists have had to make things up. The *Observer* reported recently that the paperback would not be published, and since then I've had one hundred per cent assurances from members of the entire management, from Peter Mayer down, that Penguin's position is not what was alleged. It's an incredibly difficult state of affairs, though, and it's very wrong of journalists to drive a wedge between us.

Morrison: You'd not accept that you are 'obsessive' about the paperback?

Rushdie: If I ring my publishers to talk about my book, that's not after all an unusual thing for me as an author to do. That's the basis of our relationship. There have been better moments and worse, because people have been under incredible pressure, but given that we get on very well.

I remember a time just after the book came out when I happened to be in the Penguin office and the first anonymous death-threat came through—a voice saying that I was going to be killed. The phone was answered by a secretary, who was very shaken. The level of intimidation in this affair has been extraordinary: hundreds and hundreds of telephone calls making all kinds of menacing suggestions have been received by Penguin here and in America. What has been aimed at the publishers and bookshops has been a very high-level scare campaign—I'm resisting the word terrorism only because it has other connotations. But it has certainly been a fear campaign, and one that cannot be justified simply by claiming injury. What about the injury caused to the peace of mind of those on the receiving end of this? I think many Muslims find it an embarrassment to be associated with that behaviour, and I hope that soon they might start saying: we don't like that way of carrying on.

Morrison: Would you consider the suggestion of inserting a prefatory note into the paperback?

Rushdie: I don't have strong feelings about this, but I'm not sure what that prefatory note would be or how it could be written in such a way that it didn't rapidly become outdated. People have said that *The Satanic Verses* should be identified as a work of fiction, not as a study of Islam. Well, it *is* identified as a work of fiction: it says so on the dust-jacket, even if it doesn't say so on the title page, and it's impossible to read the first page and not to be aware it's a novel.

Morrison: What about a consortium publishing the paperback, to reduce the risk to Penguin?

Rushdie: Again, I have no strong feelings about that. It's a matter for the publishers. In some countries publishers have gone down that road, in others not. If Penguin felt they needed a consortium, that would be acceptable to me.

Morrison: Should the paperback be dropped altogether as a peace gesture?

Rushdie: First of all, it's not me waging the war. Should I, therefore, be the one who is asked to make the gesture of peace? In many countries there is no division between the hardback and the paperback. In France and Spain, for instance, the book was originally published in paperback. In England and America everyone except hardback publishers would agree that the major publication of a book is its paperback edition: the real right is the paperback right. And for a simple reason: if you want to keep a book in print for any length of time, and I don't mean huge piles of books but the odd copy, then it has to be a paperback. If the paperback doesn't exist, the book has effectively been suppressed. It's the only way it can receive the judgement of posterity. It's the only way it can be studied in colleges, because hardbacks don't go on the syllabus; and any book that's been involved in a controversy such as this should be studied. Already some Muslim scholars have defended *The Satanic Verses* on the grounds of what they know about the Islamic tradition and how the book fits into it, and it's important that that process continues.

So my main reason for wanting the paperback is to prevent this book from being banned by the back door. Yes, it's sold a large number of copies, but in a few years' time if the paperback doesn't exist, the book simply won't be there for anyone who wants to read it.

Morrison: You've been under enormous psychological pressure. Have you managed to work in an ordinary way?

Rushdie: Well, I'm not working in an ordinary way, but I am working. There have been periods when I've not been able to do very much, but book-reviewing, for instance, has been useful, a way back to writing. At the moment, touch wood, it's going quite well, and there's no doubt that when it is going well it's easier to deal with the situation I'm in. When a writer is writing he feels like himself.

Morrison: This is the children's book?

Rushdie: In the last month, it has been the article 'In Good Faith', which has been this thing sitting on my shoulders, unsaid, for a whole year. It has been the most painful and difficult piece of writing I've ever done, if only because when you write as a novelist you're not writing about yourself, whereas here the subject necessarily *was* myself, my motives and personality and so on. When I finished it I felt the sort of exhaustion I would feel if I'd just finished a novel. Literally for three or four days I was completely physically exhausted, which was obviously the release of something very large. I feel much better having said it. As anyone who knows me will tell you, I'm not the kind of person who can zip up his mouth without it being quite an act of will, so it has been a difficult time.

I reckon I've now about two months' work to do on the children's book I've been writing and then it will be finished. I've also put together a selection of my essays and criticism, about ten years' work, something I've wanted to do for some time, and it's now beginning to acquire some coherence. The children's book is a fable. . .

Morrison: And has it, as I've seen suggested, anything to do with your situation now?

Rushdie: Heavens, no, that's the kind of silly thing people invent when they know nothing. I've had the story in my head for at least three years. It'll be a book of about 160 to 170 pages, aimed primarily at children in the twelve-to-fifteen-year-old age group.

My ambition is to write a book which children can enjoy but grown-ups will like as well. The great thing about children as an audience is that they tell you when they're bored: you have to make sure every paragraph is interesting. If I get that done, and the book of essays, I can at least feel that I've got something out of the year.

Morrison: And then a novel to follow?

Rushdie: Sure, I've got a novel worked out to the extent that I've written—for my own benefit really—a twenty-five-page synopsis. Even if all this hadn't happened I would not have started it: it needed time just to sit in my head and gestate. I hope that when the other two books have been completed, the essays and the children's book, that I can pull the novel out of my head, so to speak, and make a start.

Morrison: Do you foresee any change in the way you will write? Has magical realism come to a sticky end, in view of all that's happened?

Rushdie: I don't think any two of my books are alike, anyway. But the point about *The Satanic Verses* is that it's a novel that begins in a pyrotechnic high-surrealist vein and moves towards a much more emotional, inner writing. That process of putting away the magic noses and cloven hoofs is one the novel itself goes through: *it tells itself*, and by the end it doesn't need that apparatus any more. That was a direction I wanted to move in anyway, so without doubt the next novel will not have cloven hoofs or magic noses.

Morrison: All three of your major novels have been politically contentious in some way. Do you see such contentiousness as unavoidable?

Rushdie: No. It may seem fantastically naïve to say so, but I thought *The Satanic Verses* a personal, inward and spiritual novel, not a historical or political one as the previous ones had been. It's a novel about whether people can live without God, about how people change when they move across the planet. It's about how people come to terms with dying, and how they fail to learn about love. It's not a novel about religion: the subject is not faith but the loss of faith. So it seemed to me that I had already in this book moved away from politics. Obviously, that's not how it turned out [laughs]—some mistake surely—but that's what I thought I was doing. Writers can sit in a room for five years and think their processes will be understood, and most of the time they are, but sometimes, spectacularly, they're not. The idea that I planned all this is bizarre.

Morrison: What have you been reading, or watching on television?

Rushdie: I have been watching a good deal of junk television. Having had lots of late nights by myself, I've become an addict of American football over the last year. I watched the Superbowl last week right to the end. I also became very hooked on a series called *Capital City*, about yuppie bankers and money, especially as it was on at a time when my other fixes—things like *thirtysomething*, *Dynasty* and *Dallas*—were all off the air.

I have also been reading more poetry over the last few years, and have got more pleasure out of it than out of novels. The extra attention to language in poetry, the extra charge: it puts you on your mettle. I always keep Derek Walcott around, and I've been reading a lot of Miłosz. American poetry, too, even though Fenton says no American poetry is any good (perhaps even James Fenton can be wrong). I've also begun to write poetry, which I hadn't done since I was eighteen. I'm very tentative about this, and '6 March 1989', the poem that appeared in *Granta*, was the first one I'd ever published, and I felt about it like anyone would about seeing their first poem in print. And then what happens? Because of this weird situation I'm in it's read out on the *Nine O'Clock News*! I felt very sorry for it—my poor little poem, only seventeen lines—and it's a front-page story.

When the *fatwa* came, I had to leave my house in the clothes I stood in—a classic cliché of fiction—and I've never been home. So a lot of my favourite books were locked up at first. Since then at various points friends have got things out for me. I always carry *Moby Dick* around: it's a great, great masterpiece, and transgressive in a way I find very attractive. You have a universe and this little boat pursuing one kind of devil and being run by

another: that's an extraordinary metaphor—it's not surprising
the book didn't do very well when it came out. I always keep
Ulysses near me because it's the modern novel that most achieves
that charge of poetry, and I read it to be reminded what novels
can be.

I've found myself, for fairly obvious reasons, reading various
Enlightenment writers. It's very odd, when you think of how
much has been written this year about their importance in our
culture, to look at what actually happened to those guys at the
time. Rousseau's *Confessions* were not published in his lifetime
nor *Jacques le fataliste*. Voltaire kept having to skip the country
and used to say that he lived close to a frontier because that was
very useful. The fact is that, at the time the Enlightenment writers
were writing the works that we now think of as the bedrock of
European free speech, they were persecuted, banned, reviled
and accused of blasphemy. I think it would be as well for Europe
to remember that. So yes, I've been reading a lot.

Morrison: There have been consolations, then?

Rushdie: Listen, it's not great. You make the best of the situation.
The thing that's worst is the loss of ordinary life: not being able to
walk down a street, to browse in a bookshop, to go to a
movie—those sorts of trivial things that everyone—including
me, once—takes for granted, things you don't value greatly until
you don't have them. What they add up to is life. If you can't do
them, you have to do what you can, but it doesn't mean it's a
positive experience.

Morrison: Have you learned something about yourself?

Rushdie: If you had told me in advance, this and this and this is
going to happen to you over the next year, I'd not have been very
confident of my ability to stand up to it. You don't find out until
you're in the situation whether you can stand up to it or not.
Fortunately, so far, I have—but I don't recommend it. As a way
of learning about yourself, there must be better ones!

Morrison: The world has changed a lot over the last year. How does
it look to you?

Rushdie: In normal circumstances I'd have been on the first plane to Berlin. I envied my friends who did go. I have been to Berlin a few times and always found it a very exciting city, not so much in spite of but because of the Wall, and those images of people dancing on the Wall were quite extraordinary. And to miss the chance of being on it! I felt I'd missed out on one of the great moments of our time. For week after week, all the news seemed to be good: it was very strange for good news to be leading the bulletins.

Those of us who were young in 1968 used to talk of 1968 as the moment when some great shift in power towards the people took place. But actually, nothing happened in 1968: a few kids ran down a street chased by the police. This time it *actually happened*. Eighty-nine does it again: 1689, 1789, and now 1989, the greatest year in European history since the end of the Second World War.

Morrison: Do you take a particular pleasure in seeing Václav Havel as president?

Rushdie: He's clearly an extraordinary writer—apart from his plays, those prison letters to Olga are amazing—so to have a serious writer running a country, quite possibly two serious writers running countries if Vargas Llosa wins the election in Peru, well, it's a sign that perhaps the world is a less hopeless place than I thought it was. Suddenly, intelligent people seem to be in charge. It would be nice if it happened here.

Morrison: Has your attitude to the British state changed as a result of your experience?

Rushdie: Yes. It's very simple: if somebody takes steps to protect you when your life is in great danger, you feel more kindly towards them than you did before. There's no doubt, that at that personal level, my feelings about the British government have changed. And I think that's been assisted by the fact that the party I've supported and voted for all my life, the Labour Party, has been so vocal in the attack on me. There have been people in the Labour Party who have been incredibly supportive, Michael Foot especially, but I felt very shaken by the way in which certain parts of the Labour Party have abandoned positions that are important to hold—such as not playing religious politics, which is a dangerous game. I don't think there's much chance of my becoming a Conservative voter, but maybe I'd use a different kind of language if I was talking about the Conservative government now; maybe I wouldn't be quite as polemical. And I make no apologies for the fact that this is because of personal experience. I dislike this government's policies, and would argue against them, but I'd also argue that a great deal of the Labour Party's policy is mistaken too.

Contrary to public opinion, which always puts me down as a raving Lefty, I'm a very bad joiner. I've never in my life belonged to a political party, not even a local constituency party, and I've never been a hard-line zealot. I've always thought that what gave writers a role in these matters was that they couldn't be slotted into a particular category. If what a writer says can be dismissed as Thatcherite nonsense or as the work of a Labour Party stooge, you don't have to think about what he's saying.

Morrison: *The Satanic Verses* is a celebration of doubt. Do you have doubts yourself? Have there been moments of doubt—and even guilt—about the consequences of the book's publication?

Rushdie: Every day, more than once a day, of course. And if I really felt the novel is what it has been called, I wouldn't have been able to sustain my position. I've re-read the book—in a way that writers usually don't, because they hate re-reading their own work—with a view to see if I was wrong. All I can say is that, if I thought I had been, I would have done something about it. I honestly believe there isn't a sentence in this book I can't defend. And if its critics were willing to set aside threats and violence and abuse and actually talk about what's on the page—is it offensive or is it not? Why did you say this in this way and not another?—I'd be quite happy to go through the book with them. That's an open offer. It seems to me, though, that it's very difficult for any acts of conciliation to take place in an atmosphere of violence. And it's not for me to change that. The essay I've written is a way to say, I hope without bitterness or anger: let's talk to one another, not shout at each other. There has been a colossal misunderstanding and it will be a massive effort to unscramble it. What it requires is a moment of good will: that's what I've tried to offer.

Morrison: And if you had your time again and could choose not to have written the book?

Rushdie: I really don't know. As everybody says, I'm not perfect. If somebody had told me, before the book went to the press, what was going to happen, maybe I'd have chickened out; I can't say. I hope I would still have published it, because I think there are very serious reasons why the book takes the shape it does, why it uses the images it does, why it develops the language it develops, and they are reasons I can easily defend. What's very hard is to have to defend your life as well.

SALMAN RUSHDIE
CRUSOE

Let me tell you, boyo, bach: I love this place,
where green hills shelter me from fear,
jet fighters dance like dragonflies
mating over unsteady, unafraid lambs,
and in the pub a divorcée, made needy
by the Spring, talks rugby and holidays
with my protectors, drinks, and grows
more lovely with each glass. So, too, do they.
As for me, I must hide my face
from farmers mending fences, runners, ponied girls;
must frame it in these whitewashed, thickstoned walls
while the great canvas of the universe
shrinks to a thumbnail sketch. And yet
I love the place. It remembers, so it says, a time
older than chapel, druid, mistletoe and god,
and journeys still, across enchanted pools,
towards that once and future Avalon.

CHRISTOPHER
HITCHENS
ON THE ROAD TO
TIMIŞOARA

O n Christmas night, stuck in freezing fog at the Austro-Hungarian border, I had telephoned my best Budapest friend and spoken across an insufferable line, fed with near-worthless *forint* coins cadged from a friendly guard. 'Have you heard?' said Ferenc, 'Ceauşescu has been *assassinated*.' The choice of word seemed odd. 'Murdered' wouldn't do, of course, in the circumstances. 'Killed' would have been banal. 'Executed'—too correct. And Ferenc always chooses his terms with meticulous care. No, a baroque dictator who was already a prisoner, and an ex-tyrant, had somehow been 'assassinated'. I took the first of many resolutions not to resort to Transylvanian imagery. Yes, there had been King Vlad, known as the Impaler, reputed to drink blood as well as spill it. Every writer and sub-editor in the trade was going to be dusting him off. Still, I found myself wondering just how Ceauşescu had been 'assassinated' after his capture. A stake through the heart? I had read that the chief of Ceauşescu's ghastly Securitate was named General Julian Vlad, but I was determined to make absolutely nothing of it.

A sorry-looking shop-front, which was in one of the radial streets off Calvin Square in Budapest, housed the Alliance of Free Democrats (SDS), Hungary's main opposition party. It resembled the headquarters of every 'movement' I'd ever visited. The stickers and posters in haphazard pattern gave promise of an interior of clanking duplicators, overworked telephones and bearded young men in pullovers. One of the stickers was fresh and blazing with colours—the national colours in fact. It read: TIMIŞOARA=TEMESVAR. To any Hungarian, it summoned an immediate, arresting image. On the plains of Transylvania, near the town the world now knows as Timişoara, the Hungarian patriots of 1848 were scattered and cut down by the Czar's Cossack levies, lent as a favour to the Austrian emperor. Near Temesvar, as the Hungarians call it, the national poet Sandor Petofi lost his life. At nearby Arad, the thirteen generals who had sided with the 1848 revolution were put to death. Now, under its Romanian name, this lost city so well-watered with patriotic Hungarian gore was again an emblem.

Today, the first day of the post-Ceauşescu era, the office was crowded to the doors with people of every class and category, standing around wearing intense expressions. Most wore buttons reading simply: TEMESVAR. Others displayed the more reflective symbol of two ribbons, one in the Hungarian colours and one in the Romanian, arranged over a black mourning stripe. Nationalists and internationalists, they were all waiting for the Romanian border to be declared open so that they could get to the stricken field of Transylvania and the wounded city of Timişoara. A volunteer convoy was in formation, with taxi drivers, workers, housewives and students offering to donate, or to transport, food and medicine. As so often in the course of the astounding Eastern European revolution of 1989, people seemed to know what to do. And they seemed to know, what's more, without being told. My companion and I, who continually needed and sought advice and instruction, felt this keenly.

The Romanian Embassy in Budapest, scene of numerous protests (some of them cynically encouraged by the nearly defunct Hungarian Communist Party), had offered exactly the wrong kinds of reassurance. 'No problem,' said the greasy officials who had just run up a hand-stitched 'National Salvation' banner on the balcony. Had the border, sealed by Ceauşescu, been reopened by his death? 'No problem.' (I find these the two least relaxing words in the lingua franca.) Visas were said to be obtainable at the border. Or at the embassy, of course, with a wait on the cold pavement. And there would be a fee. In dollars. In cash. For some reason, we couldn't give hard currency to these soft, shifty figures, who were still dealing with the public through an insulting grille.

A s the ten cars, one truck and one taxi that together comprised the Hungarian dissident convoy prepared to set off, I got an idea of how excited and intimidated they were by the whole idea of Transylvania. We got a short and cautionary talk from Tibor Vidos, an SDS organizer, who specialized in taking the romance out of things. 'There's to be no driving at night once we cross the border . . . We pick up the blood supplies before we meet at the check-point . . . No car is to pick up hitch-hikers, however innocent-looking they are. *Secu* men have been taking lifts and getting out while leaving plastic bombs behind . . .' Carrying blood to Transylvania? No, too glib an image and indecent in the context. Dismissing Dracula once more, I went for a swift meal with

131

Miklos Haraszti, author of *The Velvet Prison*, a book which relates the trials of writers and intellectuals in the 'goulash archipelago'. He had been to Timişoara/Temesvar years before, to see the now-famous Father Laszlo Tokes, and had been detained and tortured by the *Secu*. Haraszti comes from Leninist stock; his Jewish watchmaker parents left Hungary for Palestine in order to escape fascism, but quit Palestine in 1948—the year of the proclamation of Israel—in order to come back to a people's republic. His own disillusionment had taken him through Maoism before fetching him up with the majority of Budapest's 'urbanist' intellectuals into the ranks of the liberal SDS.

Haraszti told us of something that had just happened to the convoy in front of ours. 'One of the volunteers was pulled from his car, not by the *Secu* but by the Romanian crowd. They said he looked like an Arab, and that Arab terrorists had been helping Ceauşescu's gangs.' This was an instance of the *grande peur* that infected Romania in those days, and that was to poison the inaugural moments of the revolution. Not a single Arab corpse was found, nor a single prisoner taken. Yet the presence of Libyans, Syrians, Palestinians in the degraded ranks of the *Secu* was something that 'everybody knew'. The cream of the jest, as Haraszti went on to say, was that the 'Arab-looking' volunteer seemed exotic in appearance because he was a Budapest Jew. 'One of the few New Leftists we still have. He probably does sympathize with the PLO.' Nobody knew what had become of this hapless comrade, because the convoy had been too scared to stop. As we concluded our meal, the waiter brought us the last of several predictions about the time at which Hungarian TV would transmit video pictures of the Ceauşescus' execution. At that stage, excited rumour was calling for an actual sequence of the bullets hitting the couple. Neither he nor his customers could wait for the event. I vaguely recalled seeing television pictures of the dead General Kessem after a coup in Iraq in the colonial fifties, but couldn't otherwise think of a precedent for a prime-time 'assassination' of a fallen leader. 'The genius of the Carpathians', as Ceauşescu characterized himself, hogged the stage until the very last.

I describe this hesitation on the border of Transylvania because it shows, even in small details, the way that Hungarians felt

Romania to be *in partibus infidelium*. Romania is much larger than Hungary, by virtue of having absorbed so much of it, and Ceauşescu was the perfect ogre neighbour from the point of view of the regime. Not only did he run a terrifying, hermetic police state, the weight of which was felt disproportionately by the Hungarian-speaking minority, but he flaunted a mad, grandiose, population-growth policy which overtopped the megalomania of a Mussolini. And, as he raved from his balcony, it seemed to ordinary Hungarians that the Bucharest crowd supported him, at least passively and at least in his 'Greater Romania' fantasy. I asked Haraszti if this had made him feel nationalist in turn. 'The fact that the Romanian revolution was started by Hungarians,' he said firmly, 'is a miracle.' Almost at a blow, the mutual xenophobia had been dispelled. Neither regime could ever again easily mobilize or distract its people by fear of the other. This is no small issue for Hungarian democrats, who remember that their country took the Axis side in the stupid, vainglorious hope of 'redeeming' lost Magyar territory, and instead lost most of its Jews and decades of its history as well as its national honour.

As the convoy got on the move, and as people were allocating and being allocated their tasks and their cars, I was brought the news that Queen Elizabeth II had rescinded her award of the Order of the Bath to Nicolae Ceauşescu. There were polite Hungarians who felt that I might wish to know this, and who added that the decision was taken not a minute too soon. Bloody hell, I think, it's like Chesterton's definition of journalism—telling the public that Lord X is dead when the public didn't know that Lord X had ever been alive. I'm sure most people didn't know that Ceauşescu was sporting a Windsor honour. And, by the way, for what was the Order bestowed? The brute got 'most favoured nation' status from the United States, the Order of Lenin from Moscow, the moist thanks of international bankers for exporting all his people's food, pay-offs from Israel and the Arab League and solidarity from Beijing. He was the perfect postmodern despot—a market Stalinist.

Departure was announced for two in the morning, so that all night-time driving could be done on Hungarian territory, and everyone was ready to move out on time, and did move out, without being told. Our car was the property of a man who normally drove a beer-truck, and looked like it, and drove like it (the image of the SDS as an intellectual and élitist party is misleading). The freezing fog had thickened. At first light, after frequent stops and regroupings, and a detour for the blood pick-up at the border town of Gyula, all the cars met again at the border-point. Here people started to get nervous. It would have been a good thing to have had a leader or a commander. We knew that the previous convoy had been shot up and had lost one of its Bohemian-looking members to the liberated populace.

The Romanian border guards were in the very act of revisionism when we turned up. A large blank space on the wall spoke eloquently of yesterday's *Conducator*, as Ceauşescu got himself called, and various party and state emblems were being hurriedly junked. Still, the place wore the dismal, dingy aspect of a little machine for the imposition of petty authority. Everything from the lavatories to the waiting-room was designed for insult, delay and humiliation, and there was no one-day, quick-change cosmetic to disguise the fact. The unctuous, ingratiating faces of the guards who were 'making nice' for the first time in their lives, only reinforced the impression they were trying to dispel. Eager to please, they overdid their hatred of the *Secu* to whom they had deferred the day before. They even suggested that we not proceed. 'They are firing from cars. There is no law, no authority.' Without orders, they had no idea what to do. When I said, quite absurdly and untruthfully, that I was given 'clear instructions' from the capital that visas were free of charge today, they gladly waived the fee. There was a pathetic relief in the gesture of acquiescence.

Quitting the stranded, irrelevant guardhouse, and holding perhaps the last stamps that read 'Socialist Republic of Romania', we fell back a few decades. The Hungarian town of Gyula had amenities, as Americans say. Shops and telephones, restaurants, street lamps. Across the border there were herds of pigs and geese, horse-drawn wagons and wayside hovels. The first cars to be seen were waiting in an abject queue, not because of the upheaval but because today was the day when the exiguous petrol ration was issued. The people at the side of the road looked like caricatures of

Eastern European misery, in their shapeless bundles of coats and scarves. But there was a palpable lift in the atmosphere even so, because every person raised a hand in a V-salute at the sight of the Hungarian flag (or was it our reassuring Red Cross?). These villages had been the targets for 'systematization', perhaps the nastiest political neologism since 'normalization' in Czechoslovakia, and were saved from bulldozers and unheated tower-blocks where the water-pressure sometimes got as far as the first floor, and where the official cultural activity was praise for the *Conducator* and the denunciation of fellow sufferers.

At the city of Arad, our first major stop, we found what we were to find everywhere, which was that the centre of activity had shifted to the gates of the hospital. The *Conducator*'s cops had been vicious and thorough in their last stand, whether from panic or from sheer professional pride it is hard to say.

In the street an army lorry screamed to a halt and I heard the sound of boots hitting tarmac. This forbidding noise heralded a squad of uncertain young soldiers, steel casques reassuringly askew, who held up traffic with large gestures before entering the crowd and fraternizing. In the Romanian attitude to the army there was something of the Stockholm syndrome. The soldiery had changed sides at the last minute, and some of the brass (including the excellent-sounding General Militarescu) had been in touch with Party dissidents when it was dangerous to do so. Thus there was a popular willingness to smile, to repress unease, to cry, 'Army and People.' It became an article of faith that the soldiers who had fired on crowds on Christmas Eve were not really soldiers at all, but *Secu* devils in disguise. To have armed men on your side at long last, for whatever reason, seemed worth the sacrifice of pride. So the classic photograph became that of old women handing scarce food and drink to tank crews. Which indeed happened, showing in the oddest way that Brecht was right when he said that every tank had a mechanical weakness—its driver.

The beer-truck chauffeur, who seemed a stranger to exhaustion, had had the idea of stuffing his back seat with bales of Hungarian newspapers, including the daily organ of the Communist Party he despised. To stand in the streets of Arad and hand out free copies of yesterday's Budapest editions, was to court instant

135

popularity. Every hand reached for a copy, probably because a good deal of Hungarian is spoken in these parts and probably because there hadn't been any newspapers for days, but also and undoubtedly because the front page bore the death-masks of Ceauşescu and his wife Elena. Watching people rivet themselves to this photo-exclusive, I again fought down the impulse to Transylvanian cliché. They had to see the dead monster, had to know he was dead. The Ceauşescus' 'trial' had been a shabby, panicky business with unpleasantly Freudian overtones (Elena: 'I was a mother to you all.' *BANG!*), conducted by a tribunal which feebly refused to show its members' faces; but their execution had a galvanic effect on the morale of Transylvania and a correspondingly lowering effect on the fighting spirit of the *Secu*.

All had been festivity on the way to Arad, and as we left we met bystanders who were happy and eager to point the way to Timişoara. Wayside saluting and waving seemed inexhaustible. It was like being in Orwell's Barcelona, or in Portugal in 1974, or even like being on the skirts of a liberating army. But everything changed as we approached Timişoara. There were fewer people on the roads, and they seemed less keen and animated. As we found the outlying bits of the town, we noticed that our salutes were not returned. All the window-glass in the city seemed to have gone. Except for some flags with the now famous hole cut in the centre (a borrowing from Budapest in 1956), there were no signs of anything except shell-shocked, sullen wretchedness. I felt almost cheated. Here was the town of the resistance, of the revolutionary epicentre; the town that had lived up to 1848—and won this time. Where were the garlands, the proud slogans, the maidens in national dress, the gnarled old men with fierce tears in their eyes?

How could I have been so romantic and vulgar? Timişoara was the scene not of a triumph but of an atrocity—a sort of distillate of twentieth-century horrors. The inhabitants had been strafed from the air like the people of Guernica. They had been shot down in heaps like the victims of Babi Yar, and buried like refuse in mass graves in the forest on the pattern of Katyn. Many had been raped and mutilated like the villagers of My Lai. Before he left on a state visit to, of all places, Iran, Ceauşescu had given explicit orders that the city be punished. This was his Lidice; his Ouradour. At least the people who had been through such a digest and synopsis of horror could tell themselves that they were the last carnage of the last European dictator. But this obviously was not much of a consolation on the day after.

Again, it was at the hospital that everybody gathered. Timişoara is a superficially uninteresting town with a dull, routine Stalinist design. The box-like buildings even have generic names stencilled on the outside: 'Hotel', 'Restaurant', 'Cultural Centre'. It was a surprise to learn that the fateful, desperate demonstration in support of Father Tokes had taken place in Opera Square, because Timişoara doesn't look as if it rates an Opera House. Opera Square, on the other hand, doesn't disappoint your imagination of what a Transylvanian provincial city might boast after twenty-five years of philistine despotism. What a terrible place to die, I thought grotesquely, especially if you feared you might be doing it for nothing. On the other hand, a perfect place for concluding that you had little or nothing to lose.

We entered the hospital, and were led through a morgue which perfectly misrepresented the proportions of casualties. It contained one third civilians, one third soldiers and one third *Secu* men. I had come this far to see my first dead secret policeman—a great twentieth-century experience and only partly an anti-climax. He lay in his scruffy black livery, balding but thickly furred like some once vigorous animal, and looked alarmingly intact, with no outward mark of whatever violence had taken him. One of his companions, however, had been got at by the crowd and given a thorough kicking—the more thorough, by the look of it, out of frustration at that fact that he was dead. There was a pure hatred in the way that people spoke of the fallen regime and its servants. 'Our first happy Christmas,' said Dr Istvan Balos, without affectation, when I asked him for a reaction to the shooting of the Ceauşescus. Caligula once said that he wished the Roman mob had only one head so that he might decapitate them all at one stroke. The Romanian crowd wished only that the Ceauşescus had had a million lives so that everyone could have a turn at killing them.

Just before I left New York for Eastern Europe, I had been talking and drinking with Zdeněk Urbánek, original signatory of Charter 77, friend of Václav Havel and Czech translator of Shakespeare. Most of our conversation concerned the problem of vengeance, and the argument over amnesty and prosecution in newly emancipated Prague. Urbánek took the view that there should be no retribution, and his analogy was from Rome also. Remember, he said, that *Julius Caesar* is called *Julius Caesar* even though the eponymous character disappears after a few scenes and about fifteen minutes. 'But after he is murdered his influence remains over everything, pervading everything. That is the result of blood and the effect of revenge.'

The elevated sentiments of Prague and Bratislava were alarmingly remote from the Timişoara morgue. On a slab neighbouring that of the brutish-looking *Secu* man lay a dead young soldier, his eyes wide open and very blue, and on adjacent tables were two older civilians—man and wife, we were told—who had worked at the hospital. Their corpses were being processed in some ghastly way that involved the stench of formaldehyde. If it hadn't been for this stench, in fact, I might have been spared the moment I had in the corridor outside. My nostrils only started to wrinkle just as I felt my soles getting sticky, and the smell of drying blood hit me precisely as I realized what was gumming up my feet. A blood-bath has taken place here, I thought. A fucking *blood-bath*. All these people, killed like rats after leading such miserable, chivvied existences. Life-blood on my shoes.

'We have given the *Secu* another twenty-four hours to give up,' said Dr Balos, 'after which they are subject to a popular tribunal and a summary verdict.' As he was announcing this he dropped his voice. 'Do you see that man there?'—he indicated a tall and rather handsome man in a hospital housecoat who was talking easily with colleagues—'He's *one of them*. We can do nothing now, because there is no law. But soon. . . ' He spoke as if he was still living under occupation or dictatorship.

There appeared to be a delayed reaction in the Romanian psyche. It took the form of believing, not every rumour, but every rumour that had the morbid odour of pessimism or foreboding. This was where Caesar had his posthumous revenge. There were no apparitions exactly, but an unusual number of people said that they thought the trial video was a fake, the corpses phoney, the 'live' Ceauşescu a double. In his madness, it seems Ceauşescu had commissioned a few doubles for purposes of security (or perhaps of perverted vanity or repressed self-hatred). This is only a step away from having food-tasters and granting audiences while perched on the can, but it wasn't hard to believe about the *Conducator*. I began to soften in my anti-Dracula resolve when I learned from Transylvanian historians that Ceauşescu had forbidden all mention of the Bram Stoker book or the legend. The idea that he still walked seemed implicit in his entire cult of death and in the haunting effect of his undead minions.

In Budapest, Miklos Haraszti had spoken with approval of the decision to kill the Ceauşescus and with enthusiasm of the proposal to ban the Communist Party. 'It proves that it's a real revolution,' he said decisively, adding after a pause, 'in the dirty sense as well.' As Ryszard Kapuściński once remarked, 'Hunger revolutions are the worst.' The people of Romania and especially of Transylvania were starved in every sense of the term. Kept on short rations, kept in the dark, in the cold, kept from anything that could be called culture, screaming with boredom and groaning with humiliation; forced to applaud a mad gargoyle for whom they felt puke-making hatred. In Timişoara one could see all the bitterness and futility as well as all the grandeur of a hunger revolution. One could also get premonitions of the disagreeable things that lay ahead for the country—the crowd-pleasing decision to restore capital punishment, the hasty ban on the Communist Party (the only such ban in the 1989 European revolution), the evasive answers on the make-up and origin of the Council of National Salvation, the awkward hysteria about the body count, the ambivalence about the place of the army in politics. People were—are—hopelessly rattled and furious and confused.

I had had the vague idea of finding out the true body count of the Timişoara massacre, because cynical reporters were already saying that there 'hadn't really been all that many' casualties. Nettled at this, many citizens of the town were staunchly reiterating unbelievable death-tolls. I sickened of the task, not just because of the stench of blood around the morgue but because it seemed vile to be disputing the statistics of something evidently awful and sacrificial. It gave one the same rather creepy feeling that is engendered by an argument with Holocaust revisionists about Dresden or Auschwitz. I cleaned the soles of my shoes, remembered the packets of Hungarian coffee sugar I had pocketed on leaving Budapest, distributed them to some ecstatic and unbelieving children and made ready to leave the hospital. In the reception area, patients were sitting dully watching the television. All that could be seen on it was a test card. But they sat passive and fascinated, gazing at the flickering, improvised logo that read: *Romania Libera.*

LÉONARD FREED
BUCHAREST,
26 DECEMBER 1989

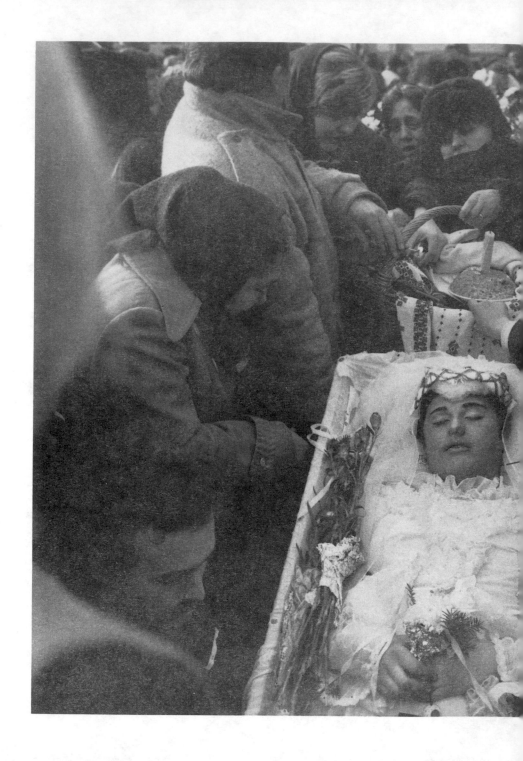

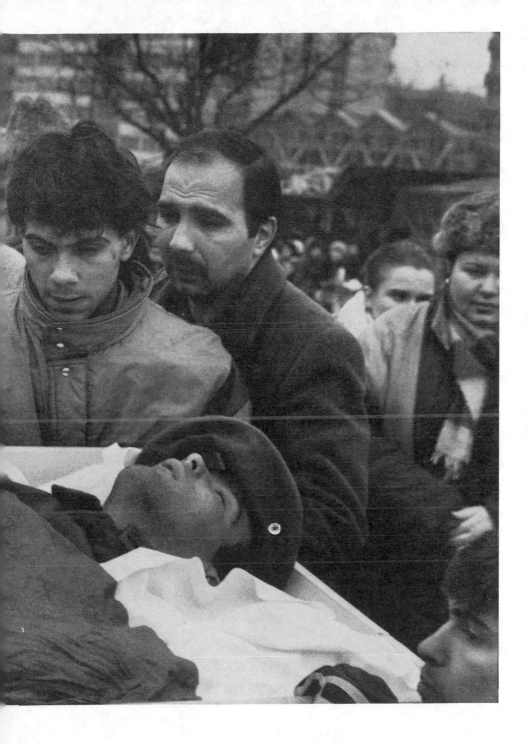

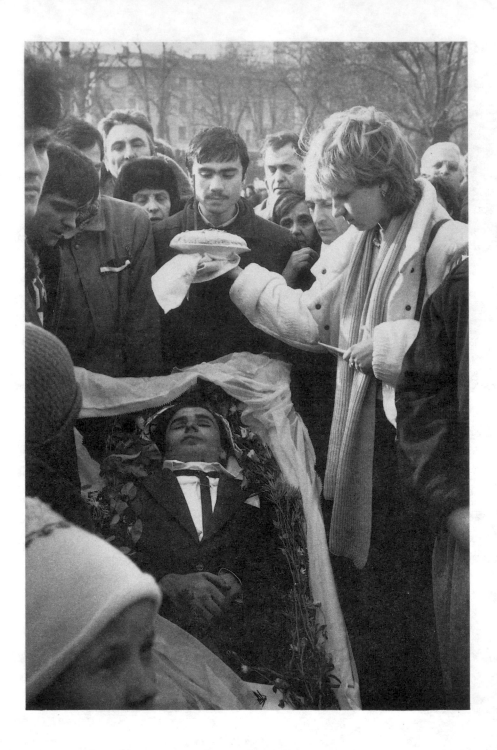

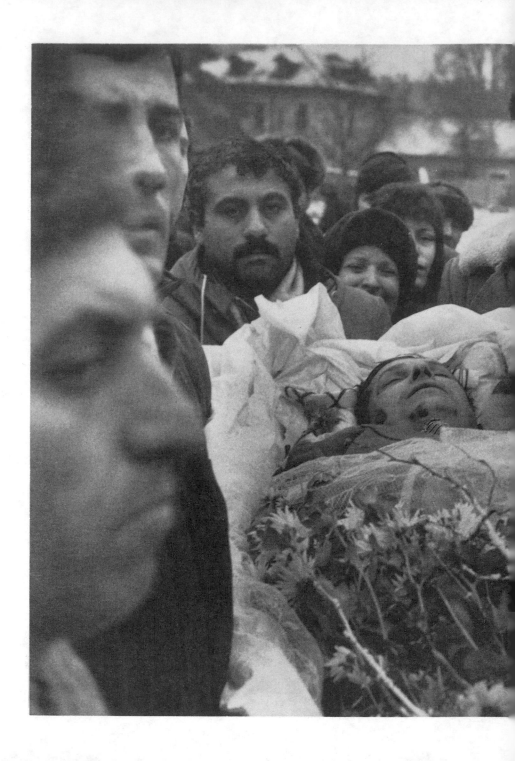

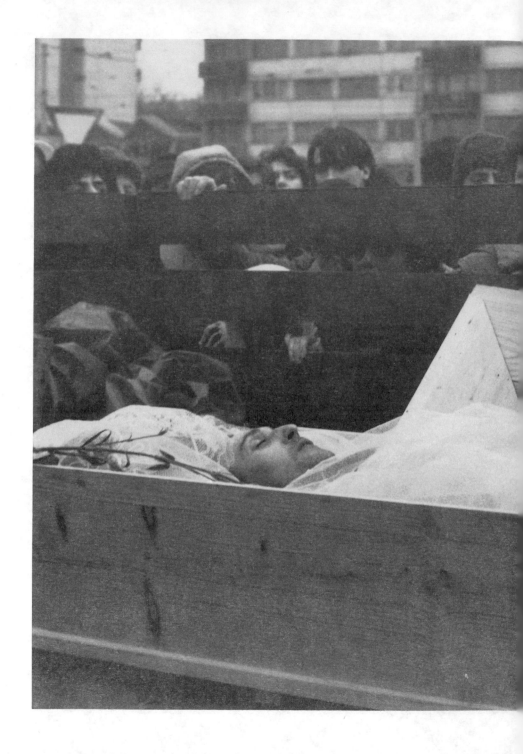

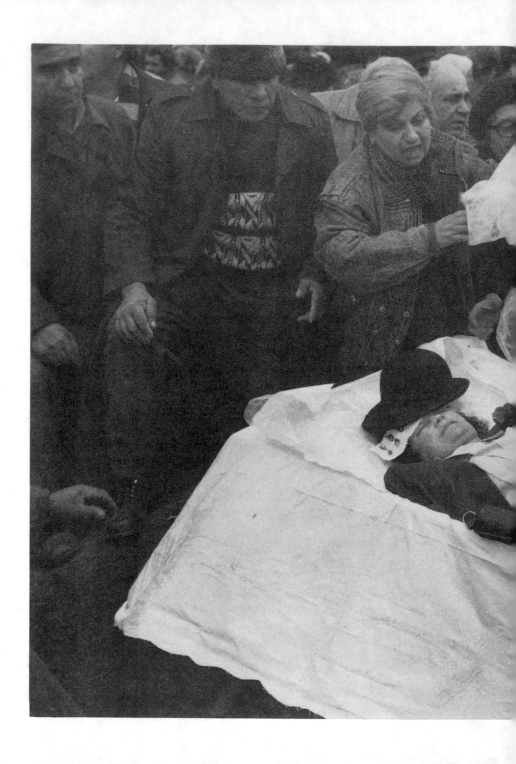

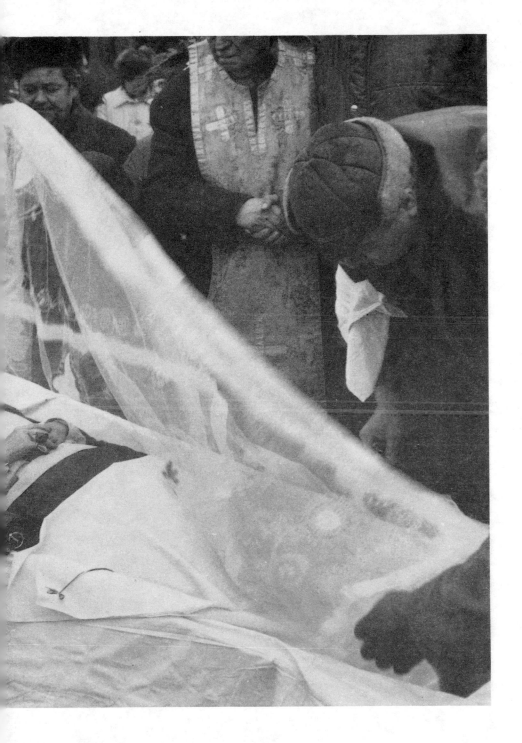

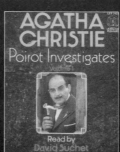

BILL BRYSON
NORTH OF NORTH

Above: Hammerfest, Norway.

Hammerfest is a thirty-hour bus ride from Oslo, though why anyone would want to go there in winter is a question worth considering. It is on the edge of the world, the northernmost town in Europe, as far from London as London is from Libya, a place of long, hard winters, where the sun sinks into the Arctic Ocean in November and does not surface again till late January.

I wanted to see the Northern Lights. I had also long harboured a curious, half-formed urge to see what life was like in such a remote and cheerless place. Sitting at home in England with a glass of whisky and a book of maps, this had seemed a good idea. But now as I picked my way through the grey, late December slush of Oslo, I was beginning to have doubts.

Things had not started well. I had overslept at the hotel in Oslo, missing breakfast, and had to leap into my clothes. I couldn't find a cab and had to drag my absurdly overweighted bag eight blocks through slush to the central bus station. (Knowing that I was about to spend three weeks in a land of darkness, I had packed masses of books and reading material, and a generous quantity of leftover Christmas foodstuffs as insurance against discovery that the diet of northern Norway was centred on herring and blubber.) I had had huge difficulty persuading the staff at the Kreditkassen Bank on Karl Johans Gate to cash sufficient traveller's cheques to pay the extortionate 1,200-kroner bus fee—they could not be made to grasp that the William McGuire Bryson on my passport and the Bill Bryson on my traveller's cheques were one and the same person—and now here I was arriving at the station two minutes before departure, breathless and steaming from the endless uphill exertion that is my life, and the girl at the ticket counter was telling me that she had no record of my reservation.

'This isn't happening,' I said. 'I'm still at home in England enjoying Christmas. Pass me a drop more port, will you, darling?'

Actually I said: 'There must be some mistake. Please look again.'

The girl studied the passenger manifest. 'No, Mr Bryson, your name is not here.'

But *I* could see it, even upside down. 'There it is, second from the bottom.'

'No,' the girl decided, 'that says Bent Bjornson. That's a Norwegian name.'

'It doesn't say Bent Bjornson. It says Bill Bryson. Look at the loop of the y, the two l's. Please.'

But she wouldn't have it.

'If I miss this bus, when does the next one go?'

'Next week at the same time.'

Oh, splendid. 'Miss, believe me, it says Bill Bryson.'

'No, it doesn't.'

'Miss, look, I've come from England. I'm carrying some medicine that could save a child's life.' She didn't buy this. 'I want to see the manager.'

'He's in Stavanger.'

'Look, I made a reservation by telephone. If I don't get on this bus I am going to write a letter to your manager that will cast a shadow over your promotion prospects for the rest of this century.' This did not alarm her. I don't suppose she was on the career fast track as it was. Then it occurred to me. 'If this Bent Bjornson doesn't show up, can I have his seat?'

'Sure.'

Why don't I think of these things in the first place and save myself the anguish? 'Thank you,' I said and lugged my bag outside.

The bus was a large double-decker, like an American Greyhound, but only the front half of the upstairs had seats and windows. The rest was solid aluminium covered with a worryingly psychedelic painting of an intergalactic landscape, like the cover of a pulp science fiction novel, and the legend 'Express 2000' emblazoned across the tail of a comet. For one giddy moment I thought the windowless back end of the bus might contain a kind of dormitory and that at bedtime we would be escorted back there by a stewardess who would invite us to choose a couchette. I was prepared to pay any amount of money for this option. But I was mistaken. The back end of the bus and all the space below us, apart from where the driver and his mate sat, was for freight. Express 2000 was really just a long-distance lorry with passengers.

We left at twelve o'clock sharp. I quickly realized that everything about the bus—everything about all modern forms of transport, come to that—was designed for discomfort. I was sitting on the heater, so that while draughts toyed with my upper extremities, my left leg grew so hot that I could hear the hairs on it crackle. The seats were designed for dwarves; there was no other explanation. The young man in front of me put his seat so far back that his head was all but in my lap. He was reading a comic book called *Tommy og Tigern* ('*Med Det Beste i Amerikansk Humor,*' which I somehow doubted). My own seat was raked at a peculiar angle that made my neck ache. There was a lever beside the seat, which I supposed might bring it back to a more tolerable position, but I knew from experience that if I touched it even tentatively the seat would fly back and break both the kneecaps of the little old lady behind me, so I left it alone. The woman beside me, who was obviously a veteran of these polar campaigns, unloaded vast quantities of magazines, tissues, throat lozenges, ointments and fruit pastilles into the seat-back pocket in front of her, and then settled beneath a blanket and slept more or less continuously through the trip.

We drove through a snowy half-light, out past the sprawling suburbs of Oslo and into the countryside. It was very agreeable. The scattered villages and farmhouses looked snug and cheery in the endless dusk. Every house had Christmas lights burning in the windows. I quickly settled into that not unpleasant state of mindlessness that tends to overcome me on long journeys.

Gradually I became aware that no one was smoking. I could see no 'No Smoking' signs, but I wasn't going to be the first person to light up and then have everyone ticking me off in Norwegian. I was certain that the man in the seat across the aisle was a smoker—he looked suitably miserable—and even more certain that the young man ahead of me must be. I have yet to meet a grown-up comic book reader who doesn't also have an affection for tobacco and tattoos. I consulted the Express 2000 leaflet that came with my seat and read with horror the line: '*Tilsammen 2,000km non-stop i 30 timer.*' I don't know Norwegian from alphabet soup but even I could figure that out. Two thousand kilometres! Non-stop! Thirty hours without a cigarette! Suddenly all the discomfort came flooding back. My neck ached, my left leg sizzled like bacon in a skillet, the young man ahead of me had his head closer to my crotch than any man had ever had before, I had less space to call my own than if I had climbed into my suitcase and shipped myself to Hammerfest, and now I was going to go thirty hours without a cigarette. This was too much.

Fortunately, it wasn't quite as desperate as that. At the Swedish border the bus stopped at a customs post in the woods and while the driver went into the hut to sort out the paperwork most of the passengers, including me and the two I'd forecast, clattered down the steps and stood stamping their feet in the snow and smoked three cigarettes in three minutes. Who could tell when we might get this chance again? Actually, after I returned to the bus and earned the bottomless disdain of the lady beside me by stepping on her foot for the second time in five minutes, I discovered from further study of the Express 2000 leaflet that three rest-stops appeared to be built into the itinerary.

The first of these came in the evening at a roadside cafeteria in Skellefteå, Sweden. It was a strange place. On the wall at the start of the food line was a menu and beside each item was a red button, which when pushed presumably alerted the people in the kitchen to start preparing that dish. Having done this, you slid your empty tray along to the check-out, pausing to select a drink, and then waited with the cashier for twenty minutes until your food was brought out. Rather defeats the purpose of a cafeteria, don't you think? As I was the last in the line and the line was going nowhere, I went outside and smoked many cigarettes beside the bus and then returned. The line was only fractionally depleted, but I took a tray and regarded the menu. I had no idea what any of the foods were and as I have a dread of *ever* inadvertently ordering liver, which I so much detest that I am going to have to leave you here for a minute and go throw up in the wastebasket from just thinking about it, I elected to choose nothing (though I thought very hard about pressing all the buttons, just to see what would happen).

Instead I selected a bottle of Pepsi and some little cakes, but when I arrived at the checkout and tried to pay, the cashier told me that my Norwegian money was no good, that I needed Swedish money. This surprised me. I had thought the Nordic peoples were all pals and freely exchanged their money, as they do between Belgium and Luxembourg. Under the cashier's heartless gaze, I replaced the cakes and Pepsi, and took instead a free glass of iced water and went to a table. Fumbling in my jacket pocket I discovered a Dan-Air cookie left over from the flight from England, and dined on that.

When we returned to the bus, sated on our lamb cutlets and potatoes and/or iced water and cookie, the driver extinguished the interior lights and we had no choice but to try to sleep. It was endlessly uncomfortable. I finally discovered, after trying all the possibilities, that the best position was to lie down on the seat more or less upside down with my legs dangling above me. In this manner, and to my considerable surprise, I fell swiftly into a deep sleep. Ten minutes after that, Norwegian coins began slipping one by one from my pocket and dropping on to the floor behind me, where (one supposes) they were furtively scooped up by the little old lady sitting there.

And thus the night passed.

We were awoken early for another rest-stop, this one in Where the Fuck, Finland. Actually it was called Muonio and it was the most desolate place I had ever seen: a filling station and lean-to café in the middle of a tundra plain. The good news was that the café accepted Norwegian money; the bad news was that it had nothing that anyone outside a famine zone would want to eat. The driver and his mate were given steaming platters of eggs, potatoes and ham, but there appeared to be nothing like that on offer for the rest of us. I took a bottle of mineral water and a slice of crispbread with a piece of last year's cheese on it, for which I was charged an astonishing twenty-five kroner, and retired to a corner booth. Afterwards, while the driver and his mate lingered over coffees and suppressed contented burps, I milled around with the other passengers in the shop part of the complex, looking at fan belts and snow shovels.

We hit the road again at seven-thirty. Only another whole day of this, I thought cheerfully. Here the landscape was inexpressibly bleak, just mile after mile of snowy waste and scraggly birch forest. Reindeer grazed along the roadside and from time to time we passed Lapp settlements looking frigid and lifeless. There were no Christmas lights in the windows here. In the distance, a sliver of sun peeked over the low hills, big and orange but as lifeless as the landscape, and then sank again. It was the last I would see of the sun for three weeks. The bus rolled on.

Just after five in the evening, we crossed a long toll-bridge on to the island of Kvaløya, an expanse of grassy rock in the Arctic Ocean, home of Hammerfest. We were now about as far north as you can get in the world by public transport. We were almost inconceivably far north—a thousand miles beyond the Shetland Islands, 800 miles north of the Faroes, 200 miles beyond the northernmost tip of Iceland. We were closer to the North Pole than to Berlin.

I was excited and pressed my nose to the cold glass. We approached Hammerfest on a winding road along the coast. It looked wonderful—a sprawl of orange street lights stretching far up into the hills and all around an expansive bay. It was much larger than I had dared hope. Maybe this would be all right, I thought. Yes, maybe this wouldn't be too bad at all.

I took a room in the Håja Hotel near the quay. It was a pleasant hotel and a pleasant room; small but spotless and comfortable, with a telephone, a small colour television and its own bathroom. I was highly pleased. I dumped my things, briefly investigated the amenities and then went out to have my first look at Hammerfest.

The city, too, seemed agreeable enough in a God-am-I-glad-I-don't-live-here sort of way. The hotel was on a small grid of streets, three blocks by three, on one edge of the main part of town. Here there were darkened shipping offices, a couple of banks and travel agents, a surprisingly large police station and a post office, with a row of telephone kiosks in front. In each of these, I noticed as I walked past, the telephone directories had been set alight by some desperate thrill-seeker and now hung charred from their chains.

It was cold out, but not nearly as cold as I had expected. This pleased me because I had very nearly bought a ridiculous Russian-style hat—one of those furry ones with ear-flaps—for 400 kroner in Oslo. Much as I hate to stand out in a crowd, I have a terrible, occasional compulsion to make myself an unwitting source of merriment for the world and I had come very close to scaling new heights with a Russian hat. Now, clearly, that would be unnecessary. The temperature was no lower, I guessed, than about twenty-five degrees Fahrenheit—not exactly basking weather, but tolerable enough.

I walked up to the main street, Strandgatan, which ran for about 300 yards along the harbour, lined on the inland side by an assortment of businesses—a bakery, a bookstore, a cinema (closed), a café called Kokken's, a bleak-looking state liquor store—and on the harbour side by the town hall, more shops and the hulking mass of a fish-processing plant. Christmas lights were strung cheerily at intervals across the street, but all the shops were shut and there wasn't a sign of life anywhere, apart from an occasional cab speeding past as if on an urgent mission.

I trudged down to where the road curved around the harbour. This was a more residential area, with houses clinging to the hillsides. Here the harbour was quite fetching, with the lights of the town smeared across the black water. Far out at the harbour's mouth the green light of a buoy blinked rhythmically. From here the town, with its large floodlit church and bright lights and houses snuggled up against the mountains, looked pleasant and welcoming, a haven of warmth and light in the Arctic darkness. Beyond me the snowy road led to a headland of industrial buildings and cranes. Across the broad harbour, a network of houses and street lights advanced towards their own headland, but they petered out about a third of the way along and the rest was darkness.

Satisfied with this initial reconnaissance, I turned up my collar and trudged back to the hotel, where I had a light but astonishingly expensive dinner and then tumbled gratefully into bed.

In the night I was awoken by a storm. I crept out of bed and peered cautiously out the window. Snow was blowing wildly and there was a howl as of banshees. Lightning lit the sky. I had never seen lightning in a snowstorm. Muttering, 'Oh, sweet Jesus, where am I?' I climbed back into bed and buried myself deep in the covers.

I don't know what time I awoke, but I dozed and tossed for perhaps two hours in the dark until it occurred to me that it never was going to get light. I got up and looked out the window. The storm was still raging. A wall of snow flew about outside the window. In the police station car-park below two squad cars marked 'Politi' were buried in drifts almost to their roof-tops.

I dressed and went downstairs to breakfast. This was a large buffet, but I appeared to be the only guest. Afterwards, I ventured out into the gale. The streets were still deserted, snow piled in the doorways. The wind was playing havoc with the town. Street lights flickered and swayed, throwing spastic shadows across the snow. The Christmas decorations rattled. A cardboard box sailed across the road ahead of me and was wafted high out over the harbour.

It was bitterly cold. On the exposed road out to the headland I began to wish again that I had bought the Russian hat. The wind was unrelenting—it must have been seventy miles an hour at least—and it drove before it wild particles of ice that seared my cheeks and made me gasp. I had a scarf with me, which I tied around my face bandit-style and trudged on, leaning into the wind.

Ahead of me out of the swirling snow appeared a figure. He was wearing a Russian hat, I was pleased to note. As he drew nearer, I pulled my scarf down to make some cheery greeting—'Bit fresh out, isn't it?' or something—but he passed by without looking at me. A hundred yards further on I passed two more people, a man and his wife tramping stolidly into town, and they too passed as if I were invisible. Strange people, I thought.

The headland proved as unpromising up close as it had looked from a distance, just a jumble of warehouses and small ship-repair yards, loomed over by creaking cranes. Tucked in among the larger buildings were a café and a hut selling newspapers and cigarettes, but both were shut. I was about to turn back when I noticed a sign pointing the way to something called the Meridianstøtten and decided to investigate. This took me down a lane on the seaward side of the headland. Here, wholly exposed to the sea, the wind was even more impossibly ferocious. I weigh nearly 200 pounds, but twice it all but picked me up and carried me a considerable distance. Only the toetips of my boots maintained contact with the ground. The lane was slick with ice and I discovered that by holding out my arms I could actually slide along, propelled by the wind. It was the most wonderful fun. Irish windsurfing, I dubbed it. I had a great time until an unexpected gust bowled me over. I fell like a man who's been hit full in the face with a frying-pan, and cracked my head so hard that I saw stars and suddenly remembered where I put the coal-shed key when we went on holiday the summer before. The pain of this event, and the thought that another gust might actually heft me into the sea, like the cardboard box I had seen earlier, made me abandon the sport.

The Meridianstøtten was an obelisk on a small elevation in the middle of a graveyard of warehouses. I later learned that it was a memorial erected to celebrate the completion of the first scientific measurement of the earth's circumference, which was concluded on this spot in 1840. (Hammerfest's other historical distinction is that it was the first town in Europe to have electric street lights.) I clambered up to the obelisk with difficulty, but the snow was blowing so much that I couldn't read the inscription, and I returned to town.

B ack at the hotel I tried once or twice to watch television. There is only one network in Norway and it's sensationally bad. It's not just that the programmes are dull—though in this respect they could win awards—but that the whole thing is so engagingly unpolished, as if they haven't quite got the hang of it yet. Films finish and you get thirty seconds of scratchy white circles like you used to get when your home movies ran out and your dad didn't get to the projector fast enough. Then the screen goes blank—you can practically hear the studio technician, ankle-deep in unwound film, shouting hysterically—before suddenly the lights come up on that day's host, looking faintly startled. The host, generally a nice-looking young man with a lively sweater and a heavy-duty hair-style, fills the time between programmes by showing trailers for the rest of the evening's highlights: a documentary on mineral extraction in Narvik, a Napoleonic costume drama in which the main characters wear moustaches that are patently not their own and strut around as if they've just had a two-by-four inserted rectally (but are trying not to let it affect their performance) and a jazz session with somebody truly hopeless and unheard of—the Sigi Würtmuller Rhythm Brigade or something.

Much of the ground floor of the hotel was given over to a restaurant and bar called the Hjelmen. Dinner was astonishingly expensive—everything in Norway is astonishingly expensive—and the portions were tiny. I had a steak that you could have hidden in a matchbox, with French fries and a kind of exotic Norwegian

177

coleslaw, plus two beers, and the bill came to thirty-five dollars. The food was excellent, but it's no wonder you don't see any fat Norwegians.

I sat for most of the evening, nursing Mack beers at fifty øre a sip, thinking that surely things would liven up in a minute. After all, it was New Year's Eve. But the Hjelmen was like a funeral parlour that served refreshments. A pair of mild-looking men in reindeer sweaters sat with beers, staring silently into space. I watched them for an hour and only once did they speak, and then only for a moment, and they hardly touched their beers. After a time I realized there was another customer, sitting alone in a darkened corner. Only the glow of his cigarette made him stand out from the gloom.

When the waiter came to take my plate away, I asked him what there was to do for fun in Hammerfest. He thought for a moment and said: 'Have you tried setting fire to the telephone directories outside the post office?'

Actually he didn't say that, because just as he was about to speak, the lone figure in the corner addressed some slurred remark to him, which I gathered was something along the lines of 'Waiter, is it true that your mother sleeps with pack animals and that you yourself are the product of an illicit liaison with a walrus?' because the waiter dropped my plate on to the table and went straight to the man and began furiously dragging him by his arm and shoulder from his seat and then pushing him with enormous difficulty to the door, where he finally heaved him out into the snow. When the waiter returned, looking flushed and disconcerted, I said brightly, 'I hope you don't show all your customers out like that!' but he clearly was in no mood for pleasantries and he retired sulkily to the bar, so I was unable to determine just what there was to do in Hammerfest to pass the time, other than set telephone books alight, speculate aloud on the parentage of menials and weep.

At 11.30, with the bar still dead, I went out to see if there was life anywhere. The wind had died but there was hardly anyone about—just scattered groups of teenagers making their way drunkenly from one house to another, pausing occasionally to set off firecrackers. I wandered up and down all the residential streets in the central part of town. Every window in every house blazed with light, but there was no sign of revelry within.

Then just before midnight an odd thing happened. Every person came out of every house and began to set off fireworks. And I don't mean those paltry little Roman candles and glorified party poppers that you get on Bonfire Night in England. I mean industrial-sized fireworks that shrieked up to the heavens and burst in a spectacular bang of colour and sparks. For half an hour, from all around the peninsula, fireworks popped and glittered over the harbour and drifted spent into the sea. And then about thirty minutes after it all began, everyone went back inside and Hammerfest slept again, but for the occasional puffs of a few die-hard fireworks in the hills and the lonely barking of a distant dog.

On New Year's Day I went for a long walk. It was snowing again, but these were big, gentle flakes, and the air was still. I discovered a cleft in the mountains and beyond it an enchanted valley, sheltered on three sides by craggy mountains. A road, lined with large, snow-decked houses, led along one side of the valley and returned to town along the other. I walked down it pleased with my discovery. The houses here were grander, more prosperous, more architecturally daring than those back in the centre of town. But it was still eerily quiet—so quiet that when I stopped I could hear the snowflakes settling one by one. This was a holiday, but where was everyone? With so little usable light each day you'd think the children would flock out to build snowmen and forts. I expected to see people walking their dogs and schlussing healthily past on cross-country skis, but there was no one. In a way, I was pleased to have it all to myself, to walk in such solitary splendour.

And then I saw it. In an empty piece of sky above the town there appeared a cloud of many colours—pinks and greens and blues and pale purples. It glimmered and seemed to swirl. Slowly, it stretched across the sky. It had a thin, oddly greasy quality about it—like the rainbows you sometimes see in a puddle of petrol. I stood transfixed.

I later learned that the Northern Lights are immensely high in the atmosphere, something like 200 miles up, but this show seemed to be suspended just above the town. There are two kinds of Northern Light—the curtains of shimmering gossamer that

179

everyone has seen in pictures and the rather rarer gas clouds that I was gazing at now. They are never the same twice. Sometimes they shoot wraithlike across the sky, like smoke in a wind tunnel, moving at enormous speed, and sometimes they hang like luminous drapes or spears of light, and very occasionally—perhaps once or twice in a lifetime—they emerge from every horizon and flow together overhead in a vast, silent explosion of light and colour. In the blackness of the countryside the lights can sometimes seem to swoop down from the sky and surround you, as if trying to take you up to the heavens. If you are driving, you find yourself repeatedly jamming on the brakes to keep from hitting them. By all accounts it's terrifying. To this day, many Lapps believe that if you show the lights a white handkerchief or sheet of paper they will come and take you away.

This display was relatively small stuff, and it lasted for only a few minutes, but it was the most beautiful thing I had ever seen and it would do me until something better came along.

The days passed. It was as if a doctor had told me to go away for a complete rest. Never had I slept so long and so well. Never had I had this kind of leisure to just potter about. Suddenly I had time to do all kinds of things: unlace my boots completely and redo them over and over until the laces were *precisely* the same length, rearrange the contents of my wallet, deal with nose hairs, make long lists of all the things I would do if I had anything to do. Sometimes I sat on the edge of the bed with my hands on my knees and just gazed about. Often I talked to myself. Mostly I went for long, cold walks through the snow and then stopped for coffee afterwards at Kokken's Café, which was warm and had steamy windows.

It occurred to me that this was just like being retired. I even began taking a small notebook with me and making pointless notes in it while I sat in Kokken's, just as my dad had done when he retired. He used to walk to a coffee-shop every day and if you passed by you would see him writing in his notebook. After he died, we found a cupboard full of these notebooks. Every one of them was filled with entries like this: 'January 4. Walked to coffee-shop. Had two cups of decaff. Weather mild.' Suddenly I understood what he was up to.

On the evening of the eighth day I was sitting in the bar of the Hjelmen reading a book and nursing a Mack at fifty øre a sip when a large, hairy, swaying figure appeared at the table and began addressing me in dark tones. He was followed a moment later by a smaller, fractionally more stable figure. I explained to them that I could not understand their Nordic sounds as I spoke only English, which they took as an invitation to join me.

Their names were Nils and Stig and they were very drunk—in fact, Stig, the hairy one, was about as drunk as it is possible to be without stopping being human. He was the sort of person that brought instantly to mind two words: stupid and dangerous. Nils explained, in English, that Stig thought I was the Swedish tourist on a Harley-Davidson who had splashed him with slush earlier in the day and that Stig had been inviting me to step outside with a view to converting me into a kind of slush. Nils assured me that Stig was now satisfied I was not that person and probably would not beat me up after all. I told him this was some comfort to me.

My two companions conferred heatedly over the menu, breaking off to give each other slaps and to shout loudly for service, and then fell into conversation in Norwegian. This, as you can imagine, was a lot of fun for me. I said: 'Look, you guys seem like a load of laughs, but there isn't much point in me sitting here listening to a conversation I can't understand, so I'm going to take my book and go to that table over there.'

But Nils wouldn't have it. He insisted that I stay with them and have some pizza and beer. In any case, Stig was blocking my way and wasn't about to move. He grabbed me intently by the arm and addressed grave, incoherent mumblings into my ear of which I understood only the words 'Harley-Davidson'. Some young people came in and joined us. They were clearly amused by Stig's condition—he sat slumped talking to himself and trying with limited success to close his lips around a cigarette—and one of them made an ill-advised joke about it. Stig, suddenly animated, rose with a leer and began stalking the young man around the room, crashing into tables. He picked up a chair and held it over his head. I looked around to see if the waiter was going to do anything about this, but he was cowering behind the bar. All you could see were his eyes, swivelling uneasily.

Pleased as I was to meet some locals at last, spending an

181

evening with a Norwegian psychopath was not my idea of a good time. I looked at my watch and said, 'Gosh, is that the time?' I explained to the young man opposite me that there was a documentary on mushroom-farming in Mörgramsdal on TV that I was dying to see and made to leave, but at that moment Nils appeared with a tray of Macks, which made Stig abandon all thoughts of violence, and he put down the chair and returned quietly to his seat beside me, precluding my escape.

I drank the beer they had bought me and listened to them jabber in an unfamiliar tongue. I made the best of things by getting Nils to teach me how to swear in Norwegian. Eventually I finished my beer and said, 'Well, it's been great. I can't remember the last time I had this much fun above the Arctic Circle, but I've really got to go. Stig, would you let me out, please?' Stig appeared not to hear me. He was mumbling to himself. 'Stig,' I said more firmly, '*hold kjaeft.*' This means 'shut up'. 'Let me out, please. I gotta go.'

Stig looked at me in a kind of dumb amazement, but slid from the table. As I slid out, he grabbed my arm and said: 'What did you say, Englishman?'

'I said, "*Hold kjaeft.*"' I patted him on the shoulder and gave him my most winning smile. 'But I was only joking.'

For a moment, I was pretty certain he was going to beat me up. It would have been an interesting contest between his diminished motor control and the absorbent capacity of my flab. But he surprised us all by giving me a big hug. We were friends for life, God help me. 'That's good—*Hold kjaeft,*' he said and sat heavily back down.

I went to the bar and urged the waiter to get up off the floor so that I could pay my bill. I considered for a moment sending two beers over to the table to repay them for the one they had bought me, but I did a quick cost-benefit analysis (cost: seventy-six kroner; benefit: the fleeting gratitude of two drunken assholes) and decided against it.

Instead I went upstairs to my lonely room and watched the last half-hour of the mushroom-farming programme, which wasn't half bad, though it would have benefited, in my view, from a couple of nude scenes.

Little by little, I began to meet more people. One evening in the Hjelmen I got to talking to a genial and urbane Dane named Olav Nielsen who had come to Hammerfest on some obscure business errand three years earlier and never quite got around to leaving. 'It's a good place to do business from,' he insisted, dismissing my observation that we were, in point of fact, on the edge of the known world. His latest venture was to try to sell a complete paint factory to the desperately paintless people of Murmansk, 200 miles to the east. 'When I came here,' he told me, 'I invited everyone on my street to my house for a little get-together. Half the people didn't come and the other half I spent the evening introducing to one another. These were people who had lived together on the same street in one little town for years and they had never got around to introducing themselves! It's crazy.'

I visited the mayor, a middle-aged man named Bjørn Johnsen. He had an undertaker's face and wore blue jeans and a work-shirt, which made him look rather like a prisoner on day release, and he smoked the sorriest-looking roll-your-own cigarettes I've ever seen, but he had a kind manner and told me much about the depressed local fishing industry.

One day in the hotel I overheard a man about my age talking to the proprietor in Norwegian but to his own children in Home Counties English. His name was Ian Tonkin. He was an Englishman who had married a Hammerfest girl and now taught English at the local high school. He and his wife Peggy invited me to their house for dinner, fed me lavishly on reindeer and cloudberries (both delicious) and were kindness itself.

Peggy told me a sad story about the town. In 1944, the retreating Germans, in an attempt to deprive the advancing Russian army of shelter, torched Hammerfest. The people were evacuated by ship to the south to live out the rest of the war with strangers. Each person was allowed to take twenty kilos of possessions—about what you could put in a pillowcase. Peggy's father, a musician, took his sheet music and a treasured violin, but her mother, too rattled to think straight, packed things like night-dresses and stationery and left behind letters and photographs and a thousand other pieces of her life. As the evacuation flotilla left the harbour, they could see the Germans setting their houses on fire.

Peggy's father took the front-door key from his pocket and dropped it into the sea. 'We won't be needing that again,' he said to his wife. After the war the people returned to Hammerfest to find nothing standing but the chapel. With their bare hands and little else they built their town again.

Bit by bit I learned more about the town—about the fishing industry, about last year's murder trial, about complaints of cronyism in the town hall and of incompetence concerning snow-removal. The odd thing was that I began to find it all thoroughly engrossing. In a way I began to feel part of it. I became a familiar face in the post office and at the bank. People honked to me on the street or joined me for coffee in Kokken's. I liked Hammerfest. I liked it a lot. It began to feel like home, and my real life in England began to feel strangely distant and dreamlike.

On my fifteenth day in the town, I went to the tourist office to pick up a report on the Northern Lights that the director of tourism had promised to get for me from the university at Tromsø, and in the course of chatting to his assistant I discovered that the bus I was supposed to be taking back to Oslo the following week had been cancelled. The only alternative was to take the bus that day, in less than an hour.

I scuttled back to the hotel, threw my things into my bag, paid the bill, said my farewells and departed. The bus was already at the station when I got there.

For one moment, I really didn't want to go. In other circumstances I might well have settled down and stayed, as Olav Nielsen and Ian Tonkin had done. But then I told myself that I was being crazy. I had a happy life of my own in England. It was time to return to Oslo and the real world. Besides, I had a hat to buy.

MARGARET ATWOOD
ISIS IN DARKNESS

How did Selena get here? This is a question Richard is in the habit of asking himself, as he sits at his desk again, shuffling his deck of filing-cards, trying again to begin.

He has a repertoire of answers. Sometimes he pictures her drifting down towards the mundane rooftops in a giant balloon made of turquoise and emerald-green silks, or arriving on the back of a golden bird like the ones on Chinese teacups. On other days, darker ones like this Thursday—Thursday, he knows, was a sinister day in her calendar—she wends her way through a long underground tunnel encrusted with blood-red jewels and with arcane inscriptions that glitter in the light of torches. For years she walks, her garments—garments, not clothes—trailing, her eyes fixed and hypnotic, for she is one of those cursed with an unending life; walks until she reaches, one moonlit night, the iron-grilled door of the Petrowski tomb, which is real, though dug improbably into a hillside near the entrance to the also-real Mount Pleasant Cemetery.

(She would love that intersection of the banal and the numinous. She once said that the universe was a doughnut. She named the brand.)

The lock splits. The iron gate swings open. She emerges, raises her arms towards the suddenly chilled moon. The world changes.

There are other plots. It just depends which mythology he's cribbing from.

A factual account exists. She came from the same sort of area that Richard came from himself: old pre-Depression Toronto, strung out along the lakeshore south of the Queen streetcar tracks, a region of small vertical houses with peeling woodwork and sagging front porches and dry, mangy lawns. Not quaint in those days, not renovated, not desirable. The sort of constipated lower-middle-class white-bread ghetto he'd fled as soon as he could, because of the dingy and limited versions of himself it had offered him. Her motivation was perhaps the same. He likes to think so.

They'd even gone to the same constricting high school, though he'd never noticed her there. But why would he? He was four years older. By the time she'd come in, a spindly, frightened Grade

Niner, he'd been almost out the door, and none too soon for him. He couldn't imagine her there; couldn't imagine her sauntering along the same faded green hallways, banging the same scratched lockers, sticking her gum underneath the same cage-like desks.

She and the high school would have been destructive opposites, like matter and anti-matter. Every time he placed her mental image beside that of the school, one or the other of them exploded. Usually it was the school's.

Selena was not her real name. She had simply appropriated it, as she'd appropriated everything else that would help her to construct her new, preferred identity. She'd discarded the old name, which was *Marjorie*. Richard has learned this by mistake, in the course of his researches, and has tried in vain to forget it.

The first time he saw her is not noted on any of his filing-cards. He only makes notes of things he is not otherwise likely to remember.

It was in 1960—the end of the fifties or the beginning of the sixties, depending on how you felt about zero. Selena was later to call it *'the white-hot luminous egg/from which everything hatches,'* but for Richard, who at the time was slogging through *Being and Nothingness*, it signalled a dead end. He was in his first year of graduate school, on a meagre grant eked out by the marking of woefully written undergraduate essays. He was feeling jaded, over-the-hill; senility was rapidly approaching. He was twenty-two.

He met her on a Tuesday night, at the coffee-house. *The* coffee-house, because as far as Richard knew there was not another one like it in Toronto. It was called The Bohemian Embassy, in reference to the anti-bourgeois things that were supposed to go on in there, and to a certain extent did go on. It sometimes got mail from more innocent citizens who had seen the listing in the phone book and thought it was a real embassy, and were writing about travel visas. This was a source of hilarity among the regulars, of whom Richard was not quite one.

The coffee-house was on a little cobbled side-street, up on the second floor of a disused warehouse. It was reached by a treacherous flight of wooden stairs with no banister; inside, it was dimly lit, smoke-filled, and closed down at intervals by the fire department. The walls had been painted black, and there were small tables with checked cloths and dripping candles. It also had an espresso machine, the first one Richard had ever seen. This machine was practically an icon, pointing as it did to other, superior cultures, far from Toronto. But it had its drawbacks. While you were reading your poetry out loud, as Richard sometimes did, Max behind the coffee-bar might turn on the machine, adding a whooshing, gurgling sound effect, as of someone being pressure-cooked and strangled.

Wednesdays and Thursdays were folk-singing, the weekends were jazz. Richard sometimes went on these nights, but he always went on Tuesdays, whether he was reading or not. He wanted to check out the competition. There wasn't a lot of it, but what there was would surely turn up at The Bohemian Embassy, sooner or later.

Poetry was the way out then, for young people who wanted some exit from the lumpen bourgeoisie and the shackles of respectable wage-earning. It was what painting had been at the turn of the century. Richard knows this now, although he did not then. He doesn't know what the equivalent is at the moment. Film-making, he'd guess, for those with intellectual pretensions. For those without, it's playing the drums in a group, a group with a disgusting name such as Animal Fats or The Living Snot if his twenty-seven-year-old son is any indication. Richard can't keep close tabs though, because the son lives with Richard's ex-wife. (Still! At his age! Why doesn't he get a room, an apartment, a job, Richard finds himself thinking, sourly enough. He understands, now, his own father's irritation with the black turtle-necks he used to wear, his scruffy attempts at a beard, his declamations, over the obligatory Sunday-dinner meat and potatoes, of *The Wasteland*, and, later and even more effectively, of Ginsberg's *Howl*. But at least he'd been interested in *meaning*, he tells himself. Or words. At least he'd been interested in words.)

He'd been good with words, then. He'd had several of his poems published in the university literary magazine, and in two little magazines, one of them not mimeographed. Seeing these poems in print, with his name underneath—he used initials, like T. S. Eliot, to make himself sound older—had given him more satisfaction than he'd ever got out of anything before. But he'd made the mistake of showing one of these magazines to his father, who was lower-middle-management with the Post Office. This had rated nothing more than a frown and a grunt, but as he was going down the walk with his bag of freshly washed laundry, on his way back to his rented room, he'd heard his old man reading one of his free-verse anti-sonnets out loud to his mother, sputtering with mirth, punctuated by his mother's disapproving, predictable voice: 'Now John! Don't be so hard on him! He's only a boy!'

The anti-sonnet was about Mary Jo, a chunky, practical girl with an off-blonde pageboy who worked at the library, and with whom Richard was almost having an affair. '*I sink into your eyes,*' his father roared. 'Old swamp-eyes! Cripes, what's he gonna do when he gets down as far as the tits?'

And his mother, acting her part in their ancient conspiracy: 'Now John! Really! Language!'

Richard told himself severely that he didn't care. His father never read anything but the *Reader's Digest* and bad paperback novels about the war, so what did he know?

By that particular Tuesday Richard had given up free verse. It was too easy. He wanted something with more rigour, more structure; something, he admits to himself now, that not everybody else could do.

He'd read his own stuff during the first set of the evening, a group of five sestinas followed by a villanelle. His poems were elegant, intricate; he was pleased with them. The espresso machine went off during the last one—he was beginning to suspect Max of sabotage—but several people said 'Shhh'. When he'd finished there was polite applause. Richard sat back down in his corner, surreptitiously scratching his neck. The black turtle-neck was giving him a rash. As his mother never ceased telling anyone who might be interested, he had a delicate skin.

After him there was a straw-haired older woman poet from the West Coast who read a long poem in which the wind was described as blowing up between her thighs. There were breezy disclosures in this poem, off-handed four-letter words; nothing you wouldn't find in Allen Ginsberg, but Richard caught himself blushing. After her reading this woman came over and sat down beside Richard. She squeezed his arm and whispered, 'Your poems were nice.' Then, staring him straight in the eye, she hitched her skirt up over her thighs. This was hidden from the rest of the room by the checked table-cloth and by the general smoky gloom. But it was a clear invitation. She was daring him to take a peek at whatever moth-eaten horror she had tucked away in there.

Richard found himself becoming coldly angry. He was supposed to salivate, jump her on the stairway like some deranged monkey. He hated those kinds of assumptions about men, about dip-stick sex and slobbery, pea-brained arousal. He felt like punching her. She must have been at least fifty.

The age he now is himself, Richard notes dejectedly. That's one thing Selena has escaped. He thinks of it as an escape.

There was a musical interlude, as there always was on Tuesdays. A girl with long, straight, dark hair parted in the middle sat on a high stool, an autoharp across her knees, and sang several mournful folk-songs in a high, clear voice. Richard was worrying about how to remove the woman poet's hand from his arm without being ruder than he wanted to be. (She was senior, she'd published books, she knew people.) He thought he might excuse himself and go to the washroom; but the washroom was just a cubicle that opened directly on to the main room. It had no lock, and Max was in the habit of opening the door when you were in there. Unless you turned out the light and pissed in the dark, you were likely to be put on exhibit, brightly lit as a Christmas crêche, hands fumbling at your crotch.

> *He held a knife against her breast,*
> *As into his arms she pressed,*

sang the girl. *I could just leave*, thought Richard. But he didn't want to do that.

> *Oh Willy Willy, don't you murder me,*
> *I'm not prepared for eternity.*

Sex and violence, he thinks now. A lot of the songs were about that. We didn't even notice. We thought it was art.

Ｉt was right after this that Selena came on. He hadn't seen her in the room before. It was as if she'd materialized out of nowhere, on the tiny stage, under the single spotlight.

She was slight, almost wispy. Like the singer, she had long, dark hair with a centre part. Her eyes were outlined in black, as was becoming the fashion. She was wearing a long-sleeved, high-necked black dress, over which was draped a shawl embroidered with what looked like blue and green dragon-flies.

Oh jeez, thought Richard, who like his father still used the laundered blasphemies of the schoolyard. *Another jeezly poetess. I suppose now we'll have more pudenda*, he added, from his graduate-school vocabulary.

Then the voice hit him. It was a warm, rich voice, darkly spiced, like cinnamon, and too huge to be coming from such a small person. It was a seductive voice, but not in any blunt way. What it offered was an entrée to amazement, to a shared and tingling secret; to splendours. But there was an undercurrent of amusement too, as if you were a fool for being taken in by its voluptuousness; as if there were a cosmic joke in the offing, a simple, mysterious joke, like the jokes of children.

What she read was a series of short connected lyrics. *Isis in Darkness*. The Egyptian Queen of Heaven and Earth was wandering in the underworld, gathering up the pieces of the murdered and dismembered body of her lover Osiris. At the same time, it was her own body she was putting back together; and it was also the physical universe. She was creating the universe by an act of love.

All of this was taking place, not in the ancient Middle Kingdom of the Egyptians, but in flat, dingy Toronto, on Spadina Avenue, at night, among the darkened garment factories and delicatessens and bars and pawnshops. It was a lament, and a celebration. Richard had never heard anything like it.

He sat back in his chair, fingering his patchy beard, trying as hard as he could to find this girl and her poetry trivial, overdone and pretentious. But he couldn't manage it. She was brilliant, and he was frightened. He felt his own careful talent shrivelling to the size of a dried bean.

The espresso machine did not go on once. After she'd finished

191

there was a silence, before the applause. The silence was because people didn't know what to make of it, how to take it, this thing, whatever it was, that had been done to them. For a moment she had transformed reality, and it took them a breath to get it back.

Richard stood up, pushing past the bared legs of the woman poet. He didn't care any more who she might know. He went over to where Selena had just sat down, with a cup of coffee brought to her by Max.

'I liked your poems,' he managed to get out.

'Liked? Liked?' He thought she was making fun of him, although she wasn't smiling. '*Liked* is so margarine. How about *adored*?'

'Adored, then,' he said, feeling like an idiot twice over—for having said *liked* in the first place, and for jumping through her hoop in the second. But he got his reward. She asked him to sit down.

Up close her eyes were turquoise, the irises dark-ringed like a cat's. In her ears were blue-green ear-rings in the shape of scarabs. Her face was heart-shaped, her skin pale; to Richard, who had been dabbling in the French Symbolists, it evoked the word *lilac*. The shawl, the darkly outlined eyes, the ear-rings—few would have been able to pull it off. But she acted as if this was just her ordinary get up. What you'd wear any day on a journey down the Nile, 5,000 years ago.

It was of a piece with her performance—bizarre, but assured. Fully achieved. The worst of it was that she was only eighteen.

'That's a lovely shawl,' Richard attempted. His tongue felt like a beef sandwich.

'It's not a shawl, it's a table-cloth,' she said. She looked down at it, stroked it. Then she laughed a little. 'It's a shawl *now*.'

Richard wondered if he should dare to ask—what? If he could walk her home? Did she have anything so mundane as a home? But what if she said no? While he was deliberating, Max the bullet-headed coffee hack walked over and put a possessive hand on her shoulder, and she smiled up at him. Richard didn't wait to see if it meant anything. He excused himself, and left.

He went back to his rented room and composed a sestina to her. It was a dismal effort; it captured nothing about her. He did what he had never before done to one of his poems. He burnt it.

192

Over the next few weeks Richard got to know her better. Or he thought he did. When he came into the coffee-house on Tuesday nights, she would greet him with a nod, a smile. He would go over and sit down, and they would talk. She never spoke about herself, her life. Instead she treated him as if he were a fellow professional, an initiate, like herself. Her talk was about the magazines by which her poems had been accepted, about projects she'd begun. She was writing a verse play for radio; she would be paid for it. She seemed to think it was only a matter of time before she'd be earning enough money to live on, though she had very little conception of how much *enough* would be. She didn't say what she was living on at the moment.

Richard found her naïve. He himself had taken the sensible course: with a graduate degree he could always make an income of some sort in the academic salt-mines. But who would pay a living wage for poetry, especially the kind she wrote? It wasn't in the style of anyone, it didn't sound like anything else. It was too eccentric.

She was like a child sleepwalking along a roof-ledge ten storeys up. He was afraid to call out in warning, in case she should wake, and fall.

Mary Jo the librarian had phoned him several times. He'd put her off with vague mumbles about overwork. On the rare Sunday when he still turned up at his parents' house to do his laundry and eat what his father called a decent meal for once, he had to endure the pained scrutiny of his mother. Her theory was that he was straining his brain, which could lead to anaemia. In fact he was hardly working at all. His room was silting up with unmarked, overdue student papers; he hadn't written another poem, another line. Instead he went out for gummy egg sandwiches or glasses of draft beer at the local beverage room, or to afternoon movies, sleazy double features about women with two heads or men who got changed into flies. Evenings he spent at the coffee-house. He was no longer feeling jaded. He was feeling desperate.

It was Selena who was causing this desperation, but he had no name for why. Partly he wanted to get inside her, find that innermost cave where she hid her talent. But she kept him at a distance. Him, and in some way everyone else.

She read several times. The poems were astonishing again,

again unique. Nothing about her grandmother, or about snow, or about childhood; nothing about dying dogs, or family members of any kind. Instead there were regal, tricky women, magical, shape-shifting men; in whom, however, he thought he could recognize the transposed outlines of some of the regulars from The Bohemian Embassy. Was that Max's white-blonde bullet head, his lidded ice-blue eyes? There was another man, a thin intense one with a moustache and a smouldering Spanish look that set Richard's teeth on edge. One night he'd announced to the whole table that he'd caught a bad case of crabs, that he'd had to shave himself and paint his groin blue. Could that be his torso, equipped with burning wings? Richard couldn't tell, and it was driving him crazy.

(It was never Richard himself though. Never his own stubby features, his own brownish hair and hazel eyes. Never even a line, about him.)

He pulled himself together, got the papers marked, finished off an essay on the imagery of mechanism in Herrick that he needed in order to haul himself safely from this academic year into the next one. He took Mary Jo to one of the Tuesday poetry evenings. He thought it might neutralize Selena, like an acid neutralizing an alkali; get her out of his head. Mary Jo was not impressed.

'Where does she *get* those tatty old clothes?' she said.

'She's a brilliant poet,' said Richard.

'I don't care. That thing looks like a table-cloth. And why does she do her eyes in that phoney way?'

Richard felt this like a cut, like a personal wound.

He didn't want to marry Selena. He couldn't imagine marriage with her. He could not place her within the tedious, comforting scenery of domesticity: a wife doing his laundry, a wife cooking his meals, a wife pouring his tea. All he wanted was a month, a week, a night even. Not in a motel room, not in the back of a car; these squalid venues left over from his fumbling youth would not do. It would have to be somewhere else, somewhere darker and infinitely more strange. He imagined a crypt, with hieroglyphics; like the last act of *Aïda*. The same despair, the same exultation, the same annihilation. From such an experience you would emerge reborn, or not at all.

It was not lust. Lust was what you felt for Marilyn Monroe, or sometimes for the strippers at the Victory Burlesque. (Selena had a poem about the Victory Burlesque. The strippers, for her, were not a bunch of fat sluts with jiggling, dimpled flesh. They were diaphanous; they were surreal butterflies, emerging from cocoons of light; they were splendid.)

What he craved was not her body as such. He wanted to be transformed by her, into someone he was not.

B y now it was summer, and the university and the coffee-house were both closed. On rainy days Richard lay on the lumpy bed in his humid, stifling room, listening to the thunder; on sunny ones, which were just as humid, he made his way from tree to tree, staying in the shade. He avoided the library. One more session of sticky near-sex with Mary Jo, with her damp kisses and her nurse-like manipulations of his body, and especially the way she sensibly stopped short of anything final, would leave her with a permanent limp.

'You wouldn't want to get me knocked up,' she would say, and she was right, he wouldn't. For a girl who worked among books, she was breath-takingly prosaic. But then, her forte was cataloguing.

Richard knew she was a healthy girl with a normal outlook. She would be good for him. This was his mother's opinion, delivered after he'd made the mistake—just once—of taking her home with him to Sunday dinner. She was like corned beef, cottage cheese, cod-liver oil. She was like milk.

O ne day he bought a bottle of Italian red wine and took the ferry over to Ward's Island. He knew Selena lived over there. That at least had been in the poems.

He didn't know what he intended to do. He wanted to see her, take hold of her, go to bed with her. He didn't know how he was going to get from the first step to the last. He didn't care what came of it. He wanted.

He got off the ferry and walked up and down the small streets of the island, where he had never been. These were summer homes, cheap and insubstantial, white clapboard or pastel, or sided with insulbrick. Cars were not permitted. There were kids on bicycles, dumpy women in swimsuits taking sunbaths on their lawns.

Portable radios played. It was not what he'd had in mind as Selena's milieu. He thought of asking someone where she lived—they would know, she'd stand out here—but he didn't want to advertise his presence. He considered turning around, taking the next ferry back.

Then, off at the end of one of the streets, he saw a minute one-storey cottage, in the shade of two large willows. There had been willows in the poems. He could at least try.

The door was open. It was her house, because she was in it. She was not at all surprised to see him.

'I was just making some peanut-butter sandwiches,' she said, 'so we could have a picnic.' She was wearing loose black cotton slacks, Oriental in tone, and a sleeveless black top. Her arms were white and thin. Her feet were in sandals; he looked at her long toes, with the toe-nails painted a light peach-pink. He noted with a wrench of the heart that the nail-polish was chipped.

'Peanut butter?' he said stupidly. She was talking as if she'd been expecting him.

'And strawberry jam,' she said. 'Unless you don't like jam.' Still that courteous distance.

He proferred his bottle of wine. 'Thanks,' she said, 'but you'll have to drink it all by yourself.'

'Why?' he said. He'd intended this to go differently. A recognition. A wordless embrace.

'If I ever started I'd never stop. My father was an alcoholic,' she told him gravely. 'He's somewhere else, because of it.'

'In the Underworld?' he said, in what he hoped was a graceful allusion to her poetry.

She shrugged. 'Or wherever.' He felt like a dunce. She went back to spreading the peanut butter, at her diminutive kitchen table. Richard, wrung dry of conversation, looked around him. There was only the one room, sparsely furnished. It was almost like a religious cell, or his idea of one. In one corner was a desk with an old black typewriter, and a bookshelf made of boards and bricks. The bed was narrow and covered with a swathe of bright-purple Indian cotton, to double as a sofa. There was a tiny sink, a tiny stove. One easy chair, Sally Ann issue. A braided, faded rug. On the walls there were no pictures at all.

'I don't need them,' she said. She'd put the sandwiches into a crumpled paper bag and was motioning him out of the door.

She led him to a stone breakwater overlooking the lake, and they sat on it and ate the sandwiches. She had some lemonade in a milk bottle; they passed it back and forth. It was like a ritual, like a communion; she was letting him partake. She sat cross-legged, with sun-glasses on. Two people went by in a canoe. The lake rippled, threw off glints of light. Richard felt absurd, and happy.

'We can't be lovers,' she said to him after a time. She was licking jam off her fingers. Richard jolted awake. He had never been so abruptly understood. It was like a trick; it made him uncomfortable.

He could have pretended he didn't know what she was talking about. Instead he said, 'Why not?'

'You would get used up,' she said. 'Then you wouldn't be there, later.'

This was what he wanted: to be used up. To burn in divine conflagration. At the same time, he realized that he could not summon up any actual, carnal desire for this woman; this *girl*, sitting beside him on the breakwater with her skinny arms and minimal breasts, dangling her legs now like a nine-year-old.

'Later?' he said. Was she telling him he was too good to be wasted? Was this a compliment, or not?

'When I'll need you,' she said. She was stuffing the waxed-paper sandwich wrapping into the paper bag. 'I'll walk you to the ferry.'

He had been circumvented, outmanoeuvred; also spied on. Maybe he was an open book and a dolt as well, but she didn't have to rub it in. As they walked, he found himself getting angry. He still clutched the wine bottle in its liquor-store bag.

At the ferry dock she took his hand, shook it formally. 'Thank you for coming,' she said. Then she pushed the sun-glasses up on to her hair, giving him her turquoise eyes full force. 'The light only shines for some,' she said, kindly and sadly. 'And even for them it's not all the time. The rest of the time you're alone.'

But he'd had enough of gnomic utterances for one day. 'Theatrical bitch,' he told himself on the ferry.

He went back to his room and drank most of the bottle of wine. Then he phoned Mary Jo. When she'd negotiated her way as usual past the snoopy landlady on the ground floor and arrived on tiptoe at his door, he pulled her inside roughly and bent her backwards in a tipsy, mocking embrace. She started to giggle, but he kissed her seriously and pushed her on to the bed. If he couldn't have what he wanted he would at least have something. The bristles of her shaved legs rasped against him; her breath smelled like grape bubble-gum. When she began to protest, warning him again of the danger of pregnancy, he said it didn't matter. She took this as a marriage proposal. In the event, it was one.

With the arrival of the baby his academic work ceased to be a thing he did disdainfully, on suffrance, and became a necessity of life. He needed the money, and then he needed more money. He laboured over his PhD. thesis, on cartographic imagery in John Donne, interrupted by infant squalling and the dentist's-drill whine of the vacuum cleaner, and by the cups of tea brought to him by Mary Jo at inappropriate moments. She told him he was a grouch, but since that was more or less the behaviour she expected from husbands she didn't seem to mind. She typed his thesis for him and did the footnotes, and showed him off to her relatives, him and his new degree. He got a job teaching composition and grammar to veterinary students at the agricultural college in Guelph.

He did not write poetry any more. Some days he hardly even thought about it. It was like a third arm, or a third eye that had atrophied. He'd been a freak when he'd had it.

Once in a while, though, he went on binges. He would sneak into bookstores or libraries, lurk around the racks where the little magazines were kept; sometimes he'd buy one. Dead poets were his business, living ones his vice. Much of the stuff he read was crap and he knew it; still, it gave him an odd lift. Then there would be the occasional real poem, and he would catch his breath. Nothing else could drop him through space like that, then catch him; nothing else could peel him open.

Sometimes these poems were Selena's. He would read them, and part of him—a small, constricted part—would hope for some lapse, some decline; but she just got better. Those nights, when he was lying in bed on the threshold of sleep, he would remember her or she would appear to him, he was never sure which; a dark-haired woman with her arms upstretched, in a long cloak of blue and dull gold or of feathers or of white linen. The costumes were variable, but she herself remained a constant. She was something of his own, that he had lost.

He didn't see her again until 1970, another zero year. By that time he'd managed to get himself hired back to Toronto, to teach graduate-level Puritan literary theory and freshman English at a new campus in the suburbs. He did not yet have tenure: in the age of publish-or-perish, he'd published only two papers, one on witchcraft as sexual metaphor, the other on *The Pilgrim's Progress* and architecture. Now that their son was in school Mary Jo had gone back to cataloguing, and with their savings they'd made a down-payment on a Victorian semi-detached in the Annex. It had a small back lawn, which Richard mowed. They kept talking about a garden, but there was never the energy.

At this time Richard was at a low point, though it was Mary Jo's contention that he was always at a low point. She fed him vitamin pills and nagged him to see a shrink so he could become more assertive, though when he was assertive with her she would accuse him of throwing his patriarchal weight around. He'd realized by now that he could always depend on her to do the socially correct thing; at the moment she was attending a women's consciousness-raising group and was (possibly) having an affair with a sandy-haired, pasty-faced linguist at the university whose name was Johanson. Whether it existed or not, this affair suited Richard, in a way: it allowed him to think badly of her.

It was April. Mary Jo was at her women's group or screwing Johanson, or possibly both; she was efficient, she could get a lot done in one evening. His son was staying overnight with a friend. Richard was supposed to be working on his book, the book that was going to do it for him, make his name, get him tenure: *Spiritual Carnality: Marvell and Vaughan and the 17th Century.* He'd hesitated between *carnal spirituality* and *spiritual carnality*, but the latter had more zing. The book was not going all that well.

There was a problem of focus. Instead of rewriting the second chapter again, he'd come downstairs to rummage in the refrigerator for a beer.

'*And tear our pleasures with rough strife through the iron gates of life, Olay!*' he sang, to the tune of *Hernando's Hideaway*. He got out two beers and filled a cereal bowl with potato chips. Then he went into the living-room and settled into the easy chair to slurp and munch, flipping through the channels on the television set, looking for the crassest, most idiotic thing he could find. He badly needed something to sneer at.

This was when the doorbell rang. When he saw who it was he was very glad he'd had the sense to click off the item he'd been watching, a tits-and-bums extravaganza posing as a detective show.

It was Selena, wearing a wide-brimmed black hat and a long, black knitted coat, and carrying a battered suitcase. 'May I come in?' she said.

Richard, amazed and a little frightened, and then suddenly delighted, stood back to let her in. He'd forgotten what delight felt like. In the last few years he'd given up even on the little magazines, preferring numbness.

He didn't ask her what she was doing at his house, or how she'd found him. Instead he said, 'Would you like a drink?'

'No,' she said. 'I don't drink, remember?' He did remember then; he remembered her tiny house on the island, in every clear detail: the pattern of small gold lions on the bedspread, the shells and round stones on the window-sill, the daisies in a jam jar. He remembered her long toes. He'd made a fool of himself that day, but now she was here it no longer mattered. He wanted to wrap his arms around her, hold her closely; rescue her, be rescued.

'Some coffee would be nice though,' she said, and he led her to the kitchen and made her some. She didn't take off her coat. The sleeves were threadbare; he could see the places where she'd stitched over the ravelled edges with mending wool. She smiled at him with the same acceptance of him she'd always shown, taking for granted that he was a friend and equal, and he was ashamed of the way he'd spent the last ten years. He must be absurd to her; he was absurd to himself. He had a paunch and a mortgage, a bedraggled marriage; he mowed the lawn, he owned sports jackets, grudgingly he raked the autumn leaves and shovelled the winter snow. He indulged his own sloth. He should have been living in an attic, eating bread and magotty cheese, washing his one shirt out at night, his head incandescent with words.

She was not noticeably older. If anything she was thinner. He saw what he thought was the fading shadow of a bruise over her right cheek-bone, but it could have been the light. She sipped at her coffee, fiddled with the spoon. She seemed to have drifted off somewhere. 'Are you writing much?' he said, seizing on something he knew would interest her.

'Oh yes,' she said brightly, returning to her body. 'I have another book coming out.' How had he missed the first one? 'How about you?'

He shrugged. 'Not for a long time.'

'That's a shame,' she said. 'That's terrible.' She meant it. It was as if he'd told her someone she'd known had died, and he was touched. It wasn't his actual poems she was regretting, unless she had no taste at all. They hadn't been any good, he knew that now and certainly she did too. It was the poems, the ones he might have written, if. If what?

'Could I stay here?' she said, putting down her cup.

Richard was taken aback. She'd meant business with that suitcase. Nothing would have pleased him more, he told himself, but there was Mary Jo to be considered. 'Of course,' he said, hoping his hesitation hadn't shown.

'Thank you,' said Selena. 'I don't have anywhere else right now. Anywhere safe.'

He didn't ask her to explain this. Her voice was the same, rich and tantalizing, on the edge of ruin; it was having its old devastating effect on him. 'You can sleep in the rec room,' he said. 'There's a sofa that folds out.'

'Oh good.' She sighed. 'It's Thursday.' Thursday, he recalled, was a significant day in her poetry, but at the time he couldn't remember whether it was good or bad. Now he knows. Now he has three filing-cards with nothing but Thursdays on them.

When Mary Jo got home, brisk and defensive as he'd decided she always was after furtive sex, they were still sitting in the kitchen. Selena was having another cup of coffee, Richard another beer.

Selena's hat and mended coat were on top of her suitcase. Mary Jo saw them and scowled.

'Mary Jo, you remember Selena,' Richard said. 'From the Embassy?'

'Right,' said Mary Jo. 'Did you put out the trash?'

'I will,' said Richard. 'She's staying overnight.'

'I'll put it out myself then,' said Mary Jo, stomping off towards the glassed-in back porch where they kept the garbage cans. Richard followed her and they fought, at first in whispers.

'What the hell is she doing in my house?' Mary Jo hissed.

'It's not just your house, it's my house too. She's got nowhere else to go.'

'That's what they all say. What happened, some boy-friend beat her up?'

'I didn't ask. She's an old friend.'

'Look, if you want to sleep with that weird flake you can do it somewhere else.'

'As you do?' said Richard, with what he hoped was bitter dignity.

'What the hell are you talking about? Are you accusing me of something?' said Mary Jo. Her eyes were bulging out, as they did when she was really angry and not just acting. 'Oh. You'd love that, wouldn't you. Give you a voyeuristic thrill.'

'Anyway I'm not sleeping with her,' said Richard, reminding Mary Jo that the first false accusation had been hers.

'Why not?' said Mary Jo. 'You've been leching after her for ten years. I've seen you mooning over those stupid poetry magazines. *On Thursdays you are a banana*,' she intoned, in savage mimicry of Selena's deeper voice. 'Why don't you just screw her and get it over with?'

'I would if I could,' Richard said. This truth saddened him.

'Oh. Holding out on you? Tough shit. Do me a favour, just rape her in the rec room and get it out of your system.'

'My, my,' said Richard. 'Sisterhood *is* powerful.' As soon as he said it he knew he'd gone too far.

'How dare you use my feminism against me like that?' said Mary Jo, her voice up an octave. 'That is so cheap! You always were a cheap little prick!'

Selena was standing in the doorway watching them. 'Richard,' she said, 'I think I'd better go.'

'Oh no,' said Mary Jo, with a chirpy parody of hospitality. 'Stay! It's no trouble! Stay a week! Stay a month! Consider us your hotel!'

Richard walked Selena to the front door. 'Where will you go?' he said.

'Oh,' she said, 'there's always somewhere.' She stood under the porch light, looking up the street. It *was* a bruise. 'But right now I don't have any money.'

Richard dug out his wallet, emptied it. He wished it was more.

'I'll pay you back,' she said.

If he has to date it, Richard pinpoints this Thursday as the day his marriage was finally over. Even though he and Mary Jo went through the form of apologizing, even though they had more than a few drinks and smoked a joint and had dislocated, impersonal sex, nothing got fixed. Mary Jo left him soon after, in quest of the self she claimed she needed to find. She took their son with her. Richard, who hadn't paid that much attention to the boy, was now reduced to nostalgic, interminable weekends with him. He tried out several other women, but couldn't concentrate on them.

He looked for Selena but she'd disappeared. One magazine editor told him she'd gone out west. Richard felt he'd let her down. He had failed to be a place of refuge.

Ten years later he saw her again. It was 1980, another year of the nothing, or of the white-hot egg. He notes this coincidence only now, laying out the filing-cards like a fortune-teller across the surface of his particle-board desk.

He'd just got out of his car, having returned through thickening traffic from the university, where he was still clinging on by his finger-nails. It was mid-March, during the spring melt, an irritating and scruffy time of year. Mud and rain and scraps of garbage left over from the winter. His mood was similar. He'd recently had the manuscript of *Spiritual Carnality* returned to him by a publisher, the fourth rejection. The covering letter informed him that he'd failed sufficiently to problematize the texts. On the title page someone had written, in faint, semi-erased pencil, *fatuously romantic*. He suspected that shrike Johanson, who was one of their readers, and who'd had it in for him ever since Mary Jo had left. After a brief interval of firm-chinned single coping she'd moved in on Johanson and they'd lived together for six months of blitzkreig. Then she'd tried to hit him up for half the value of his house. Johanson had been blaming this on Richard ever since.

He was thinking about this, and about the batch of student papers in his briefcase: James Joyce from a Marxist perspective, or garbled structuralism seeping in from France to dilute the student brain yet further. The papers had to be marked by tomorrow. He had a satisfying fantasy of laying them all out in the muddy street and running over them with his car. He would say he'd been in an accident.

Coming towards him was a short, thickish woman in a black trench coat. She was carrying a large, brown tapestry bag; she seemed to be looking at the numbers on the houses, or possibly the snowdrops and crocuses on the lawns. Richard did not understand that it was Selena until she'd almost passed him.

'Selena,' he said, touching her arm.

She turned up to him a blank face, the turquoise eyes dull. 'No,' she said. 'That's not my name.' Then she peered more closely. 'Richard. Is that you?' Either she was feigning pleasure, or she really felt it. Again, for him, there was a stab of unaccustomed joy.

He stood awkwardly. No wonder she'd had trouble recognizing him. He was prematurely grey, overweight; Mary Jo had told him, on the last, unpleasant occasion on which he'd seen her, that he was slug-coloured. 'I didn't know you were still here,' he said. 'I thought you'd moved out west.'

'Travelled,' she said. 'I'm through with that.' There was an edge to her voice he'd never heard before.

'And your work?' he said. It was always the thing to ask her.

'What work?' she said, and laughed.

'Your poetry.' He was beginning to be alarmed. She was more matter-of-fact than he'd ever known her to be, but somehow this struck him as crazy.

'Poetry,' she said with scorn. 'I hate poetry. It's just this. This is all there is. This stupid city.'

He went cold with dread. What was she saying, what had she done? It was like a blasphemy, it was like an act of desecration. Though how could he expect her to maintain faith in something he himself had so blatantly failed?

She'd been frowning, but now her face wrinkled in anxiety. She put a hand on his arm, stood on tiptoe. 'Richard,' she whispered. 'What happened to us? Where did everyone go?' A mist came up with her, an odour. He recognized sweetish wine, a whiff of cat.

He wanted to shake her, lead her to safety, wherever that might be. 'We just changed, that's all,' he said gently. 'We got older.'

'Change and decay in all around I see,' she said, smiling in a way he did not like at all. 'I'm not prepared for eternity.'

It wasn't until she'd walked away—refusing tea, hurrying off as if she couldn't wait to see the last of him—that he realized she'd been quoting from a folk-song. It was the same one he'd heard sung to the autoharp in the coffee-house, the night he'd first seen her, standing under the single spotlight in her dragon-fly shawl.

That, and a hymn. He wondered whether she'd become what his students called 'religious'.

Months later he heard she was dead. Then there was a piece in the paper. The details were vague. It was the picture that caught his eye: an earlier picture of her, from the jacket of one of her books. Probably there was nothing more recent, because she hadn't published anything for years. Even her death belonged to an earlier time; even the people in the small closed world of poetry had largely forgotten about her.

Now that she's dead, however, she's become newly respectable. In several quarterly reviews the country has been lambasted for its indifference towards her, its withholding of recognition during her lifetime. There's a move afoot to name a parkette after her, or else a scholarship, and the academics are swarming like bot-flies. A thin volume has appeared, of essays on her work, shoddy stuff in Richard's opinion, flimsy and superficial; another one is rumoured to be in the offing.

This is not the reason Richard is writing about her, however. Nor is it to cover his professional ass: he's going to be axed from the university anyway, there are new cut-backs, he lacks tenure, his head is on the block. It's merely because she's the one thing left he still values, or wants to write about. She is his last hope.

Isis in Darkness, he writes. *The Genesis*. It exalts him simply to form the words. He will exist for her at last, he will be created by her, he will have a place in her mythology after all. It will not be what he once wanted: not Osiris, not a blue-eyed god with burning wings. His are humbler metaphors. He will only be the archaeologist; not part of the main story, but the one who stumbles upon it afterwards, making his way for his own obscure and battered reasons through the jungle, over the mountains, across the desert, until he discovers at last the pillaged and abandoned temple. In the ruined sanctuary, in the moonlight, he will find the Queen of Heaven and Earth and the Underworld lying in shattered white marble on the floor. He is the one who will sift through the rubble, groping for the shape of the past. He is the one who will say it has meaning. That too is a calling, that also can be a fate.

He picks up a filing-card, jots a small footnote on it in his careful writing, and replaces it neatly in the mosaic of paper he is making across his desk. His eyes hurt. He closes them and rests his forehead on his two fisted hands, summoning up whatever is left of his knowledge and skill, kneeling beside her in the darkness, fitting her broken pieces back together.

THE USES OF ADVERSITY
Timothy Garton Ash

Ten years ago Timothy Garton Ash came to East Berlin to find out from the archives what the Berliners had done under Hitler. Instead he found out – from the streets – what 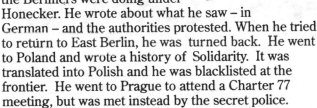 the Berliners were doing under Honecker. He wrote about what he saw – in German – and the authorities protested. When he tried to return to East Berlin, he was turned back. He went to Poland and wrote a history of Solidarity. It was translated into Polish and he was blacklisted at the frontier. He went to Prague to attend a Charter 77 meeting, but was met instead by the secret police.

Ten years ago Timothy Garton Ash began to discover Central Europe, **The Uses of Adversity** records what he found.

'A passionate case for the liberation and cultural survival of Central Europe, pursued with wit and discrimination. Since the book came out in September, events have nudged its status up from Useful to Essential.'
Anthony Lane, *Independent*

'A collection of brilliant articles which not only describe but participate in the current metamorphosis of the Eastern European countries, Timothy Garton Ash's excellent **The Uses of Adversity** shows that a British writer can still take the world for scope.'
Clive James, *Observer*

Hardback, £13.95 paperback, £5.99.

ISBN: 0 140 14018 2

BOOKS *etc.*
has arrived in Covent Garden.

26 James Street
Covent Garden
Tel: 01-379 6947

RICHARD FORD
ELECTRIC CITY

I n the fall of 1960, when I was sixteen and my father was for a time not working, my mother met a man named Warren Miller and fell in love with him. This was in Great Falls, Montana, at the time of the Gypsy Basin oil boom, and my father had brought us there in the spring of that year up from Lewiston, Idaho, in the belief that people—small people like him—were making money in Montana or soon would be, and he wanted a piece of that good luck before all of it collapsed and was gone in the wind.

My father was a golfer. A teaching pro. He had been to college though not to the war. And since 1944, the year when I was born and two years after he married my mother, he had worked at that—at golf—at the small country clubs and public courses in the towns near where he'd grown up, around Colfax and the Palouse Hills of eastern Washington State. And during that time, the years when *I* was growing up, we had lived in Coeur d'Alene and McCall, Idaho, and in Endicott and Pasco and Walla Walla, where both he and my mother had gone to college and where they had met and gotten married.

My father was a natural athlete. His own father had owned a clothing store in Colfax and made a good living, and he had learned to play golf on the kinds of courses he had taught on. He could play every sport—basketball and ice hockey and throw horseshoes, and he had played baseball in college. But he loved the game of golf because it was a game other people found difficult and that was easy for him. He was a smiling, handsome man with dark hair—not tall but with delicate hands and a short fluid swing that was wonderful to see but never strong enough to move him into the higher competition of the game. He was good at teaching people to play golf though. He knew how to discuss the game patiently, in ways to make you think you had a talent for it, and people liked being around him. Sometimes he and my mother would play together and I would go along with them and pull their cart, and I knew he knew how they looked—good-looking, young, happy. My father was soft-spoken and good-natured and optimistic—not slick in the way someone might think. And though it is not a usual life to be a golfer, to make your living at it the way anyone does who is a salesman or a doctor, my father was in a sense not a usual kind of man: he was innocent and he was honest, and it is possible he was suited perfectly for the life he had made.

In Great Falls my father took a job two days a week at the air base, at the course there, and worked the rest of the time at the club for-members-only, across the river. The Wheatland Club that was called. He worked extra because, he said, in good times people wanted to learn a game like golf, and good times rarely lasted long enough. He was thirty-nine then, and I think he hoped he'd meet someone there, someone who'd give him a tip, or let him in on a good deal in the oil boom, or offer him a better job, a chance that would lead him and my mother and me to something better.

We rented a house on Eighth Street North in an older neighborhood of single-storey, brick-and-frame houses. Ours was yellow and had a low, paled fence across the front of it and a weeping birch tree in the side yard. Those streets are not far from the train tracks and are across the river from the refinery where a bright flame burned at all hours from the stack above the metal tank buildings. I could hear the shift whistles blow in the morning when I woke up, and late at night the loud whooshing of machinery processing crude oil from the wildcat fields north of us.

My mother did not have a job in Great Falls. She had worked as a book-keeper for a dairy concern in Lewiston, and in the other towns where we had lived she had been a substitute teacher in math and science—subjects she enjoyed. She was a pretty, small woman who had a good sense for a joke and who could make you laugh. She was two years younger than my father, had met him in college in 1941 and liked him, and simply left with him when he'd taken a job in Spokane. I do not know what she thought my father's reasons were for leaving his job in Lewiston and coming to Great Falls. Maybe she noticed something about him—that it was an odd time in his life when his future had begun to seem different to him, as if he couldn't rely on it just to take care of itself as it had up until then. Or maybe there were other reasons, and because she loved him she went along with him. But I do not think she ever wanted to come to Montana. She liked eastern Washington, liked the better weather there, where she had been a girl. She thought it would be too cold and lonely in Great Falls, and people would not be easy to meet. Yet she must've believed at the time that this was a normal life she was living, moving, and working when she could, having a husband and a son, and that it was fine.

The summer of that year was a time of forest fires. Great Falls is where the plains begin, but south and west and east of there are mountains. You could see mountains on clear days from the streets of town—sixty miles away the high eastern front of the Rocky Mountains themselves, blue and clear-cut, running to Canada. In early July, fires started in the timber canyons beyond Augusta and Choteau, towns that were insignificant to me but that were endangered. Fires began by mysterious causes. They burned on and on through July and August and into September when it was thought that an early fall would bring rains and possibly snow, though that is not what happened.

Spring had been a dry season and lasted dry into summer. I was a city boy and knew nothing about crops or timber, but we all heard that farmers believed dryness forecasted dryness, and read in the paper that standing timber was drier than wood put in a kiln, and that if farmers were smart they would cut their wheat early to save losses. Even the Missouri River dropped to a low stage, and fish died, and dry mud flats opened between the banks and the slow stream, and no one boated there.

My father taught golf every day to groups of airmen and their girlfriends, and at the Wheatland Club he played foursomes with ranchers and oilmen and bankers and their wives, whose games he was paid to improve upon and tried to. In the evenings through that summer he would sit at the kitchen table after work, listening to a ball game from the East and drinking a beer, and read the paper while my mother fixed dinner and I did school work in the living-room. He would talk about people at the club. 'They're all good enough fellows,' he said to my mother. 'We won't get rich working for rich men, but we might get lucky hanging around them.' He laughed about that. He liked Great Falls. He thought it was wide open and undiscovered, and no one had time to hold you back, and that it was a good time to live there. I don't know what his ideas for himself were then, but he was a man, more than most, who liked to be happy. And it must've seemed as though, just for that time, he had finally come to his right place.

By the first of August the timber fires to the west of us had not been put out, and a haze was in the air so that you could sometimes not see the mountains or where the land met the sky. It was a haze you wouldn't detect if you were inside of it, only if you were on a mountain or in an airplane and could see Great Falls from above. At night I stood at the window and looked west up the valley of the Sun River toward the mountains that were blazing, I could believe that I saw flames and hills on fire and men moving, though I couldn't see that, could only see a brightening, wide and red and deep above the darkness between the fire and all of us. At night I would wake up and taste smoke and smell it. Twice I even dreamed our house had caught fire, a spark travelling miles on a wind and catching in our roof, consuming everything. Though I knew even in this dream that the world would spin on and we would survive, and the fire did not matter so much. I did not understand, of course, what it meant not to survive.

Such a fire could not help changing things, and there was a feeling in Great Falls, some attitude in general, that was like discouragement. There were stories in the paper, wild stories. Indians were said to have set fires to get the jobs putting them out. A man was seen driving a loggers road throwing flaming sticks out his truck window. Poachers were to blame. A peak far back in the Marshall Mountains was said to have been struck by lightning a hundred times in an hour. My father heard on the golf-course that criminals were fighting the fire, murderers and rapists from Deer Lodge, men who'd volunteered but then slipped away and back to civilized life.

No one, I think, thought Great Falls would burn. Too many miles separated us from the fire, too many other towns would have to go first—too much bad luck falling one way. But people wet the roofs of their houses, and planes took off every day carrying men to jump into the flames. West of us smoke rose like thunderheads, as if the fire itself could make rain. And as the wind stiffened in the afternoon, we all knew that the fire had jumped a trench line or rushed forward or exploded into some untouched place, and that we were all affected, even if we never saw flames or felt the heat.

I was then beginning the eleventh grade in Great Falls High School and was trying to play football, a game I did not like and wasn't good at, and tried to play only because my father thought I could make friends by playing. There were days, though, that we sat out football practice because the doctor said smoke would scar our lungs and we wouldn't feel it. I would go on those days and meet my father at the Wheatland Club—the base course having closed because of the fire danger—and hit practice balls with him late in the day. My father began to work fewer days as the summer went on, and was home more. People did not come to the club because of the smoke and the dryness. He taught fewer lessons, saw fewer of the members he had met and made friends with the spring before. He worked more in the pro-shop, sold golf equipment and clothes and magazines, rented carts, spent more time collecting balls along the edge of the river by the willows where the driving range ended.

On an afternoon in late September, two weeks after I had started school and the fires in the mountains west of us seemed to be lasting forever, I walked with my father out on the driving range with wire baskets. One man was hitting balls off the practice tee far back and to the left of us. I could hear the thwock of the club and a hiss as the balls arched out into the twilight, hit and bounced toward us. At home, the night before, he and my mother had talked about the election that was coming. They were Democrats. Both their families had been. But my father said on that night that he was considering the Republicans now. Nixon, he said, was a good lawyer. He was not a personable man, but he would stand up to the labor unions.

My mother laughed at him and put her hands over her eyes as if she didn't want to see him. 'Oh, not you, too, Jerry,' she said. 'Are you becoming a right-to-work advocate?' She was joking. I don't think she cared who he voted for, and they did not talk about politics. We were in the kitchen and food was already set out on the table.

'Things feel like they've gone too far in one direction,' my father said. He put his hands on either side of his plate. I heard him breathe. He still had on his golf clothes, green pants and a yellow nylon shirt with a red club emblem on it. There had been a railroad strike during that summer but he had not talked about unions, and I didn't think it had affected us.

My mother was standing and drying her hands at the sink. 'You're a working man, I'm not,' she said. 'I'll just remind you of that, though.'

'I wish we had a Roosevelt to vote for,' my father said. 'He had a feel for the country.'

'That was just a different time then,' my mother said, and sat down across the metal table from him. She was wearing a blue and white checked dress and an apron. 'Everyone was afraid then, including us. Everything's better now. You forget that.'

'I haven't forgotten anything,' my father said. 'But I'm interested in thinking about the future now.'

'Well,' she said. She smiled at him. 'That's good. I'm glad to hear that. I'm sure Joe's glad of it, too.' And then we ate dinner.

The next afternoon, though, at the end of the driving range by the willows and the river, my father was in a different mood. He had not given a lesson that week, but wasn't tense and didn't seem mad at anything. He was smoking a cigarette, something he didn't ordinarily do.

'It's a shame not to work in warm weather,' he said, and smiled. He took one of the golf balls out of his basket, drew back and threw it through the willow branches toward the river where it hit down in the mud without a sound. 'How's your football going?' he asked me. 'Are you going to be the next Bob Waterfield?'

'No,' I said. 'I don't think so.'

'I won't be the next Walter Hagen, either,' he said. He liked Walter Hagen. He had a picture of him wearing a broad-brimmed hat and a heavy overcoat, laughing at the camera as he teed off some place where there was snow on the ground. My father kept that picture inside the closet door in his and my mother's bedroom.

He stood and watched the lone golfer who was driving balls out on to the fairway. We could see him silhouetted. 'There's a man who hits the ball nicely,' he said, watching the man take his club back smoothly, then sweep through his swing. 'He doesn't take chances. Get the ball in the middle of the fairway, then take the margin of error. Let the other guy foul up. That's what Walter Hagen did. The game came naturally to him.'

'Isn't it the same with you?' I asked, because that's what my mother had said, that my father had never needed to practice.

'Yes it is,' my father said, smoking. 'I thought it was easy. There's probably something wrong with that.'

'I don't like football,' I said.

My father glanced at me and then stared at the west where the fire was darkening the sun, turning it purple. 'I liked it,' he said in a dreamy way. 'When I had the ball and ran up the field and dodged people, I liked that.'

'I don't dodge enough,' I said. I wanted to tell this to him

215

because I wanted him to tell me to quit football and do something else. I liked golf and would've been happy to play it.

'I wasn't going to not play golf, though,' he said, 'even though I'm probably not cagey enough for it.' He was not listening to me, now, though I didn't hold it against him.

Far away at the practice tee I heard a thwock as the lone man drove a ball up into the evening air. There was a silence as my father and I waited for the ball to hit and bounce. But the ball actually hit my father, hit him on the shoulder above the bottom of his sleeve— not hard or even hard enough to cause pain.

My father said, 'Well. For Christ's sake. Look at that.' He looked down at the ball beside him on the ground, then rubbed his arm. We could see the man who'd hit the ball walking back toward the clubhouse, his driver swinging beside him like a walking cane. He had no idea where the balls were falling. He hadn't dreamed he'd hit my father.

My father stood and watched the man disappear into the long white clubhouse building. He stood for a while as if he was listening and could hear something I couldn't hear—laughing, possibly, or music from far away. He had always been a happy man, and I think he may simply have been waiting for something to make him feel that way again.

'If you don't like football,'—and he suddenly looked at me as if he'd forgotten I was there—'then just forget about it. Take up the javelin throw instead. There's a feeling of achievement in that. I did it once.'

'All right,' I said. And I thought about the javelin throw— about how much a javelin would weigh and what it was made of and how hard it would be to throw the right way.

My father was staring toward where the sky was beautiful and dark and full of colors. 'It's on fire out there, isn't it? I can smell it.'

'I can too,' I said, watching.

'You have a clear mind, Joe.' He looked at me. 'Nothing bad will happen to you.'

'I hope not,' I said.

'That's good', he said, 'I hope so, too.' And we went on then picking up golf balls and walking back toward the clubhouse.

When we had walked back to the pro-shop, lights were on inside, and through the glass windows I could see a man sitting alone in a folding chair, smoking a cigar. He had on a business suit, though he had the jacket over his arm and was wearing brown and white golf shoes.

When my father and I stepped inside carrying our baskets of range balls, the man stood up. I could smell the cigar and the clean smell of new golf equipment.

'Hello there, Jerry,' the man said, and smiled and stuck out his hand to my father. 'How'd my form look to you out there?'

'I didn't realize that was you,' my father said, and smiled. He shook the man's hand. 'You have a blueprint swing. You can brag about that.'

'I spray 'em around a bit,' the man said, and put his cigar in his mouth.

'That's everybody's misery,' my father said, and brought me to his side. 'This is my son, Joe, Clarence. This is Clarence Snow, Joe. He's the president of this club. He's the best golfer out here.' I shook hands with Clarence Snow, who was in his fifties and had long fingers, bony and strong, like my father's. He did not shake my hand very hard.

'Did you leave any balls out there, Jerry?' Clarence Snow said, running his hand back through his thin, dark hair and casting a look at the dark course.

'Quite a few,' my father said. 'We lost our light.'

'Do you play this game, too, son?' Clarence Snow smiled at me.

'He's good,' my father said before I could answer anything. He sat down on the other folding chair that had his street shoes under it, and began unlacing his white golf shoes. My father was wearing yellow socks that showed his pale, hairless ankles, and he was staring at Clarence Snow while he loosened his laces.

'I need to have a talk with you, Jerry,' Clarence Snow said. He glanced at me and sniffed his nose.

'That's fine,' my father said. 'Can it wait til' tomorrow?'

'No it can't,' Clarence Snow said. 'Would you come up to the office?'

'I certainly will,' my father said. He had his golf shoes off and he raised one foot and rubbed it, then squeezed his toes down. 'The tools of ignorance,' he said, and smiled at me.

217

'This won't take much time,' Clarence Snow said. Then he walked out the front door, leaving my father and me alone in the lighted shop.

My father sat back in his folding chair, stretched his legs in front of him, and wiggled his toes in his yellow socks. 'He'll fire me,' he said. 'That's what this'll be.'

'Why do you think that?' I said. And it shocked me.

'You don't know about these things, son,' my father said. 'I've been fired before. These things have a feel to them.'

'Why would he do that?' I said.

'Maybe he thinks I fucked his wife,' my father said. I hadn't heard him say that kind of thing before, and it shocked me, too. He was staring out the window into the dark. 'Of course, I don't know if he has a wife.' My father began putting on his street shoes, which were black loafers, shiny and new and thick-soled. 'Maybe I won some money from one of his friends. He doesn't have to have a reason.' He slid the white shoes under the chair and stood up. 'Wait in here,' he said. And I knew he was mad, but did not want me to know he was. He liked to make you believe everything was fine and for everybody to be happy if they could be. 'Is that OK?' he said.

'It's OK,' I said.

'Think about some pretty girls while I'm gone,' he said, and smiled at me.

Then he walked, almost strolling, out of the little pro-shop and up toward the clubhouse, leaving me by myself with the racks of silver golf clubs and new leather bags and shoes and boxes of balls— all the other tools of my father's trade, still and silent around me like treasures.

When my father came back in twenty minutes he was walking faster than when he'd left. He had a piece of yellow paper stuck up in his shirt pocket, and his face looked tight. I was sitting on the chair Clarence Snow had sat on. My father picked up his white shoes off the green carpet, put them under his arm, then walked to the cash register and began taking money out of the trays.

'We should go,' he said in a soft voice. He was putting money in his pants pocket.

'Did he fire you?' I asked.

'Yes he did.' He stood still for a moment behind the open cash register as if the words sounded strange to him or had other meanings. He looked like a boy my own age doing something he shouldn't be doing and trying to do it casually. Though I thought maybe Clarence Snow had told him to clean out the cash register before he left and all that money was his to keep. 'Too much of a good living, I guess,' he said. Then he said, 'Look around here, Joe. See if you see anything you want.' He looked around at the clubs and the leather golf bags and shoes, the sweaters and clothes in glass cases. All things that cost a lot of money, things my father liked. 'Just take it,' he said. 'It's yours.'

'I don't want anything,' I said.

My father looked at me from behind the cash register. 'You don't want anything? All this expensive stuff?'

'No,' I said.

'You've got good character, that's your problem. Not that it's much of a problem.' He closed the cash register drawer. 'Bad luck's got a sour taste, doesn't it?'

'Yes sir,' I said.

'Do you want to know what he said to me?' My father leaned on the glass countertop with his palms down. He smiled at me, as if he thought it was funny.

'What?' I said.

'He said he didn't require an answer from me, but he thought I was stealing things. Some yokel lost a wallet out on the course, and they couldn't figure anybody else who could do it. So I was elected.' He shook his head. 'I'm not a stealer. Do you know it? That's not me.'

'I know it,' I said. And I didn't think he was. I thought I was more likely to be a stealer than he was, and I wasn't one either.

'I was too well liked out here, that's my problem,' he said. 'If you help people they don't like you for it. They're like Mormons.'

'I guess so,' I said.

'When you get older,' my father said. And then he seemed to stop what he was about to say. 'If you want to know the truth don't listen to what people tell you,' was all he said.

He walked around the cash register, holding his white shoes, his pants pockets full of money. 'Let's go now,' he said. He turned off the light when he got to the door, held it open for me, and we walked out into the warm summer night.

When we'd driven back across the river into Great Falls and up Central, my father stopped at the grocery a block from our house, went in and bought a can of beer and came back and sat in the car seat with the door open. It had become cooler with the sun gone and felt like a fall night, although it was dry and the sky was light blue and full of stars. I could smell beer on my father's breath and knew he was thinking about the conversation he would have with my mother when we got home, and what that would be like.

'Do you know what happens,' he said, 'when the very thing you wanted least to happen happens to you?' We were sitting in the glow of the little grocery store. Traffic was moving behind us along Central Avenue, people going home from work, people with things they liked to do on their minds, things they looked forward to.

'No,' I said. I was thinking about throwing the javelin at that moment, a high arching throw into clear air, coming down like an arrow, and of my father throwing it when he was my age.

'Nothing at all does,' he said, and he was quiet for several seconds. He raised his knees and held his beer can with both hands. 'We should probably go on a crime spree. Rob this store or something. Bring everything down on top of us.'

'I don't want to do that,' I said.

'I'm probably a fool,' my father said, and shook his beer can until the beer fizzed softly inside. 'It's just hard to see my opportunities right this minute.' He didn't say anything else for a while. 'Do you love your dad?' he said in a normal voice, after some time had passed.

'Yes,' I said.

'Do you think I'll take good care of you?'

'Yes,' I said. 'I think so.'

'I will,' he said.

My father shut the car door and sat a moment looking out the windshield at the grocery, where people were inside moving back and forth behind the plate-glass windows. 'Choices don't always feel exactly like choices,' he said. He started the car then, and he put his hand on my hand just like you would on a girl's. 'Don't be worried about things,' he said. 'I feel calm now.'

'I'm not worried,' I said. And I wasn't, because I thought things would be fine. And even though I was wrong, it is still not so bad a way to set your mind toward the unknown just when you are coming into the face of it.

After that night in early September things began to move more quickly in our life and to change. Our life at home changed. The life my mother and father lived changed. The world, for as little as I'd thought about it or planned on it, changed. When you are sixteen you do not know what your parents know, or much of what they understand and less of what's in their hearts. This can save you from becoming an adult too early, save your life from becoming only theirs lived over again—which is a loss. But to shield yourself—as I didn't do—seems to be an even greater error, since what's lost is the truth of your parents' life and what you should think about it, and beyond that, how you should estimate the world you are about to live in.

On the night my father came home from losing his job at the Wheatland Club, he told my mother about it straight out and they both acted as if it was a kind of joke. My mother did not get mad or seem upset or ask him why he had gotten fired. They both laughed about it. When we ate supper my mother sat at the table and seemed to be thinking. She said she could not get a job substituting until the term ended, but she would go to the school board and put her name in. She said other people would come to my father for work when it was known he was free, and that this was an opportunity in disguise—the reason we had come here—and that Montanans did not know gold when they saw it. She smiled at him when she said that. She said I could get a job, and I said I would. She said maybe she should become a banker, though she would need to finish college for that. And she laughed. Finally she said, 'You can do other things, Jerry. Maybe you've played enough golf for this lifetime.'

After dinner, my father went into the living-room and listened to the news from a station we could get from Salt Lake after dark and went to sleep on the couch still wearing his golf clothes. Late in the night they went into their room and closed the door. I heard their voices, talking. I heard my mother laugh again. And then my father laughed and said, loudly, still laughing, 'Don't threaten me. I can't be threatened.' And later on my mother said, 'You've just had your feelings hurt, Jerry, is all.' After a while I heard the bathtub

221

running with water, and I knew my father was sitting in the bathroom talking to my mother while she took her bath, which was a thing he liked doing. And later I heard their door close and their light click off and the house become locked in silence.

And then for a time after that my father did not seem to take an interest in working. In a few days the Wheatland Club called—a man who was not Clarence Snow said someone had made a mistake. I talked to the man, who gave me the message to give to my father, but my father did not call back. The air base called him, but again he did not accept. I know he did not sleep well. I could hear doors close at night and glasses tapping together. Some mornings I would look out my bedroom window, and he would be in the backyard in the chill air practising with a driver, hitting a plastic ball from one property line to the next, walking in his long easy gait as if nothing was bothering him. Other days he would take me on long drives after school, to Highwood and to Belt and Geraldine, which are the towns east of Great Falls, and let me drive the car on the wheat prairie roads where I could be no danger to anyone. And once we drove across the river to Fort Benton and sat in the car and watched golfers playing on the tiny course there above the town.

Eventually, my father began to leave the house in the morning like a man going to a job. And although we did not know where he went, my mother said she thought he went downtown, and that he had left jobs before and that it was always scary for a while, but that finally he would stand up to things and go back and be happy. My father began to wear different kinds of clothes, khaki pants and flannel shirts, regular clothes I saw people wearing, and he did not talk about golf anymore. He talked some about the fires, which still burned late in September in the canyons above Allen Creek and Castle Reef—names I knew about from the *Tribune*. He talked in a more clipped way then. He told me the smoke from such fires went around the world in five days and that the amount of timber lost there would've built 50,000 homes the size of ours. One Friday he and I went to the boxing matches at the City Auditorium and watched boys from Havre fight boys from Glasgow, and afterward in the street outside we could each see the night glow of the fires, pale in the clouds just as it had been in the summer. And my father said, 'It could rain up in the canyons now, but the fire wouldn't go out. It would smoulder then start again.' He blinked as the boxing crowd shoved around us. 'But here we are,' he said, and smiled, 'safe in Great Falls.'

It was during this time that my mother began to look for a job. She left an application at the school board. She worked two days at a dress shop, then quit. 'I'm lacking in powerful and influential friends,' she said to me as if it was a joke. Though it was true that we did not know anyone in Great Falls. My mother knew the people at the grocery store and the druggist's, and my father had known people at the Wheatland Club. But none of them ever came to our house. I think we might've gone someplace new earlier in their life, just picked up and moved away. But no one mentioned that. There was a sense that we were all waiting for something. Out of doors, the trees were through with turning yellow and leaves were dropping onto the cars parked at the curb. It was my first autumn in Montana, and it seemed to me that in our neighborhood the trees looked like an eastern state would and not at all the way I'd thought Montana would be. No trees is what I'd expected, only open prairie, the land and sky joining almost out of sight.

'I could get a job teaching swimming,' my mother said to me on a morning when my father left early and I was looking through the house for my school books. She was standing drinking coffee, looking out the front window, dressed in her yellow bathrobe. 'A lady at the Red Cross said I could teach privately if I'd teach a class, too.' She smiled at me and crossed her arms. 'I'm still a life-saver.'

'That sounds good,' I said.

'I could teach your dad the backstroke again,' she said. My mother had taught me to swim, and she was good at that. She had tried to teach my father the backstroke when we lived in Lewiston, but he had tried and failed at it, and she had made a joke about it afterwards. 'The lady said people want to swim in Montana. Why do you think that is? These things always signify a meaning.'

'What does it mean?' I said, holding my school books.

She hugged her arms and turned herself a little back and forth as she stood in the window frame watching out. 'Oh, that we're all going to be washed away in a big flood. Though I don't believe that. So. Some of us will *not* be washed away and will float to the top. That's better, isn't it?' She took a drink of coffee.

'It should have a happy ending for the right people,' I said.

223

'That's easy,' she said. 'Everyone doesn't do it that way, though.' She turned and walked away back into the kitchen then to start my breakfast before school.

In the days after that, my mother went to work at the YWCA in Great Falls, at the brick building that is gone now on Second Street North, near the courthouse. She walked to work from our house and carried her swimming-suit in a vanity case, with a lunch to eat and some makeup articles for when she came home in the afternoon. My father said he was glad if she wanted to work there, and that I should find a job, too, which I had not done. But he didn't mention himself working or how he was spending his days or what he thought about our future or any plans he had made for things. He seemed out of reach to me, as if he had discovered a secret he didn't want to tell. Once, when I walked home from football practice, I saw him inside the Jack 'n' Jill cafe, sitting at the counter drinking coffee and eating a piece of pie. He was wearing a red plaid shirt and a knitted cap, and he hadn't shaved. A man I didn't know was sitting on a stool beside him, reading the *Tribune*. They seemed to be together. Another time, on a day when the wind was blowing hard, I saw him walking away from the court-house wearing a woollen jacket and carrying a book. He turned the corner at the library and disappeared, and I did not follow him. And one other time I saw him go into a bar called the Pheasant Lounge where I thought Great Falls city policemen went. This was at noon, and I was on my lunch hour and couldn't stay to see more.

When I told my mother that I had seen him these times she said, 'He just hasn't had a chance to get established, yet. This will be all right finally. There's no lack in him.'

But I did not think things were all right. I don't believe my mother knew more than I did then. She was simply surprised, and she trusted him and thought she could wait longer. But I wondered if my parents had had troubles that I didn't know about, or if they had always had their heads turned slightly away from each other and I hadn't noticed. I know that when they shut the door to their bedroom at night and I was in my bed waiting for sleep, listening to the wind come up, I would hear their door open and close quietly, and my mother come out and make a bed for herself on the couch in the living-room. Once I heard my father say, as she was leaving,

'You've changed your thinking now, haven't you, Jean?' And my mother say 'No.' But then the door closed and she did not say anything else. I do not think I was supposed to know about this, and I don't know what they could've said to each other or done during that time. There was never yelling or arguing involved in it. They simply did not stay together at night, although during the day when I was present and life needed to go on normally there was nothing to notice between them. Coming and going was all. Nothing to make you think there was trouble or misunderstanding. I simply know there was, and that my mother for her own reasons began to move away from my father then.

After a time I quit playing football. I wanted to find a job, though I thought that when spring came, if we were still in Great Falls, I would try to throw the javelin as my father had said. I had taken the book, *Track and Field for Young Champions*, out of the library and had found the equipment cage in the school basement and inspected the two wooden javelins there, where they were stored against the concrete wall in the shadows. They were slick and polished and thicker than I thought they'd be. Though when I picked one up, it was light and seemed to me perfect for the use it had. And I thought that I would be able to throw it and that it might be a skill—even if it was a peculiar one—that I might someday excel at in a way my father would like.

I had not made friends in Great Falls. The boys on the football team lived farther downtown and across the river in Black Eagle. I had had friends in Lewiston, in particular a girlfriend named Iris, who went to the Catholic school and who I had exchanged letters with for several weeks when we had come to Great Falls in the spring. But she had gone to Seattle for the summer and had not written to me. Her father was an Army officer, and it could be her family had moved. I had not thought about her in a while, did not care about her really. It should've been a time when I cared about more things—a new girlfriend or books—or when I had an idea of some kind. But I only cared about my mother and my father then, and in the time since then I have realized that we were not a family who ever cared about much more than that.

The job I found was in the photographer's studio on Third Avenue. It was the place that took airmen's photographs, and engagement and class pictures, and what I did was clean up when school was over, replace bulbs in the photographer's lamps, and rearrange the posing furniture for the next day.

I finished work by five o'clock, and sometimes I would walk home past the YWCA and slip through the back door and down into the long tiled pool room where my mother taught her classes of adults until five, and from five to six was free to teach privately and be paid for it. I would stand at the far end behind the tiers of empty bleachers and watch her, hear her voice, which seemed happy and lively, encouraging and giving instruction. She would stand on the side in her black bathing suit, her skin pale, and make swimming motions with her arms for the students standing in the shallow water. Mostly they were old women, and old men with speckled bald heads. From time to time they ducked their faces into the water and made the swimming motions my mother made—slow, jerky grasps—without really swimming or ever moving, just staying still, standing and pretending. 'It's so easy,' I would hear my mother say in her bright voice, her arms working the thick air as she talked. 'Don't be afraid of it. It's all fun. Think about all you've missed.' She'd smile at them when their faces were up, dripping and blinking, some of them coughing. And she would say, 'Watch me now.' Then she'd pull down her bathing cap, point her hands over her head to a peak, bend her knees and dive straight in, coasting for a moment, then breaking the surface and swimming with her arms bent and her fingers together, cutting the water in easy reaching motions to the far side and back again. The old people—ranchers, I thought, and the divorced wives of farmers—watched her in envy and silence. And I watched, thinking as I did that someone else who saw my mother, not me or my father, but someone who had never seen her before, would think something different. They would think: 'Here is a woman whose life is happy'; or 'Here is a woman with a nice figure to her credit'; or 'Here is a woman I wish I could know better, though I never will.' And I thought to myself that my father was not a stupid man, and that love was permanent, even though sometimes it seemed to recede and leave no trace at all.

On the first Tuesday in October, the day before the World Series began, my father came back to the house after dark. It was chill and dry outside, and when he came in the back door his eyes were bright and his face was flushed and he seemed as if he had been running.

'Look who's here now,' my mother said, though in a nice way. She was cutting tomatoes at the sink board and looked around at him and smiled.

'I've got to pack a bag,' my father said. 'I won't have dinner here tonight, Jean.' He went straight back to their room. I was sitting beside the radio waiting to turn on some baseball news, and I could hear him opening a closet door and shoving coat hangers.

My mother looked at me, then she spoke toward the hallway in a calm voice. 'Where are you going, Jerry?' She was holding a paring knife in her hand.

'I'm going to that fire,' my father said loudly from the bedroom. He was excited. 'I've been waiting for my chance. I just heard thirty minutes ago that there's a place. I know it's unexpected.'

'Do you know anything about fires?' My mother kept watching the empty doorway as if my father was standing in it. 'I know about them,' she said. 'My father was an estimator. Do you remember that?'

'I had to make some contacts in town,' my father said. I knew he was sitting on the bed putting on different shoes. The overhead light was on and his bag was out. 'It's not easy to get this job.'

'Did you hear me?' my mother said. She had an impatient look on her face. 'I said you don't know anything about fires. You'll get burned up.' She looked at the back door, which he'd left partway open, but she didn't go to close it.

'I've been reading about fires in the library,' my father said. He came down the hall and went into the bathroom where he turned on the light and opened the medicine cabinet. 'I think I know enough not to get killed.'

'Could you have said something to me about this?' my mother said.

I heard the medicine cabinet close and my father stepped into the kitchen doorway. He looked different. He looked like he was sure that he was right.

'I should've done that,' he said. 'I just didn't.' He had his shaving-bag in his hand.

'You're not going out there.' My mother looked at my father across the kitchen, across over my head in fact, and seemed to smile. 'This is a . . . stupid idea,' she said, and shook her head.

'No it's not,' my father said.

'It isn't your business,' my mother said, and pulled up the front of her blue apron and wiped her hands on it, though I don't think her hands were wet. She was nervous. 'You don't have to do this. I'm working now.'

'I know you are,' my father said. He turned and went back into the bedroom. I wanted to move from where I was but I didn't know where a better place was to be, because I wanted to hear what they would say. 'We're going to dig firebreaks up there,' he said from the bedroom. I heard the locks on his bag snap closed. He appeared again in the doorway, holding a gladstone bag, a bag his father had given him when he had gone away to college. 'You're not in any danger,' he said.

'I might die while you're gone,' my mother said. She sat down at the metal table and stared at him. She was angry. Her mouth looked hardened. 'You have a son here,' she said.

'This won't be for very long,' my father said. 'It'll snow pretty soon, and that'll be that.' He looked at me. 'What do you think, Joe? Is this a bad idea?'

'No,' I said. And I said it too fast, without thinking what it meant to my mother.

'You'd do it, wouldn't you?' my father said.

'Will you like it if your father gets burned up out there and you never see him again?' my mother said to me. 'Then you and I go straight to hell together. How will that be?'

'Don't say that, Jean,' my father said. He put his bag on the kitchen table and came and knelt beside my mother and tried to put his arms around her. But she got up from her chair and walked back to where she had been cutting tomatoes and picked up the knife and pointed it at him, where he was still kneeling beside the empty chair.

'I'm a grown woman,' she said, and she was very angry now. 'Why don't you act like a grown man, Jerry?'

'You can't explain everything,' my father said.

'I can explain everything,' my mother said. She put the knife down and walked out the kitchen door and into the bedroom, the one she had not been sleeping in with my father, and closed the door behind her.

My father looked at me from where he was still beside her chair. 'I guess my judgement's no good now,' he said. 'Is that what you think, Joe?'

'No,' I said. 'I think it is.'

And I thought his judgement was good, and that going to fight the fire was a good idea even though he might go and get killed because he knew nothing about it. But I did not want to say all of that to him because of how it would make him feel.

My father and I walked from home in the dark down to the Masonic Temple on Central. A yellow Cascade County school bus was parked at the corner of Ninth, and men were standing in groups waiting to go. Some of the men were bums. I could tell by their shoes and their coats. Though some were just regular men who were out of work, I thought, from other jobs. Three women who were going waited together under the street-light. And inside the bus, in the dark, I could see Indians were in some of the seats. I could see their round faces, their slick hair, the tint of light off their eye-glasses in the darkness. No one would get in with them, and some men were drinking. I could smell whiskey in the night air.

My father put his bag on a stack of bags beside the bus, then came and stood next to me. Inside the Masonic Temple—which had high steps up to a glass centre door—all the lights were on. Several men inside were looking out. One, who was the man I had seen with my father in the Jack 'n' Jill, held a clipboard and was talking to an Indian man beside him. My father gestured to him.

'People categorize other people,' my father said. 'But you shouldn't do that. They should teach you that in school.'

I looked at the men around me. Most of them were not dressed warmly enough and were shifting from foot to foot. They looked like men used to work, though they did not seem glad to be going to fight a fire at night. None of them looked like my father, who seemed eager.

'What will you do out there?' I said.

'Work on a fire line,' my father said. 'They dig trenches the fire won't cross. I don't know much more, to tell you the truth.' He put his hands in his jacket pockets and blew down into his shirt. 'I've got this hum in my head now. I need to do something about it.'

'I understand,' I said.

'Tell your mother I didn't mean to make her mad.'

'I will,' I said.

'We don't want to wake up in our coffins, though, do we? That'd be a rude surprise.' He put a hand on my shoulder and pulled me close to him and squeezed me and laughed an odd little laugh, as if the idea had actually given him a scare. He looked across Central Avenue at the Pheasant Lounge, the place I had seen him go into the week before. On the red neon sign over the door a big cock pheasant was busting up into the night air, its wings stretched into the darkness—escaping. Some men waiting at the Masonic Temple had begun to go across the street into the bar. 'I'm only thinking about right this minute now,' he said. He squeezed my shoulder again, then put his hands back into his jacket pockets. 'Aren't you cold?'

'I'm a little cold,' I said.

'Then go back home,' he said. 'You don't need to watch me get on a bus. It might be a long time. Your mother's probably thinking about you.'

'All right,' I said.

'She doesn't need to get mad at you. She's mad enough at me.'

I looked at my father. I tried to see his face in the streetlight. He was smiling and looking at me, and I think he was happy for that moment, happy for me to be with him, happy that he was going to a fire now to risk whatever he cared about risking. It seemed strange to me, though, that he could be a man who played golf for a living and then one day become a man who fought forest fires. But it's what was happening, and I thought I would get used to it.

'Are you too old now to give your old dad a kiss?' my father said. 'Men love each other, too. You know that, don't you?'

'Yes,' I said. And he took my cheeks in his hands and kissed me on the mouth, and squeezed my face. His breath smelled sweet to me and his face was rough.

'Don't let what your parents do disappoint you,' he said.

'All right,' I said, 'I won't.' I felt afraid then for some reason, and I thought if I stayed there I would show him that I was, so I turned around and started back up Central in the dark and the growing cold. When I got to the corner I turned to wave good-bye. But my father was not in sight, and I thought that he had already gotten onto the bus and was waiting in his seat among the Indians.

JONATHAN RABAN
NEW WORLD

Above: Charles Lindbergh in 1941.

Come Fly the Friendly Skies!—slogan for United Airways, 1989.

This is an American airport. I mean, it is a particular airport in the United States. It has its own name—Logan, or Bates Field, or William B. Hartsfield, or Sky Harbor, or O'Hare— but in my fear of flying I've forgotten what it's called. As for where it is, anyone can see that it is just *here*; a place with a character more powerfully redolent and oppressive than any of the cities to which the airport might be nominally attached.

Entering *here*, you must abandon almost everything you have. The cheerful Spirit was dumped long ago at one of the place's eggbox-concrete outposts; the black zippered bag containing my travelling life went off on a journey of its own down some long dark tunnel at Check-In; my groin and armpits have been immodestly fingered in a search for firearms; my sponge-bag has been X-rayed, and a uniformed woman *here* now knows (if she cares) that I'm down to my last two Ativans. Maybe she read a few lines of my manuscript too, when it went past, and gave it a derisory thumbs-down. She had the face of a *New York Magazine* book-strangler.

At every point, I have managed to meet reproof. At the car-rental office, I tried to amuse a man called Wayne with the story of how the driver's-side seat-belt had been eaten by a jealous dog. He fined me 100 dollars, told me the incident would be reported as an act of malicious damage, and said his company kept a blacklist of customers like me.

Checking in, I said, 'Window seat in Smoking, if there is one, please.' A woman called Marsha sniffed and made a face. Now I'd confessed, she could smell my habit on me, and intended to make me feel the stink of my own polluted clothes in her nostrils. 'There *is* no smoking on Domestic flights,' she said, her expression warming sharply into a vindictive smile.

The phrase had kept on coming back to me during these last two hours. A cat is a domestic animal. A saucepan is a domestic utensil. To Marsha, jetting across a continent in a 747 was just pottering tamely about the house. I marvelled at the size of Marsha's house.

Ticketed, disencumbered, searched and cleared for boarding, we are babyishly dependent on the controllers of the place.

Sometimes they tell us to do things; mostly they leave us to fret. Every ten minutes I go and stare morosely at the nearest VDU display. An hour ago we were due to board half an hour ago at Gate B6; now we're due to board in forty minutes at Gate C14. As I watch, one of the invisible controllers adds an extra twenty minutes for luck.

An hour and a half later we're getting somewhere—at least I thought so fifty minutes ago when I buckled in to 38F and began looking out through the lozenge of scratched, multiplex plastic at the men in ear-muffs and storm-gear on the ground below. Since then we haven't budged. We've suffered faint, pastiche imitations of Scott Joplin, Count Basie and Glenn Miller on the muzak system. My neighbour in 38E, who is careless of the usual rules of body space, has worked her way slowly through four pages of the *National Inquirer*, moving her lips as she reads. In the seats ahead, there has been a good deal of scuffing and refolding of copies of *Business Week* and the *Wall Street Journal*. Still no one seems much disconcerted except me. The inside of the plane is hot and getting hotter. The stewards, flirting routinely among themselves, are proof against any damn-fool questions from me.

The muzak clicks off. A voice clicks on.

'Hi!'—and that seems to be it for a good long time. Then, 'I'm, uh, Billy Whitman, and I'm going to be your pilot on this flight here to . . . ' I think I can hear Mr Whitman consulting his clipboard. ' . . . uh, Sea-Tac this morning. Well—it was meant to be this morning, but it looks to me now to be getting pretty damn close to afternoon . . . '

He's read *The Right Stuff*, and he's doing it—the entire cow-licked, gum-shifting country boy performance.

'I guess some of you folks back there may be getting a little antsy 'bout this delay we're having now in getting airborne . . . Well, we did run into a bit of a glitch with Control up there, getting our flight-plan sorted . . . '

We haven't got a flight-plan? Is Mr Whitman waiting for someone to bring him a *map*?

'But they got that fixed pretty good now, and in, uh, oh, a couple or three minutes, we should be closing the doors, and I'm planning on getting up into the blue yonder round about ten minutes after that. So if you all sit tight now, we'll be getting this show right on the road. Looks pretty nice up there today . . . no weather problems that I can see so far . . . at least, once we get atop this little local overcast . . . and I'm looking for a real easy trip today. Have a good one, now, and I'll be right back to you just as soon as we go past something worth looking out the window for. OK?'

Click.

After the video and the stewards' dumb show about what to do in 'the unlikely event' of our landing on water (where? the Mississippi?), Captain Whitman takes us on a slow ramble round the perimeter of the airport. We appear to be returning to the main terminal again when the jet takes a sudden deep breath, lets out a bull roar, and charges down the runway, its huge frame shuddering fit to bust. Its wings are actually flapping now, trying to tear themselves out at their roots in the effort to achieve lift-off. It bumps and grinds. The plastic bulkheads are shivering like gongs. Rain streams past the window, in shreds and gobbets, at 200 miles an hour.

This is the bit I hate. We're not going fast enough. We're far too heavy to bring off this insanely dangerous trick. We're breaking up. To take this flight was tempting fate one time too many. We're definitely goners this time.

But the domestic fliers remain stupidly oblivious to our date with death. They go on reading. They're lost in the stock-market prices. They're learning that the human soul has been proved to exist and weighs exactly three-quarters of an ounce; that Elvis Presley never died and has been living as a recluse in Dayton, Ohio. These things engage them. These guys are—bored. The fact, clear enough to me, that they are at this moment rocketing into eternity is an insufficiently diverting one to make them even raise their eyes from their columns of idiot print.

As a European child I used to think that Americans were somehow possessed of a lower specific gravity than we were. I envied them for it—for the way they seemed to be able to detach themselves from the ground with so much more

235

ease than anyone I knew. Distant members of my family had occasionally been known to travel by aeroplane; and each of these ascents was spoken of for weeks beforehand, remembered for years after. 'That was the year that Uncle Peter *flew* to Geneva.' Americans were different. They took to the sky with hardly more forethought or apprehension than swallows launching themselves from a telegraph-wire. 'Going up in an aeroplane', in British English, was quite a different kind of venture from 'taking an airplane' in American. *Aero-* retained the Greek dignity of the word, gave it a dash of Icarian daring and danger. To my eyes, *airplane* always looked impertinently casual on the page; it robbed the amazing machine of its proper mystery.

Flying did mean something different to Americans—even though the aviation industry was at least as much a European as an American creation. It was Louis Blériot who first crossed the Channel by plane in 1909; it was two Englishmen, John Alcock and Arthur Whitten Brown, who first crossed the Atlantic, from Newfoundland to Ireland, in 1919. In the design and manufacture of aircraft, Germany, France and Britain were as active as the United States, and in the early days of passenger flying it was a British firm, Imperial Airways, which commanded the longest and richest routes in the world.

Yet none of our nations learned to fly—not with the insouciance of these Americans who had managed to absorb the whole alarming business of airports, flight numbers, take-offs and landings into the ordinary fabric of their daily culture. In 38F, and hardly a novice in the scary tedium of long-distance air travel, I feel leadenly European in the company of these natural fliers.

38E's elbow is in my ribs. She is shouting into my deafened left ear. '*She* says you want a cocktail?'

The steel bulk of the mobile ice-and-drinks canteen has always bothered me. Suppose we hit an unexpected pocket of turbulence . . . suppose that thing takes wing from the aisle and hits the ceiling of the fuselage? Suppose a sharp-angled hundredweight truck of miniatures of Jack Daniels, London Gin, Stolichnaya, Californian Cabernet and Chablis, plus ice, tonic, soda, *etcet* slams into the roof of this elongated eggshell . . . ?

But the steward's waiting, and not conspicuously patiently. I settle, sadly, for a mineral water. I've learned the hard way about high-altitude dehydration. Trying to work out the controls of a strange car at the entrance to a strange city, with a fox-fur mouth and a blinding headache, cured me of my old game of trying to see just how many empty twenty-five-centilitre champagne bottles it was possible to secrete behind the airline magazine and the Emergency Procedure card in the netting pocket on the back of the seat in front of you. Eight was my record. Now it's mineral water all the way. Plus, there's no smoking on domestic flights. I have to make do with the consolations of history.

When Charles Lindbergh scooped the Orteig Prize of 25,000 dollars for the first non-stop flight between Paris and New York on 21 May 1927, he did something that would, almost certainly, have been done by someone else within the next few days—or hours. Two rival planes, the *Columbia* and *America*, were waiting in their hangars on Roosevelt Field when Lindbergh took off in *The Spirit of St Louis*. A fortnight before, a French contender, *L'Oiseau Blanc*, had been lost somewhere over the Atlantic; and in September 1926 a big three-engine Sikorsky piloted by René Fonck with a crew of three had crashed on take-off at the end of the Roosevelt Field runway.

Despite the crashes, the technology of aviation in 1927 was clearly up to the challenge set by Raymond Orteig, a French national who owned two New York hotels. Alcock and Brown had flown the Atlantic (by a much shorter route) eight years before; America had been crossed coast-to-coast; planes with a cruising speed of around 130 miles per hour and a fuel capacity for forty hours of flying were being built on both sides of the Atlantic. Someone was going to do the thing, and it happened to be Lindbergh.

It was the aftermath of the flight, not the flight itself, that was extraordinary—the transformation of Lindy, the Lone Eagle, the Flying Fool into the American hero who, for a few years, would shine in the popular imagination as the greatest American hero in history. His fame was majestically out of proportion to his actual achievement; and it is that disproportion which makes Lindbergh so fascinating a figure.

Here one has to forget about the facts and read the newspapers. By the time that Lindbergh arrived back in New York on 13 June, to be showered (they said) with 1,800 tons of ticker-tape, all the essential ingredients of the Lindbergh Story were in place. He was 'the lanky demon of the skies from the wide open spaces'; a solitary country boy (forget that he was born in Detroit), from Little Falls, Minnesota, on the banks of the Mississippi. He was a child of nature, raised in woods by Fenimore Cooper on water by Mark Twain.

Like Huck, Lindy ran away from school (correct: he flunked out of the University of Wisconsin, Madison); but he never smoked a corn-cob pipe or touched a drop of liquor. In bootleg America, Lindy was incorruptibly teetotal and (like this damned plane) smoke-free. He was also chaste. Mother was his only girl.

Even the most admiring of Lindbergh's later biographers have left a picture of a priggish and sexually backward young man with a questionable taste in male rough-housing and practical jokes (he is supposed to have placed a live poisonous snake in the bed of a room-mate who'd been dating a girl). In 1927, this sort of thing may, I suppose, have passed for cleaner fun than it does now. Certainly Lindbergh the Virgin Boy was the Lindbergh that America then wanted, and his irritable shrugging-off of the girls who tried to cling to him at parades was a famous part of his charm.

The skies had been billed as 'the new frontier' and Lindbergh was groomed by his image-makers into the most perfect of old-fashioned, literary-sentimental frontiersmen. His truest ancestor was Natty Bumppo, wise in the woods, innocent in towns. Natty's aliases—Hawkeye, Pathfinder—fitted Lindbergh beautifully; and the best-known alias of all—Leatherstocking—has a spooky aptness when one looks at photographs of Lindbergh in his triumphal year. In flying gear, Lindy *is* Leatherstocking, from the coonskin hat of his undone airman's helmet down through the trapper's leather coveralls to the fur-lined boots. Leatherstocking's sole concession to technology is his trusty musket; Lindy's is *The Spirit of St Louis*, in front of which he stands, one hand behind his back resting gently on the plane's propeller.

In the spirit of Leatherstocking, Lindy, in the Lindbergh Story at least, walked alone. Not only was his flight a single-handed one, in contrast to the two- and four-man crews of most of the rival planes, but he represented the unaided individual talent, battling against the syndicate and the corporation. He was the barnstormer, employed to take folks up for a spin at five dollars a ride at country fairs; the lone pilot, flying the night mail to Chicago for a tinpot outfit in St Louis. As the house poet of the New York *Sun* put it:

> *. . . no kingly plane for him;*
> *No endless data, comrades, moneyed chums;*
> *No boards, no councils, no directors grim—*
> *He plans ALONE . . . and takes luck as it comes.*

This was to forget rather a lot, including the backing of the St Louis *Globe-Democrat*, and several individual members of its board, a St Louis bank, a St Louis insurance company and a St Louis aviation business, along with the services of an enterprising PR man called Dick Blythe, who was assigned to promote Lindbergh by the mammoth Wright Aeronautical Corporation. In fact, Lindbergh was impressively efficient at persuading the various boards, councils and directors of St Louis that his attempt on the Orteig Prize would bring glory to the city, and managed to raise 15,000 dollars before commissioning a plane from the Ryan Aircraft Company in San Diego at a price of 10,580 dollars. But it's true that these sums were small compared with the 100,000 dollars spent on the *America* by Admiral Byrd, and Lindbergh's corporate loneliness rang with at least metaphorical conviction.

Alone (or rather ALONE, *Sun*-style), tall, young, pure, a creature of the Heartland and the wide open spaces, the very incarnation of the folk-hero of the frontier, Lindbergh made flying an airplane into something that America had been doing all through the sweetest and best years of its own history. It wasn't something new, like driving an automobile or dancing the black bottom; it was something old, and Lindbergh was teaching America to remember it.

The Atlantic flight established the myth, but it was later in the summer of 1927 that Lindbergh drove America wild with the domestic flight of all time. He took *The Spirit of St Louis* on a 22,350-mile tour of all forty-eight states, and led grand parades in eighty-two cities. Leonard Mosley, in *Lindbergh*, writes:

He was paid 50,000 dollars for making the tour, but he did it less for the money than because he earnestly believed that showing himself and the *Spirit* to the people, and always arriving on time no matter what the weather, would prove to them that the air age had arrived and they should become part of it.

Showing himself and the Spirit *to the people* . . . These were the manifestations of a god making himself flesh. His robe was touched, as souvenir hunters snipped away fragments of the sacred fabric from the fuselage.

In that summer, Lindbergh knitted the land mass of North America together in a great web of inter-city air routes. Until now, flying had been a sport, a method of warfare, a means of carrying mail. There were a few passenger services—the earliest had been started in 1914, when the Benoist Company set up regular flights between Tampa and St Petersburg in Florida. Even in the middling-late 1920s, though, passengers, insofar as there were any passengers, were usually expected to fit themselves between the mail-bags and muddle in as best they could. Lindbergh's second, domestic flight articulated a vision of the whole of the United States seen from the air. He connected up a mass of scattered dots and made a thrilling picture of them.

Here, resting in its moulded beige niche, under a silky veil of polythene, is something that the airline, in a shaft of facetious wit, calls breast of chicken. 38E has already wolfed hers down and has started in on the red Jello. My bit of bird yields to the prodding of a baby plastic knife and fork with unbecoming cowardice. It goes to pieces. It seems to be as bad at air travel as I am myself. I lunch like an anchorite on a sprig of cold broccoli and a salteena. Face pressed against the chilly perspex of the window, I count the disintegrating jet trails in the sky; four of them, shredding to bits like tufts of wet cotton wool. Below them lie some thin, violet streaks of cirrus, and below the clouds, a land too witchy-dark to make much sense of. Is that a mountain or a city? I'm not sure. The occasional fuse-wire glints are rivers, I think. From six miles up, in hazy visibility, the earth unspools without incident, without much interest, like an underexposed home movie.

After Lindbergh, the big money poured into American aviation. In 1928, C. M. Keys, the asset-stripping, merger-making president of Transcontinental Air Transport, paid the flying god 250,000 dollars for—being the flying god, having the ear of President Hoover, and allowing his name to be associated, if vaguely, with TAT. The terms of the agreement between Keys and Lindbergh were made public in 1934 when, under Roosevelt, the Black Committee was investigating graft in the allocation of government mail contracts to the airlines. It appeared that Keys was mainly interested in explaining to Lindbergh what he need *not* do in return for his quarter-million down and 10,000 dollars a year.

> You will not, until you express a desire to do so, become a director of the company. It is not my desire or intention, nor is it yours, that this work shall prevent you from carrying on other activities for the general advancement of aviation in which you have so deep an interest. Nor will it prevent you from carrying on other business activities not competitive with those of Transcontinental Air Transport Inc. . .

What the money essentially represented was the price set, in June 1928, by a tough businessman, on the picture painted a year before by the Leatherstocking of the skies. Keys's advertising men set out to educate America into calling TAT 'The Lindbergh Line'.

The speed of events from then on can be measured by the advance order books for the Boeing 247D, which came into production in 1933. The 247 was the first twin-engined, all-metal airliner. It carried ten passengers, a pilot, co-pilot and one flight attendant. It flew at 200 miles an hour and had a range of a little over 600 miles. Before the mock-up stage of the aircraft had been completed, sixty orders had been placed for it by US airlines. It went coast to coast (with refuelling stops) and shuttled between cities like New York and Chicago and Los Angeles and San Francisco.

It is, I imagine, a Boeing 247 in which the first chapter of Scott Fitzgerald's *The Last Tycoon* is set, and in which two distinctively new types of American make their appearance. One is Monroe

Stahr, the movie producer closely based on Irving Thalberg. The other is Cecilia Brady, the novel's narrator and a rather self-consciously precocious junior at Bennington College in Vermont. Her newness resides in the fact that she is going back to her parents' Hollywood home at the end of a semester, and she is flying.

'The world from an airplane I knew,' she says, and the grammatical inversion is a nice Bennington-girlism, just this side of arch.

> Father always had us travel back and forth that way from school and college. After my sister died when I was a junior, I travelled to and fro alone, and the journey always made me think of her, made me somewhat solemn and subdued. Sometimes there were picture people I knew on board the plane, and occasionally there was an attractive college boy—but not often during the depression. I seldom really fell asleep during the trip, what with thoughts of Eleanor and the sense of that sharp rip between coast and coast—at least not till we had left those lonely little airports in Tennessee.

This is post-Lindbergh geography, beautifully phrased: the mere 'sharp rip' between coast and coast, a black and lonely canyon, barely inhabited between the two bright points of American civilization. Here is *flyoverland*—that region of disregarded spaces where the lesser mortals live.

In the novel, a brewing storm in the Mississippi valley forces the plane to make an unscheduled landing at Nashville. ('Nashville!' says Wylie White, a Hollywood scriptwriter and fellow-passenger; 'My God! I was born in Nashville.') During the descent (' . . . going down, down, down, like Alice in the rabbit hole . . .'), Cecilia looks out of the window at the distant city and meditates on airports and on her own grandeur as an airborne American:

> I suppose there has been nothing like the airports since the days of the stage-stops—nothing quite as lonely, as sombre-silent. The old red-brick depots were built right into the towns they marked—people didn't get off at those isolated stations unless they lived there. But airports lead

you way back into history like oases, like the stops on the great trade routes. The sight of air travelers strolling in ones and twos into midnight airports will draw a small crowd any night up to two. The young people look at the planes, the older ones look at the passengers with a watchful incredulity. In the big trans-continental planes we were the coastal rich, who casually alighted from our cloud in mid-America.

Grounded in the small hours, the Californians might as well have been suddenly tipped into Thailand or Tuscany. They are innocent tourists in their own country. A railroad line, a highway, would have prepared them for Tennessee, but the high night sky has equipped them with no clues or presentiments. They commission a taxi driver to take them to the Andrew Jackson home, the Hermitage; a drive that takes longer in the book (two hours, or thereabouts) than it looks on the map (eleven miles). On the way, they see a Negro driving three cows (the South!); Cecilia is impressed, even in the darkness, by the lush green of the Tennessee woods. They reach the Hermitage at dawn, when, not surprisingly, it turns out to be closed to the public. They go back to the airport, leaving one of their number behind to take the Andrew Jackson tour. Within six pages of dialogue, and back into darkness again, they are landing at Glendale airport, returned to the real, important, coastal world.

The Cecilia Brady approach to Nashville is a prophetic model of a new kind of relationship between Americans and their landscape. Casually to alight from a cloud, to taste a city in a spirit of lofty and alienated connoisseurship, was to become *the* American way of travelling, and it was to have enormous consequences for the social and family life of the nation.

As the planes got bigger and ticket prices went down, air travel stopped being the prerogative of the coastal rich. One of the perks of the job for almost every middle-class corporate employee was to fly, several times a year, to the trade fair, the sales conference, the professional convention (Funeral Directors of America . . . The American Society of Anaesthesiologists). The airport-cities built Convention & Trade Centers in their mouldering downtowns and leafletted the country with extravagant advertisements for themselves. Lifeless dumps rechristened themselves with the names of precious stones (The Ruby City, The Emerald City, The Sapphire City) or proclaimed that they were the Gateway to The Great Lakes. The West, The Orient, the Sunbelt. Colour photographs of a recently cleaned-up slum showed gas-lamps, cobbles, a gallery, an open-air café ('Shoppers take a needed break to enjoy Blandville's world-famous *croissants* and *capuccino*').

In corporate offices high over New York and Chicago, marketing directors and their assistants went into conference. 'We gave the beach people Miami back in January; now we owe the golfers one. How about Phoenix? You got anything on golf in Phoenix?'

For the corporate tourists, the nature of cities abruptly changed. Now they swam up to meet you from below the cloud-ceiling; out of context, exotic, phenomenal. Their only hinterland was the pale speedway that linked them to their airport. They had no reason for being. Whatever had originally created them was hidden from the visitor from the air. They had no human geography.

In the crowded programme of the conventioneer there was no time to find out the *why* of *here*. Cities had to make themselves instantly memorable by means of some totem or icon. St Louis was that place where the Arch was. Philadelphia was the Liberty Bell. In the one-hour guided tour, you needed a single novelty or monument to put the city on your private map of the United States. We went to sales-conference there—that was the Alamo; *that* was the Paul Revere House; *that* was the Space Needle; *that* was the Grand Ole Opry; *that* was Astroworld; *that* was Preservation Hall.

Touting for custom, the cities were marvellously resourceful at dreaming up ways to imprint themselves on the memories of these jaded and blasé air travellers. In Chambers of Commerce, fiction-writers were set to construct local-colour 'regional cuisine' recipes. Who could forget, say, a traditional dish of succulent North Dakotan grasshoppers in a tangy blueberry sauce? Where no ready-made icons existed, the city fathers raised money to build them—constructions so tall and bizarre that (like Portland, Oregon's Public Service Building) they would figure in the subsequent nightmares of even the most absent-minded of short-stay visitors.

This constant jetting about between convention centres had created an extraordinary body of misleading knowledge. Almost every American I knew who worked for a large company seemed to have visited almost every American city I could name for a period of, on average, about thirty-six hours. Wherever I was going, they knew it.

'Oh, but you *have* to try those tiny oysters there, more flavour than food . . . you *have* to go to the Pike Place Market . . . you *have* to take the elevator up to the top of the Space Needle for the view . . . and there's a hotel there (I didn't stay in it myself) where you can fish right out your window . . .'

'But what's the *place* like?'

That was the trouble. They hadn't been to a place. There hadn't been time for that. They had dropped out of the sky in order to be shown a tight cluster of artfully manufactured symbols.

Yet there was something very different in all this from the usual tourists' whirl through the Great Cities of Europe. These were domestic flights, and these were domestic fliers, beating the bounds of their enormous home patch. If you flew, coast to coast and Lakes to Gulf, as often, and as indifferently, as these people, the experience would eventually give you a landowner's sense of possession. All the cities you have nibbled at, as if each one was an éclair, they are *yours*. Maybe one day, when you're shown the swing door, or the kids are in college, you'll come back and take up your inheritance for a while, in the Topaz City or the Gateway to the Rockies.

It is a thought that comes easily, and comfortingly, at six miles up. You are not really half so heavy as you feel. You think of the house and garden, the neighbours (you never liked their cats, or their children)—that brick albatross with its leaky roof and unmended fence. On the ground, *home* is a word like *fate*; it's what you've got, what you probably deserved. In the air, it has a different ring. It's a disposable asset. *I quit the office, sold my home and my car, and took the plane . . .*

My seat-back's on full tilt. I'm indulging myself in American thoughts, looking sleepily out over my great estate. The land below has brightened up since the last time I inspected it. It's agribusiness territory, in some Midwestern state; a flat checker-board, the colours burned out of it by the sun. We're flying over the close cross-hatching of a town, and I can pick out its water tower, a silver button-mushroom, and the heliographic wink of what I take to be the herded pick-ups on the lot of the local auto-dealership.

We're sustaining the right height. There's a war on down there—silos full of unsold corn, debt, foreclosures, repo men moving in on family farms. From here, the unhappy heartland still looks orderly and fat, but the news is bad. I remember (in this detached, Cecilia Bradyish way) the story of a respectable Iowa farmer who got out his old Remington shotgun one morning, blew his wife's heart clean out of her body, drove down to the bank and shot his personal banker, killed a neighbouring farmer with whom he was in dispute, then, sitting in his pick-up, pointed the gun barrel at his own chest and pulled the trigger. This story, so it was said at the time, fairly represented the despair in the farming communities of the Midwest in the 1980s. Dale Burr of Lone Tree had only done what thousands of farmers like him were on the brink of doing now.

I search the landscape for signs, but find none. I think of the farmers' sons and daughters, booking their flights out.

GRANTA

NOTES FROM ABROAD

On a Boat to Tangier
Tahar Ben Jelloun

I like travelling by ship. In these times of speed and crowded skies, ships are a luxury. You can take your time moving around. It is an opportunity to create space and prepare yourself to get into a new rhythm.

This summer I was on the *Marrakesh*, a magnificent steamer that sails the crossing between Sète in southern France and Tangier in northern Morocco.

No sooner had we set off than a short man in his fifties came up, arms open wide, and greeted me with a hug. I had never seen this man before. I was rather taken aback and said nothing. It must surely be a misapprehension, I had been mistaken for someone else. No, it was nothing like that at all. The man reassured me.

'My name's Hadj Abdelkrim, I was born in Marrakesh on an exceptionally hot day; I'm married to a Sicilian woman and have three children who know and love you. Unfortunately, I don't read. My wife has to read for me. I don't read but I am experienced in life, in what's visible and what isn't. What's my job? Getting foreigners to love my country, introducing it in all its beauty and complexity. That's what brought me to you: I've been waiting a long time for this moment—there's a story I've wanted to tell you; a true story. You're a writer, aren't you? Now listen to me: This is the story of Brahim, a man without a story, a fine man who tries to support his family. It is the story of a destiny that found itself on the road to Evil. Listen.'

Hadj Abdelkrim stood in the middle of the lounge; travellers had gathered from all sides to listen to him . . .

t had been a long time since a tourist had stopped to watch Brahim and his snakes. The snakes were tired, too old and lacked all conviction. They had ceased to respond to the unchanging music from their master and charmer. Brahim had swapped his flute and his music in vain: they barely showed their heads, just lay in their chest, disturbed or asleep. There seemed only one way for Brahim to make his performance attractive again: renew his stock. Brahim made the sacrifice and bought, in a village renowned for its snakes, a glistening, blue viper full of life. He stroked and teased it, then played a passage of his tune. The snake proved an exceptional dancer, writhing at will, closely following the rhythm, flicking out its tongue to mark the beat. Brahim regained confidence in himself. His other snakes were seduced by the beautiful blue viper.

That night Brahim had a strange dream: the big square was empty and lit up by a full moon. He was sitting cross-legged in the middle of the square. He couldn't move. You might have said he was stuck to the ground by a special glue. Opposite him appeared the viper in the guise of a young blue woman. He could not be sure whether she was wearing a blue veil or whether blue was the colour of her skin. She had a woman's body and a viper's head. She spoke to him while she circled around him.

'This afternoon I showed you what I was capable of. I played along with your game. But you are not going to sentence me to a life of writhing to amuse your tourists. I deserve better than that; I am young, I want to live, to be free to roam, have feelings, pleasures and memories for my old age. If your tourists want unique sensations, they have only to go to the Amazon or the country where the stones have memories. I warn you, if you turn me into a spectacle, you'll be sorry . . . but I'm not sure you'll have time to be sorry for anything at all.'

As she spoke, she moved around him, brushing against his hand or hip. He tried to reply. The words were trapped in his throat. He was hypnotized. Sure of herself, she continued: 'Don't try to tell me your problems and win my pity. Let me go and you will have peace. I have too much to do. It is harvest-time; I must go back under the stones. I like the fresh hands of the young girls who bend down to gather the corn. Your tourists disgust me. They are ugly. Their paltry tips are enough to satisfy you. Have a little dignity.

'Now you can leave. The square will soon be full; the sun will rise and you will go and think it over, but if you want your peace of mind, return to me my freedom.'

Brahim woke up with a start, trembling and feverish. He inspected the chest where the snakes slept. There was the viper, quiet, in a deep sleep. Reassured, he washed and said his morning prayers. That day, he joined his hands to ask God for help and protection: 'Allah, you are the greatest, the most merciful; keep from me Evil and the unscrupulous. I'm a weak man. I earn my living with treacherous animals. I've no means to combat Evil, or change my job. Times are hard. My father was a snake-charmer. I was born and raised surrounded by snakes. I never wholeheartedly trusted them. They are perfidious. As a good Muslim I don't believe in reincarnation; but sometimes I come across people whose hypocrisy and sneering smiles make me think their hearts and souls were formerly those of vipers.'

It wasn't his habit to justify himself in prayer. He had been practising this profession for years without asking any questions. That night's dream had shaken him. It was in some way real. Brahim was afraid, afraid of an accident, afraid of having another attack of epilepsy, afraid of the evil eye.

That day he had to charm his snakes in a big hotel before a group of tourists who had paid a supplement to be present at a spectacle whose exoticism was guaranteed; the sight of a viper dancing to the music of a man from the hills. Brahim said a prayer before leaving home, did not take his bicycle, tied a silver clasp round his neck. In principle his fears were exorcized. He arrived at the hotel right on time. The tourists had just eaten a couscous. They had drunk rosé wine and beer. They were full and sleepy. Their courier introduced Brahim.

'Ladies and gentlemen, here before your eyes what you have often heard about but never seen, here you have the difference between North and South, here you have not magic but poetry, here you have the most famous charmer in the square, here you have the man that will risk his life to give you a thrill, here for you are Brahim and his snakes . . .'

Cameras were made ready. Some tourists looked unimpressed—Brahim appeared frail and hesitant—they drank their mint tea and ate their gazelle horns. Brahim greeted his audience with a bow. As he bent down, he thought he saw the blue woman from his dream. She had the head of a bird and was wearing a blue *djellaba* that sculpted her body. She had almost no breasts. She sat on a tree branch swinging her legs like a child. Brahim played his flute, putting off the moment he would open the snake chest. The tourists no longer nodded off; they were all staring at the chest. Brahim pushed up the lid and sunk his hand inside. He caught the viper—in fact, it clung to his wrist. Just when he was about to stroke its head, it bit him. The snake still had all its venom, despite the fact that Brahim had seen its venom drained the day he had bought it. He fell down dead on the spot, frothing at the mouth with blood and whitish foam. It was a poisonous foam. The tourists thought it was a joke in bad taste. Some were annoyed and protested; others were taken aback by this live death and threw up their lunch. Photos were taken. Snapshot souvenir of a sudden death, souvenir of the artist dying on stage.

Brahim's body was carried to the main morgue and placed in drawer number 013.

Hadj Abdelkrim paused: 'Friends of the Righteous! That's not the end of the story. Don't be impatient. At the beginning I spoke of a thwarted destiny. You'll soon see; life goes on; don't forget what I've just told you, and now listen to the other side of the night . . .

Ali and Fatima—the two children holding hands on the way to school on the cover of the learn-to-read text-book—have grown up. From childhood they had been promised to each other, they made a nice quiet couple, no drama, faithful to the benign image in the dreams of thousands of school children. They got married because they were in love and nobody could have prevented that marriage. But despite appearances, too many things separated them: Ali had been able to pursue his studies and worked for a private company. Fatima came from a humble background and could hardly read or write. Ali was what is called 'a man whose look can fell a bird in full flight'; people also said—with reference to his passion for women—that he had 'green eyes'. His eyes were dark. He liked drinking, fast driving and stealing other men's wives. His wife, Fatima, was a domesticated woman, looking after the home, totally dedicated to her husband, whom she attended to constantly, and their two children. She was a woman resigned to her lot, not at all devious, offering her husband no surprises, having no more mystery for him, a woman full of good faith and good will, a defenceless woman trapped in kindness that quickly turned into a kind of stupidity. Like her mother and grandmother, Fatima had acquiesced until the day when she decided to react, to do something to keep Ali close to her. But his life was elsewhere. There was apparently nothing to keep him in a home where routine ruled alongside sadness. When Fatima dared to protest, Ali slapped her a couple of times and slammed the door behind him. He did not hide his many adventures. He ran after whores. He did not deny it and thought he had no obligation to render accounts to anyone. That only exacerbated Fatima's jealousy. A sickly jealousy. Her doctors could not give her back her husband. They prescribed tranquillizers for her.

Fatima did not dare to confide in her family. But she did consult a clairvoyant.

'Your husband is handsome,' she was told. 'He deceives you and will always deceive you; it is stronger than he is. I can see a crowd of pretty women surrounding him, wanting to kiss him. He enjoys great potency; he can give women what other men can't. You could say he was born to satisfy all those whom chance has paired with weaklings. His role is to repair the damage. You can't do anything. This kind of man is not made for marriage and family life. Even if you hide him away in prison, the women will come and liberate him and take him away. Be brave. That's all I can say to you, my dear!'

Fatima was in despair. She confided in Khadouj, a neighbour and a nurse in the municipal hospital. Khadouj was well-qualified to be Fatima's advisor. She had tried, unsuccessfully, to attract Ali herself. She not only understood her friend's jealousy and disarray, but shared them. She suggested they go and see a witch, a woman well-known for solving married couples' problems. Her office was in a magnificent apartment and she only consulted by appointment. She was a young, modern woman, and had studied applied psychology. She was not at all like those alarming, one-eyed witches. She asked Fatima to explain her problem, took notes and asked detailed questions.

'Do you want your husband back, just for yourself and nobody else? I could prescribe some pills to dissolve in his morning coffee, but I can't be sure they will work. You could also mix a certain herb in his bread; but that carries risks of poisoning. I suppose you want him back healthy, not sick.'

Fatima whispered something to Khadouj then addressed the practitioner: 'I don't want him to become impotent or limp. I want him as I knew him, as I love him, very loving and tender.'

'In that case I am going to prescribe a well-tried recipe, from our ancestors: a ball of unleavened dough that has spent a whole night in a dead man's mouth, preferably a recent death, not a corpse forgotten in the morgue. Your husband will only have to bite the dough, eat it and he will change and come back to you as in your dreams. In a word, the dough must pass from the dead man's mouth into his. It can be done whilst he is sleeping, in case you can't get him to eat it.'

Fatima commented on the difficulty of finding a corpse. Khadouj winked at her. Fatima settled the fee with the secretary whose office was in the entrance, next to the waiting-room.

That very afternoon the dough was ready. Khadouj wrapped it in a handkerchief and went off to the hospital. She went down to the morgue, opened a few drawers, looking for the last corpse to arrive, and put the dough in his mouth. Number thirteen was still warm. His mouth was half-open. It was still whitish with foam and blood. The nurse had no difficulty in squeezing the dough between the dead man's teeth. She was on duty that night. Chance occasionally gets things right. Early in the morning she brought the dough back in the same handkerchief. Ali was in a deep sleep. Fatima gently opened his mouth and put the dough in place. He bit on it unaware. Ali did not wake up. He was dead. The snake venom was still active.

Fatima fainted. The blue viper-headed woman appeared to her and spoke thus: 'Witchcraft doesn't exist. Stupidity does. One person wanted to keep me against my wish. He died as a result. The other tried to go against the current of the river and she lost everything. One lacks dignity, the other, pride. In both cases, I can draw the moral of the story: you must beware of vipers especially when cursed by the moon, on an evening when it has been full of bitterness and loathing. Farewell, my daughter. At last you can sleep in peace and for eternity. As you can see, I am not all bad.'

Translated from the French by Peter Bush

Notes on Contributors

Isabel Hilton has been writing about Latin America since 1982. She is the co-author, with Magnus Linklater and Neal Ascherson, of *The Fourth Reich*, a biography of Klaus Barbie, and contributed to *The Falklands War* by the *Sunday Times* Insight Team. She is the European Affairs Editor of the *Independent* in London. **Gabriel García Márquez**'s new novel, *The General in his Labyrinth*, based on the life of Simon Bolívar, will be published in the autumn in the United States by Random House. He lives in Mexico. **Salman Rushdie**'s *The Satanic Verses* has now been translated into fifteen languages, and there are five further translations about to be completed. A paperback edition of the novel is to be published in Norway shortly (the first publication in France, Spain, Greece and Holland was in paperback). 'In Good Faith', the article mentioned in the interview, is available as a pamphlet from *Granta* at £3.00. **Blake Morrison** is the Literary Editor of the *Independent*. A collection of **Christopher Hitchens**'s essays entitled *Prepared for the Worst* was published last year. A new book, *Blood, Class and Nostalgia, a Study of Anglo-American Ironies* will be published in July. He lives in Washington D. C. **Léonard Freed** was in Romania throughout the revolution. He has been a member of Magnum Photographers since 1956. He is based in New York. **Bill Bryson** is the author of *The Lost Continent*. His previous contributions to Granta, 'Fat Girls in Des Moines' and 'More Fat Girls in Des Moines' appeared in issues 23 and 26. He is currently writing a book retracing a journey made hitch-hiking through Europe twenty years ago. He lives in North Yorkshire. **Richard Ford**'s first story in *Granta* was 'Rock Springs', published in issue 8, 'Dirty Realism'. 'Electric City' is taken from his new novel, *Wildlife*, which will be published this summer by Collins Harvill in Britain and the Atlantic Monthly Press in the United States. He now lives in New Orleans. **Margaret Atwood** lives in Toronto, Canada. Her novels include *Lady Oracle*, *The Handmaid's Tale* and, most recently, *Cat's Eye*, which was short-listed for the 1989 Booker Prize. **Jonathan Raban** has just returned from the United States and, as we go to press, he is writing his final instalment of 'New World'. **Tahar Ben Jelloun** is completing a trilogy of novels, the second of which, *La Nuit Sacrée*, received the Prix Goncourt in 1987. He lives in Paris.

SALMAN RUSHDIE

IN GOOD FAITH

On 4 February 1990, Salman Rushdie produced a powerful public statement, ending a year of silence.

'In Good Faith' is Salman Rushdie's answer to the critics of *The Satanic Verses*. Michael Foot, writer and former leader of the British Labour Party, described it as 'The most brilliant piece of polemical writing I have read in my life.'

It is available from Granta as a special edition pamphlet.

For your copy (post free) send a cheque or postal order of £3.00 and the coupon below (or with details written on a separate sheet of paper).

Name _____

_____

_____ Postcode _____

Send to Granta, Freepost, Cambridge CB1 1BR. Foreign orders add £1 for postage.